Education and Training in Canada

Education and Training in Canada

A Research Report prepared by:

Keith Newton, Director
Patrice de Broucker
Gilles Mcdougall
Kathryn McMullen
Thomas T. Schweitzer
Tom Siedule

1992

© Minister of Supply and Services Canada 1992

All rights reserved. No part of this publication may be reproduced, stored in
a retrieval system or transmitted in any form or by any means, electronic, mechanical,
photocopying, recording, or otherwise without prior written permission of the
Minister of Supply and Services Canada.

ISBN 0-660-14681-9
DSS Catalogue No. EC22-188/1992E

Available in Canada through your local bookseller or by mail from:
Canada Communication Group — Publishing
Ottawa, Canada K1A 0S9

Publishing Co-ordination: Ampersand Communications Inc.

Printed in Canada

Canadian Cataloguing in Publication Data

Main entry under title:

Education and training in Canada

> Issued also in French under title: Éducation
> et formation professionnelle au Canada.
> ISBN 0-660-14681-9
> DSS cat. no. EC22-188/1992E
>
> 1. Career education -- Canada. 2. Education,
> Secondary -- Canada. 3. Vocational education --
> Canada. I. Economic Council of Canada. II. Title.
>
> LC1035.8.C2E38 1992   373'.0113'0971   C92-099745-7

Note

This report, *Education and Training in Canada*, is the companion piece to *A Lot to Learn*, a Statement on Education, published in April 1992 by the Economic Council of Canada. The research underlying the two reports is the same; the main difference is that thedetails of the research are reported here. The conclusions and policy recommendations from *A Lot to Learn* have not changed and reflect the concensus views of the Economic Council of Canada. They are reproduced here as Chapter 7.

Contents

	Foreword	*vii*
1	**Introduction**	
	Return on Investment in Human Capital	1
	Contribution of Education to Economic Growth	3
	The Education "Industry"	4
2	**The Issue of Quality**	7
	Assessing the Quality of Education	7
	International Comparisons	11
	Interprovincial Comparisons	18
	Intertemporal Comparisons	22
	Crucial Aspects of Educational Achievement	23
	Opportunity to Learn and Related Questions	31
	Avenues for Future Research	37
	Appendix: Is Educational Testing a Valid Tool?	39
3	**The Learning Continuum**	41
	Adult Education and Training in Canada	41
	Full-time Training	41
	Short-term Courses and Part-time Training	46
	Barriers to Training	49
	Apprenticeship	51
	The National Picture	55
	Summary	57
	Conclusion	65
4	**The Economics of the Teaching Profession**	67
	A Profile of Teachers in Canada	68
	Teacher Supply and Demand	69
	Teacher Training	74
	Teachers' Earnings	75
	The Professionalization of Teaching	82
	Summary	82
5	**The Cost and Funding of Education**	87
	Canada's Situation	89
	Intraprovincial Comparison	97
	Appendix: Definitions of Educational Levels	102

6	**Education and Training: An International Perspective**	103
	Education, the Labour Market and the Economy:	
	How does Canada Rate?	103
	Competitiveness and the Coherence of Socio-Economic Systems	113
	Some Lessons for Enhancing Coherence in Canada	127
	Bibliography	130
7	**Conclusions and Policy Recommendations**	131
	Targets	133
	Indicators	134
	Directions for Change	134
	Towards a Comprehensive System	134
	Towards an Open System	137
	Towards a Responsive System	139
	Towards a Relevant System	140
	Concluding Remarks	142
	Bibliography	143
	Authors and Consultants	145

Foreword

Education and training issues have long been of concern to the members of the Economic Council. Education was the subject of the Second Annual Review in 1965 and a number of Council reports published in the 1970s, 1980s, and early 1990s emphasized the critical role of education and training for Canada's future. They demonstrated its importance in maintaining the competitiveness of the Canadian economy in an increasingly globalized trading environment, in strengthening its ability to adapt to changes in the industrial structure and in technology, and in improving the distribution of income and unemployment.

In recognition of the essential role played by the education and training systems in the social and economic spheres of Canadian life, the Economic Council decided to undertake a comprehensive examination of the way in which primary and secondary schools and the training system in Canada prepare young people for adult life. Based on its research, the Council released its Statement on Education, titled *A Lot to Learn,* in April 1992. This companion report sets out some of the analytical underpinnings of that statement.

Education is a cumulative process — skills that are learned well in the early years provide the foundation for future success. And early setbacks in learning are hard to correct, often leading to dropping out, followed by a lifetime of low wages and unstable employment patterns.

Our research also shows that employers and parents — and indeed, society as a whole — give conflicting signals to students and teachers. This lack of "coherence" is most evident in the transition from school to work. Large numbers of young Canadians do not value education. They cannot see clear pathways from school to work and therefore follow a process of trial and error that is in stark contrast to the clear pathways laid out in other industrial countries, particularly Japan and Germany.

We are very much aware that the task facing schools and teachers is much harder than it used to be: social institutions such as the family and the church have been weakened, and the student population has become more diverse. At the same time, the need for a strong education and training system has increased because the level of skills required in the world of work has escalated as a result of the transition to an information society.

It is our hope that these research findings will shed new light on the system's weaknesses and that the targets and policy directions proposed here will help Canadians to make education and training more effective and more responsive to their needs.

This is the last research report prepared for the Economic Council of Canada since, in February 1992, the federal Minister of Finance announced the decision to abolish the Council. The Council closed its doors on June 30, 1992. It is therefore fitting that this final report treats a topic that directly affects the lives of all Canadians and that requires all to work together in partnership so that real improvements to the system can be made.

Judith Maxwell

Chairman
Economic Council of Canada

1
Introduction

Education and training in Canada are currently under intense scrutiny. The reasons behind the rapidly-mounting debate vary but all are familiar. Contextual factors include globalization, technological change, trade liberalization, demographic shifts, fiscal restraint and privatization. The implications of these factors – with respect to the future needs of Canadians for knowledge and skills and the ability of the system to satisfy those needs – have become a matter of national concern and a major public policy issue.

Responses have been varied. Virtually all provinces have undertaken evaluations of their educational systems. The Council of Ministers of Education (CMEC) embarked on an ambitious project to compile and standardize tests of educational achievement. Indicators resulting from this project may include standardized achievement tests. Learning institutions, school boards and researchers – all are engaged in some form of critical evaluation.

At the national level, the Canadian Labour Force Development Board has been established to forge closer and more systematic links between the labour market and learning institutions. The learning dimensions of the federal Prosperity Initiative also reflect a conviction that skills development and a strategy to enhance productivity and competitiveness are central to Canada's future.

The intent of this report is to contribute to the debate by reporting empirical research on major aspects of education and training, and to evaluate the Canadian education system critically as to its past performance and future prospects. Human resource development is an important component of increased productivity and economic growth and education and training. In addition to being crucial to self-fulfillment and a variety of social goals, they constitute a large and important sector of economic activity. For these reasons alone a Council study is appropriate. Also, Canadians have a clear sense of urgency regarding education, training, and learning as a whole. Simply stated, "learning" is now a major public policy issue. Our hope is that the facts and figures generated by our program of research will contribute to public understanding in this important debate.

Return on Investment in Human Capital

In economic terms, education constitutes an investment in human capital — an investment with associated costs and benefits. The rate of return to education can be established by comparing the costs with the benefits. More precisely, the rate of return to education is determined by: *the average annual rate by which benefits exceed costs over a time period represented by an individual's active life.*

This method of calculating the rate of return is based on a particular view of education as a process — a view based on the theory of human capital. According to this theory, an individual will continue to invest in his or her own human capital (i.e., will continue studying) until such time as the marginal cost of the educational investment equals the marginal benefit. This benefit includes the increased earnings that are assumed to arise from the productivity increases that are directly related to the number of years spent in the educational system. However, this raises some interesting questions.

Does education actually increase individual productivity or does it simply act as a filter serving to identify those individuals who are already more productive? If the latter, then some individuals who are progressing through the educational system are already highly productive, and the educational system merely helps to point out who they are. It is argued that employers pay these individuals higher wages not because of the knowledge they have gained through their studies, but because they have demonstrated that they have the "right stuff" to earn a diploma. Generally speaking, research does not support this argument; it does, however, support the first interpretation: that education is an investment in human capital.

The education-as-filter theory implies that there are no private returns to education until graduation. Yet, comparisons of the productivity rates of drop-outs and graduates indicate that there are no significant differences. In fact, sometimes the former group outperforms the latter! The filter theory also suggests that, since a diploma serves primarily as an identifier, private returns should decline with years of experience.

Again, however, studies of productivity rates suggest that, far from declining with experience, private returns to education increase with years of experience. This contradicts the education-as-filter theory and supports the contention that education represents an investment in human capital with long-term benefits.

Lastly, it is not unreasonable to suppose that if the educational system serves no other purpose than to identify individuals who are already productive, other, less-costly filter mechanisms would have appeared over time. That has not happened. The fact is that, while it is possible for education to act as a filter for certain occupations, this phenomenon has not had any significant influence on decisions affecting education. For our purposes, therefore, the rate of return to education is defined in accordance with the theory of human capital.

According to the theory of human capital, two different productivity rates can be calculated: the private return to education, (i.e., the return an individual receives from his or her investment in education); and the public return to education, (i.e., the benefit society as a whole receives from individuals, institutions, and governments as a result of their combined investments in education).

Income is the variable used to measure the benefits of education. Net after-tax income is used to calculate the private rate of return to education; gross income is the basis for calculating the public rate of return. In the latter case, taxes are considered to benefit society as a whole rather than the individual who pays them. There are two kinds of costs: direct expenditures, made by an individual or by society; and indirect expenditures, which consist mainly of the income foregone during the time spent in school. For example, a student's private direct expenditure might include tuition fees and book purchases. Total direct public expenditures are obtained by adding public subsidies to this amount. Indirect expenditures are based essentially on estimates of foregone income, (i.e., the income an individual sacrifices in order to attend school). This foregone income is estimated as net income for an individual and as gross income for society as a whole.

Table 1.1 compares rates of return to education in 1985 by region for males and females who completed high school relative to those who did not. It should be noted that these figures reflect the return of an "additional" investment in education. High school students planning to obtain a diploma have to evaluate their potential additional gains from earning that diploma

Table 1.1
Private and Public Returns to Education, School Graduates vs Dropouts, Canada and Regions, 1985

	Men		Women	
	Private	Public	Private	Public
Canada	29.0	11.2	33.2	8.4
Atlantic Provinces	28.5	12.9	19.6	2.7
Quebec	11.3	4.4	21.8	7.4
Ontario	31.7	12.9	32.6	8.8
Manitoba/ Saskatchewan	39.4	16.1	47.3	12.3
Alberta	28.7	10.7	40.1	10.0
British Columbia	4.0	13.9	45.5	10.6

Source: Vaillancourt, François, "Private and Public Monetary Returns to Schooling in Canada, 1985," Working Paper, (forthcoming)

relative to dropping out, then deduct their "additional" costs, (e.g., tuition, book purchases, etc.) plus the amounts they stand to lose by not entering the labour market immediately.

What is immediately apparent from Table 1.1 is that, relative to dropping out, high-school graduation yields very high returns to both men and women. For Canada as a whole in 1985, males who completed high school could expect lifetime earnings 29 per cent higher than males who dropped out before completing high school. For females, the returns to high school completion compared to dropping out were 33 per cent. This highlights the value and importance of obtaining a high-school diploma for the individual, and underlines the adverse effects of dropping out. The jobs obtainable through possession of a high-school diploma generally pay much better than those obtainable without. Furthermore, private rates of return to high school completion are consistently higher than public rates of return. This is partly because students enjoy a subsidy. Direct private expenditures on education are actually extremely low compared with public expenditures because there are no tuition fees associated with public elementary and secondary school in Canada.

With the exception of the Atlantic provinces, private rates of return to high school completion relative to dropping out are higher for women than for men. It would seem, then, that female drop-outs are at a particular disadvantage in the labour market.

Interprovincial differences in private rates of return in 1985 were large and reflected differences in industrial structure and labour-force composition. The lowest rates were found in Quebec, particularly for men; the highest rates were found in Manitoba, Saskatchewan and British Columbia.

Contribution of Education to Economic Growth

The contribution of education to economic growth is most often measured using the growth-accounting method. This method assumes that there are basically three sources of growth: labour, capital and all other sources. The last of these — the residual component — includes the contributions made by such factors as general improvement in knowledge, better allocation of resources, improvements to infrastructure, technological change and, lastly, education. The variable most commonly used to measure the contribution of education is the average number of years of schooling achieved by the workforce. Theoretically, this variable should be "corrected" for variations in the quality of education. For instance, if it is true that the quality of education has declined over the past three or four decades, the growth-accounting method will overestimate the contribution of education to economic growth. However, the lack of adequate data on educational quality makes such an adjustment impossible.

The growth-accounting method has been used by many researchers to estimate the contribution of education to economic growth over a variety of time periods. The conclusion has always been that education contributes positively to growth. On average, research shows that on an annual basis education contributes approximately one-half a percentage point to economic growth. Table 1.2 illustrates the size of that contribution.

Some studies, however, have found that since the early 1980s the contribution of education to economic

Table 1.2
Contribution of Education to Economic Growth, 1909-1988, Canada (%)
(First Line – Absolute Contribution to Output Growth; Second Line – Relative Contribution)

Study	1909–1929	1928–1957	1950–1962	1962–1973	1973–1981	1981–1988
Bertram	0.35	0.67	—	—	—	—
	12.4	22.9	—	—	—	—
Lithwick	—	0.35	—	—	—	—
	—	11.0	—	—	—	—
Walters	—	—	0.2	—	—	—
	—	—	4.7	—	—	—
Kendrick[1]	—	—	—	0.5	0.6	—
	—	—	—	8.8	2.0	—
Macdonald Commission	—	—	—	0.5	0.8	—
	—	—	—	8.8	26.7	—
CLMPC	—	—	—	—	—	0.54
	—	—	—	—	—	16.2

[1] The 1962-1973 period refers to 1960-1973; the 1973-1981 period refers to 1973-1979.
Source: Based on CLMPC, "The Linkages Between Education and Training and Canada's Economic Performance", in *Quarterly Labour Market and Productivity Review*, Winter 1989-90

growth has been declining relative to the 1970s. Several factors may help explain this. First, demographic changes have contributed to a decline in the number of new entrants to the labour market. Following the baby-boom of the 1950s and 1960s, birth rates decreased. However, young people tend to have more years of formal education than the population as a whole — declining birth rates meant that fewer young people entered the labour force than in previous years, causing a decrease in the rate at which average education levels increased.

The decline in the contribution of education to economic growth can also be traced to the recession of the early 1980s and to the fact that labour-market imbalances have gradually increased since then. These imbalances were reflected in the simultaneous persistence of high levels of unemployment and labour shortages in certain sectors. At some point during the 1980s the education and training system appears to have faltered; it became less efficient at supporting economic growth. Today many employers are still experiencing difficulty in finding workers with the skills they need.

The Education "Industry"

The discussion so far has focussed on the contribution of education to growth in individual and national productivity. This contribution has long been regarded as important. As early as 1776, Adam Smith characterized education as a kind of capital formation in *The Wealth of Nations*. In addition, however, the education sector is a major contributor to the level of gross domestic product (Table 1.3).

Over the last thirty years, the education sector has accounted for between 5 and 8 per cent of real gross domestic product (in 1986 dollars). Education therefore constitutes a major Canadian "industry". Table 1.3 also shows the fluctuations in the education sector over the last 30 years. These were due to a multitude of causes including: the movement of the baby-boom and the subsequent baby-bust through the school system, the increase in the teacher/student ratio, the introduction of the community colleges and CEGEPs, the expansion of the university system in post-secondary education and the various educational reforms of the period. All of these influenced the size of the education sector.

Education is a highly labour-intensive industry. In 1991, over 850,000 persons — one out of every fourteen persons employed — worked in the education industry (Table 1.4). Although this ratio has not changed much over the last 15 years, the absolute number of employees in the education sector increased by 195,000 — or by approximately 30 per cent — between 1976 and 1991. This is all the more noteworthy because total school enrolment (all levels) has

Table 1.3
Gross Domestic Product (in Millions of 1986 dollars)

	1961 $	1961 %	1971 $	1971 %	1981 $	1981 %	1991 $	1991 %
Total	156,428	100.0	267,060	100.0	397,090	100.0	502,080	100.0
Non-business Sector[1]	20,991	13.4	27,446	10.3	37,124	9.3	42,918	8.5
Education[2]	9,392	6.0	21,716	8.1	24,856	6.3	28,067	5.6
Health[2]	8,528	5.5	15,871	5.9	23,821	6.0	31,860	6.3
Construction	13,809	8.8	17,318	6.5	27,158	6.8	31,804	6.3
Primary Industries	18,993	12.1	28,897	10.8	28,057	7.1	34,789	6.9
Transportation, Communication and Utilities	11,809	7.5	23,676	8.9	40,857	10.3	57,322	11.4
Trade	16,873	10.8	29,722	11.1	42,110	10.6	56,922	11.3
Manufacturing	31,127	19.9	56,669	21.2	77,896	19.6	84,971	16.9
Finance and Community Services	31,539	20.2	52,102	19.5	94,998	23.9	134,592	26.8
Adjusting Entry[3]	-6,632	-4.2	-6,357	-2.4	-213	0.1	-1,165	-0.2

[1] Nonprofit sector, excluding health and education.

[2] Including both public and private components.

[3] For the Technical description of this item, see Statistics Canada Catalogue 15-512, pp. 17-20.

Source: Statistics Canada Catalogue No. 15-512, 15-001 June 1991, December 1991

Table 1.4
Employment by Sector

	1976		1981		1986		1991	
	Thousands	%	Thousands	%	Thousands	%	Thousands	%
Total	9,477	100.0	11,001	100.0	11,531	100.0	12,340	100.0
Public Administration	678	7.2	767	7.0	796	6.9	832	6.7
Other Services	1,219	12.9	1,711	15.5	1,996	17.3	2,314	18.8
Education	661	7.0	709	6.4	771	6.7	856	6.9
Health	693	7.3	841	7.6	999	8.7	1,205	9.8
Construction	635	6.7	651	5.9	619	5.4	695	5.6
Primary Industries	707	7.5	809	7.4	752	6.5	728	5.9
Transportation, Communication and Utilities	823	8.7	910	8.3	889	7.7	916	7.4
Trade	1,644	17.3	1,884	17.1	2,064	17.9	2,169	17.6
Manufacturing	1,921	20.3	2,124	19.3	1,989	17.2	1,865	15.1
Finance, Insurance and Real Estate	496	5.2	594	5.4	657	5.7	760	6.2

Note: Percentages may not total 100 due to rounding.

Source: Statistics Canada 71-220

remained relatively stable since 1976 (Table 1.5), although its composition has changed.

Elementary and secondary enrolments continued to decline throughout the period, while post-secondary enrolment increased dramatically as a result of several factors. First, the baby-boom generation was the first to pursue post-secondary studies on a large scale, in terms of both absolute numbers and the percentage of that age group that went on to college and university. Since 1960, full-time post-secondary enrolment in Canada has increased more than eight-fold. Second, in an attempt to address this demand for further education and to provide alternative types of post-secondary education, provincial governments created the community college system. (In Quebec, students completing Grade 11 may then go on to attend a CEGEP.) Third, part-time enrolment at the post-secondary level also has increased substantially. At present, one in four Canadians is enrolled in school on a full- or part-time basis.

These demographic and institutional changes, plus the forces of inflation unleashed in the late '70s and early '80s, precipitated an increase in total educational expenditure of more than twenty-times the amount spent in 1988/89 compared to 1961 (Table 1.6). The relative share of expenditures on the primary and secondary sectors declined substantially between 1961 and 1971. After 1971, however, the spending shares in these sectors stabilized, even though student enrolments continued to decline in both absolute and relative terms. The impressive increases in post-secondary enrolment since 1971 have not been matched by corresponding increases in expenditures. Fiscal stringency, arising in part out of federal and provincial budget deficits, continues to act as a rein on educational spending.

Our knowledge of vocational training in Canada is much less precise: much of that training takes place informally, on the job. However, the federal government alone spends over $1 billion annually on training, and the recent Human Resource Development and Training Survey undertaken by Statistics Canada estimates that Canadian employers also spend about $1.4 billion each year on formal training courses.

All in all, the learning sector is large and economically very important. But lately, in mounting public debate, its effectiveness is increasingly being called into question. For this reason, the Economic Council of Canada embarked upon a program of research that culminated in the publication in April 1992, of *A Lot to Learn*. That statement contains a summary of the Council's major research findings as well as a set of recommended policy directions. The present volume contains the detailed analytical underpinnings of those findings and, in some cases, new research that goes beyond what was reported earlier.

Table 1.5
School Enrolment by Level of Study

	1960-61 Thousands	%	1965-66 Thousands	%	1970-71 Thousands	%	1975-76 Thousands	%	1980-81 Thousands	%	1985-86 Thousands	%	1989-90 Thousands	%
Total	4,367.5	100.0	5475.0	100.0	6,520.4	100.0	6,371.8	100.0	5,994.8	100.0	6,167.4	100.0	6,408.8	100.0
Elementary-secondary	4,204.4	96.3	5201.4	95.0	5,888.3	90.3	5,594.7	87.8	5,106.3	85.2	4,927.8	79.9	5085.5	79.4
CEGEPs[1]	—	—	—	—	74.4	1.1	117.7	1.8	135.4	2.3	224.3[3]	3.6	216.0[3]	3.4
Community Colleges[1]	49.4	1.1	69.4	1.3	91.7	1.4	103.3	1.6	125.4	2.1	263.1[4]	4.3	288.4[4]	4.5
University[2]	113.7	2.6	204.2	3.7	466.0[5]	7.1	556.1[5]	8.7	627.7[5]	10.5	752.2[5]	12.2	819.0[5]	12.8
Total full-time enrolment	4,367.5	100.0	5,475.0	100.0	6,375.8	100.0	6,186.8	100.0	5,749.7	100.0	5,717.2	100.0	5927.1	100.0

[1] Data prior to 1985-86 do not include part-time CEGEP and Community College students.
[2] Data prior to 1970-71 do not include part-time University students.
[3] Of which 60.1 were part-time in 1985-86, 61.7 in 1989-90.
[4] Of which 105.1 were part-time in 1985-86, 115.4 in 1989-90.
[5] Of which 144.6 were part-time in 1970-71, 185.0 in 1975-76, 245.1 in 1980-81, 285.0 in 1985-86, 304.6 in 1989-90.

Source: Statistics Canada Catalogue No. 81-229

Table 1.6
Expenditure on Education by Level, Canada ($ Millions)

	1961 $	%	1971 $	%	1980-81 $	%	1988-89 $	%
Total	1,930.7	100.0	8,349.7	100.0	22,188.6	100.0	41,791.6	100.0
Elementary-Secondary	1,499.5	77.7	5,389.3	64.6	14,568.0	65.7	26,475.1	63.4
Colleges	58.4	3.0	530.0	6.3	1,850.2	8.4	3,311.2	7.9
Universities	310.6	16.1	1,864.5	22.3	4,438.3	20.0	8,548.7	20.5
Vocational Training Schools	62.2	3.2	565.9	6.8	1,332.2	6.0	3,456.7	8.3

Percentages may not total 100 due to rounding.

Source: Statistics Canada Catalogue No. 81-229 Annual

2

The Issue of Quality

Schooling in Canada has all the characteristics of a monopolistic industry. There are, of course, some differences among the provinces, but it is generally compulsory between the ages of 6 and 15 at the primary and secondary levels, and it is provided almost entirely by the public school system. (Fewer than 5 per cent of the total elementary and secondary school population is enrolled in private schools).

In the absence of market pressure, monopolies tend to pay less attention to the quality of their products than might otherwise be the case. Indeed, there has been growing concern about the quality of public education in Canada among people in business, politics, the media, and the education sector itself. According to a survey undertaken by the Canadian Labour Market and Productivity Centre in 1990, only 42 per cent of the business leaders and 60 per cent of the labour leaders surveyed believe that Canada's elementary and secondary schools play an adequate role in educating and training Canadians; 36 and 51 per cent, respectively, consider illiteracy to be "very significant" or "somewhat significant" among Canadian workers. What can be done to improve Canadian education?

Assessing the Quality of Education

In order to assess the quality of an educational system, one must have a clear view of what education is expected to achieve. This is not a simple issue: philosophical discussions centering on the goals of education have been ongoing since at least the days of Plato and Aristotle. An exhaustive list has been provided by Goodlad (see The Goals of Education). It is unlikely that any education system has ever been systematically assessed against all of Goodlad's criteria; indeed, it may be impossible to do so. Equally problematic, however, is the question of how to measure success by weighing one criterion against another. In this chapter, three major methods of assessing the quality of education are reviewed: public opinion polls; quality indicators; and comparisons among systems or through time. Factors which influence educational achievement are also discussed.

Public Opinion Polls

One way to assess the quality of the educational system is through public opinion polls. This technique involves at least two problems when it is applied to questions concerning education: the responses may be inconsistent; and adult respondents may judge the current system by colouring it with recollections of their own past schooling rather than by assessing present conditions and the qualities needed for the future success of today's students.

To illustrate: the Canadian Education Association commissioned public opinion polls in 1979, 1984 and 1990 (Williams and Millinoff, 1990; Flower, 1984, CEA Task Force on Public Improvement in Educational Decisions, 1979). In 1984 the largest groups of respondents said that schools were better than they were in 1979 (Figure 2.1) but the second largest group said they were worse. In a follow-up poll taken in 1990 most respondents said either that there had been no change since 1984 or that schools had improved. When asked to assign a grade to the school system, however, declining proportions rated the school system as very good, while the proportions assigning schools grades of C, D or F increased (Figure 2.2).

As for students' intellectual development, public opinion appears to be reasonably well satisfied with schools teaching science, mathematics, and technology: the "satisfied" responses exceeded the "dissatisfied" responses by 48 percentage points. At the same time, those satisfied exceeded those dissatisfied by 37 percentage points with respect to students' ability to solve problems, 25 per cent with respect to their desire for lifelong learning, and 24 per cent with respect to their ability to read, write, and speak properly. (There is a curious inconsistency here: it is unlikely that young people will excel in science and technology or become good at problem-solving if their reading and writing skills are only mediocre.)

Should another interpretation be applied to these findings? Is it possible that public opinion is unduly influenced by the responses of parents whose knowledge of science and mathematics is inferior to that of

The Goals of Education

I ACADEMIC GOALS

1 Mastery of Basic Skills and Fundamental Processes

    1.1   Learn to read, write, and handle basic arithmetical operations.
    1.2   Learn to acquire ideas through reading and listening.
    1.3   Learn to communicate ideas through writing and speaking.
    1.4   Learn to utilize mathematical concepts.
    1.5   Develop the ability to utilize available sources of information.

2 Intellectual Development

    2.1   Develop the ability to think rationally, including problem-solving skills, application of principles of logic, and skill in using different modes of inquiry.
    2.2   Develop the ability to use and evaluate knowledge, i.e., critical and independent thinking that enables one to make judgments and decisions in a wide variety of life roles - citizen, consumer, worker, etc. - as well as in intellectual activities.
    2.3   Accumulate a general fund of knowledge, including information and concepts in mathematics, literature, natural science, and social science.
    2.4   Develop positive attitudes toward intellectual activity, including curiosity and a desire for further learning.
    2.5   Develop an understanding of change in society.

II VOCATIONAL GOALS

3 Career Education/Vocational Education

    3.1   Learn how to select an occupation that will be personally satisfying and suitable to one's skills and interests.
    3.2   Learn to make decisions based on an awareness and knowledge of career options.
    3.3   Develop salable skills and specialized knowledge that will prepare one to become economically independent.
    3.4   Develop habits and attitudes, such as pride in good workmanship, that will make one a productive participant in economic life.
    3.5   Develop positive attitudes toward work, including acceptance of the necessity a living and an appreciation of the social value and dignity of work.

III SOCIAL, CIVIC, AND CULTURAL GOALS

4 Interpersonal Understandings

    4.1   Develop a knowledge of opposing value systems and their influence on the individual and society.
    4.2   Develop an understanding of how members of a family function under different family patterns as well as within one's own family.
    4.3   Develop skill in communicating effectively in groups.
    4.4   Develop the ability to identify with and advance the goals and concerns of others.
    4.5   Learn to form productive and satisfying relations with others based on respect, trust, cooperation, consideration, and caring.
    4.6   Develop a concern for humanity and an understanding of international relations.
    4.7   Develop an understanding and appreciation of cultures different from one's own.

5 Citizenship Participation

    5.1   Develop historical perspective.
    5.2   Develop knowledge of the basic workings of the government.
    5.3   Develop a willingness to participate in the political life of the nation and the community.
    5.4   Develop a commitment to the values of liberty, government by consent of the governed, representational government, and one's responsibility for the welfare of all.
    5.5   Develop an understanding of the interrelationships among complex organizations and

5.8 Develop an understanding of the basic interdependence of the biological and physical resources of the environment.
5.9 Develop the ability to act in light of this understanding of interdependence.

6 **Encultur ation**

6.1 Develop insight into the values and characteristics, including language, of the civilization of which one is a member.
6.2 Develop an awareness and understanding of one's cultural heritage and become familiar with the achievements of the past that have inspired and influenced humanity.
6.3 Develop understanding of the manner in which traditions from the past are operative today and influence the direction and values of society.
6.4 Understand and adopt the norms, values, and traditions of the groups of which one is a member.
6.5 Learn how to apply the basic principles and concepts of the fine arts and humanities to the appreciation of the aesthetic contributions of other cultures.

7 **Moral and Ethical Character**

7.1 Develop the judgment to evaluate events and phenomena as good or evil.
7.2 Develop a commitment to truth and values.
7.3 Learn to utilize values in making choices.
7.4 Develop moral integrity.
7.5 Develop an understanding of the necessity for moral conduct.

IV PERSONAL GOALS

8 **Emotional and Physical Well-being**

8.1 Develop the willingness to receive emotional impressions and to expand one's affective sensitivity.
8.2 Develop the competence and skills for continuous adjustment and emotional stability, including coping with social change.
8.3 Develop a knowledge of one's own body and adopt health practices that support and sustain it, including avoiding the consumption of harmful or addictive substances.
8.4 Learn to use leisure time effectively.
8.5 Develop physical fitness and recreational skills.
8.6 Develop the ability to engage in constructive self-criticism.

9 **Creativity and Aesthetic Expression**

9.1 Develop the ability to deal with problems in original ways.
9.2 Develop the ability to be tolerant of new ideas.
9.3 Develop the ability to be flexible and to consider different points of view.
9.4 Develop the ability to experience and enjoy different forms of creative expression.
9.5 Develop the ability to evaluate various forms of aesthetic expression.
9.6 Develop the willingness and ability to communicate through creative work in an active way.
9.7 Seek to contribute to cultural and social life through one's artistic, vocational, and avocational interests.

10 **Self-realization**

10.1 Learn to search for meaning in one's activities, and develop a philosophy of life.
10.2 Develop the self-confidence necessary for knowing and confronting one's self.
10.3 Learn to assess realistically and live with one's limitations and strengths.
10.4 Recognize that one's self-concept is developed in interaction with other people.
10.5 Develop skill in making decisions with purpose.
10.6 Learn to plan and organize the environment in order to realize one's goals.
10.7 Develop willingness to accept responsibility for one's own decisions and their consequences
10.8 Develop skill in selecting some personal, life-long learning goals and the means to attain them.

Source: Goodlad, *A Place Called School: Prospects for the Future*, (1984)

Figure 2.1
Changes in the Quality of Schools, 1979, 1984 and 1990, Canada

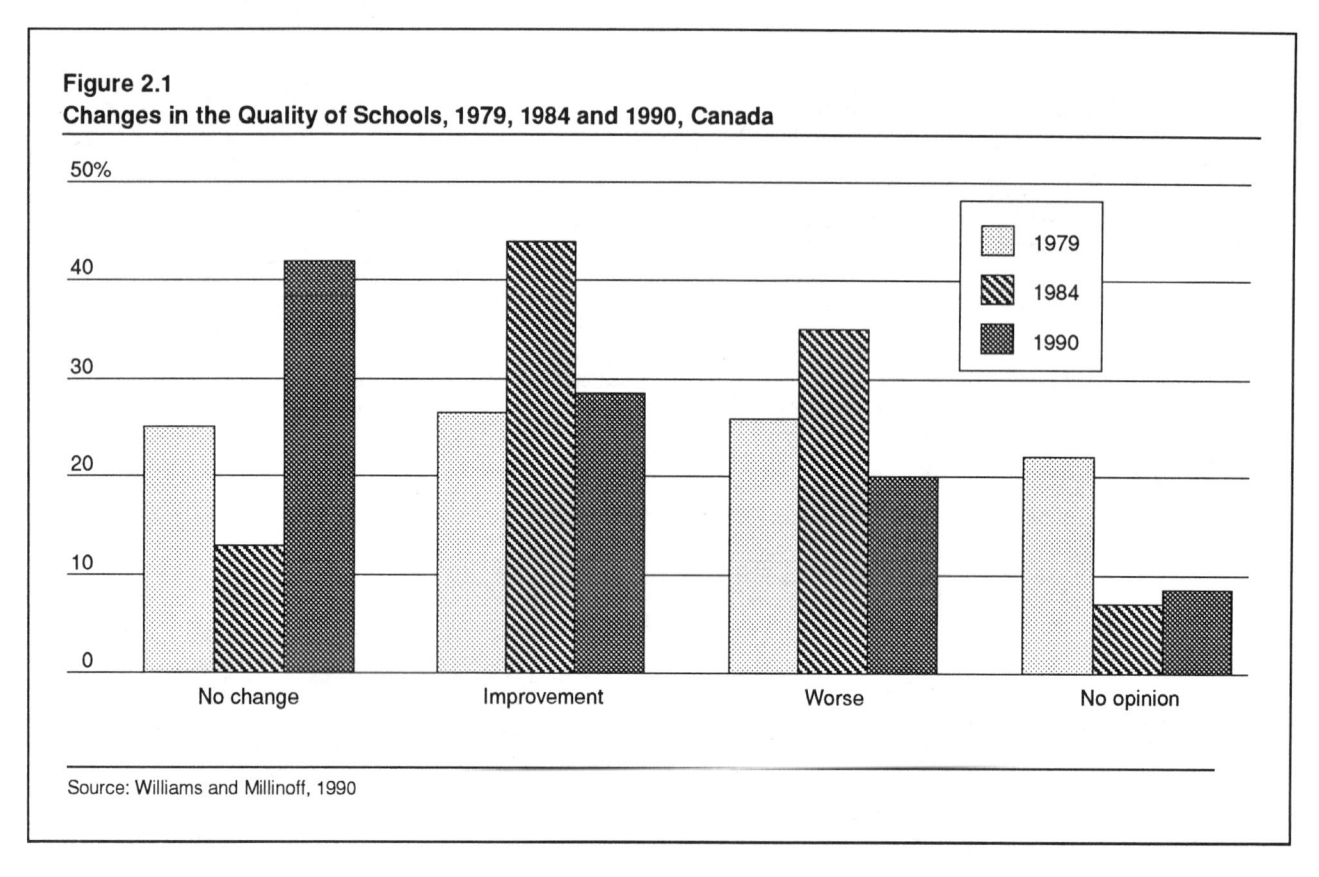

Source: Williams and Millinoff, 1990

Figure 2.2
Grades Assigned to Community Schools, 1979, 1984 and 1990, Canada

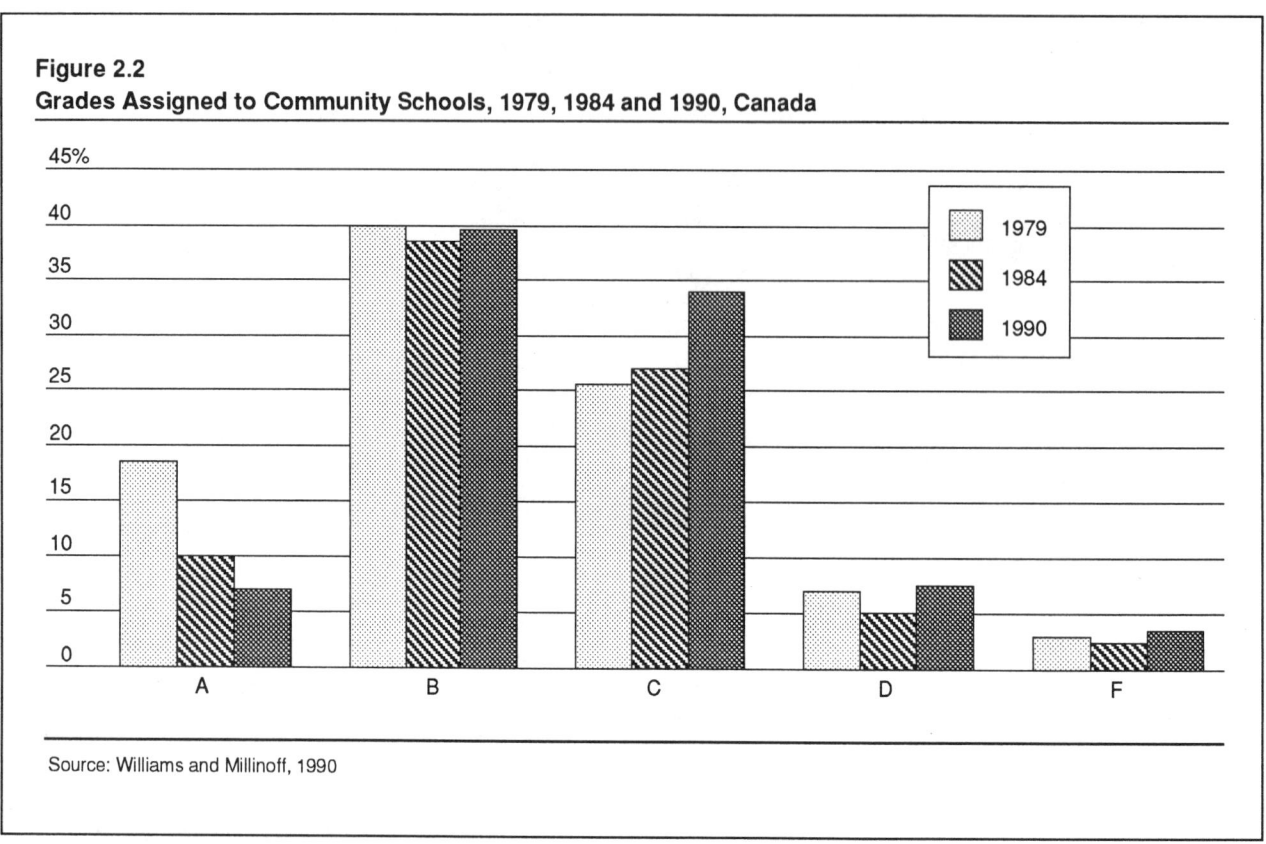

Source: Williams and Millinoff, 1990

their children, even though the scientific/mathematical knowledge of young Canadians is inferior to that of young people in other countries? It is much easier for most parents to recognize poor performance in reading, writing and language.

Public opinion concerning the human and social development of young people is also contradictory. For example, there is far more satisfaction than dissatisfaction with students' racial tolerance (a difference of 47 per cent), but the difference with respect to students' ability to "tolerate, respect and co-operate with others" is much smaller (21 per cent). "Self-worth and confidence" are supposed to be rooted in "personal discipline", yet, while the former scored 44 per cent, the latter rated only 24 per cent.

Opinions about teaching staff are relatively positive: the proportion of respondents who gave staff an A or a B for effectiveness was 59 per cent; for responsiveness to parents' concerns, 58 per cent; and for the adequate preparation of girls in science, mathematics, and technology, 45 per cent. This last result is remarkably close to reality: according to the Second International Mathematics Study (Robitaille and Garden, 1989), girls make up about 40 per cent of the total number of Canadian students taking advanced mathematics in the last year of high school; in addition, boys tended to score higher than girls in mathematics. Similarly, in the Second International Science Study (International Association for the Evaluation of Educational Achievement, 1988), Canadian boys tended to outperform girls.

How should these findings be interpreted? Are Canadians satisfied with the lower performance of girls? Do they consider this to be unavoidable under present social circumstances, or are they simply poor judges of teachers' achievement.

Some of the other results of the opinion survey are closer to expert judgment in these matters. In the Canadian Education Association poll, 53 per cent of respondents gave teachers an A or a B for "preparing students adequately for post-secondary education", but only 36 per cent did so for "preparing them adequately for the work force". Public opinion judges that the Canadian school system does not serve well the 60 to 70 per cent of young people who cannot or will not go on to post-secondary studies.

Indicators of Quality

The level of participation in schooling and measures of cognitive achievement are among the most important indicators of the quality of an education system.

Accessibility is the first of these indicators. In this respect, Canada compares very well with other industrial countries. In terms of such criteria as median years of formal schooling, high-school enrolment and graduation rates, and the level of participation in post-secondary education, Canada is among the top nations of the world. These are important indicators of the accessibility of the system, but they do not, in themselves, demonstrate its quality. For example, a system cannot be described as good or efficient if it requires 12 years of schooling to teach what other systems manage to teach in 10 years. Similarly, there is little virtue in post-secondary schooling if it serves as an expensive (and much delayed) remedial instruction in subject matter that should have been acquired or otherwise mastered earlier. In one Canadian university, for example, 18.4 per cent of first-year students did not go on to their second year because of academic failure or because they left the post-secondary system permanently (Gilbert, Evers, and Auger, 1989): in such situations, the first year at university serves as a very expensive screening method.

Information concerning achievement with respect to most of the goals of education listed by Goodland (1984) is unavailable. Some information is available on cognitive achievement (what students know), based on test results, but the evidence is fragmentary and is not easy to interpret. Also, because education is a jealously guarded provincial responsibility, it is difficult to obtain a coherent *total* picture of Canadian educational achievement. The following pages constitute an attempt to assemble the pieces of that jigsaw puzzle and to interpret the picture that emerges through comparisons over time between Canadian provinces and with other countries.

International Comparisons
Mathematics

SECOND INTERNATIONAL MATHEMATICS STUDY, 1980-82
The International Association for the Evaluation of Educational Achievement (IEA) conducted a number of studies of educational outcomes in the mid-1960s. ("Outcomes" in this context refers primarily to scores on

achievement tests — i.e., students' marks.) No Canadian province participated in that first set of studies.

The tests of the Second International Mathematics Study (SIMS) were administered in 1980-82. Two Canadian provinces — British Columbia and Ontario — participated in SIMS (Robitaille and Garden, 1989; Robitaille, 1990). This survey investigated the mathematics achievements of two "populations", described below. Internationally agreed-upon sets of mathematical test problems were administered to scientifically-selected samples of students in each participating system, and the results were evaluated.

Population A

Population A consisted of all students in the grade (year level) in which the majority of students were between 13 years and 13 years, 11 months old by the middle of the school year; in most participating countries, this corresponded to Grade 8.

Twenty systems participated. The achievements of 16 of those in industrialized countries are summarized in Table 2.1. Of the systems not included in the table, three are in countries (Nigeria, Swaziland, and Thailand) that cannot be regarded as industrialized, and one is in a country (Luxembourg) that, while industrialized, is also heavily agricultural and thus is not typical of the group selected.

The evaluation of the SIMS Population A is relatively simple. In almost all industrialized countries, schooling is still compulsory at this level, as is mathematics a required subject. Nevertheless, some caveats are necessary: 1) in Japan and Hong Kong, the test material was deemed too easy for Grade 8 students and so the test was administered to students in Grade 7; and 2) while compulsory schooling begins at age 6 in most countries, in Scandinavia it begins at age 7. It follows, therefore, that the Population A students from Japan, Hong Kong, Finland and Sweden had one year less schooling than those in the other systems.

The following results of Table 2.1 are noteworthy:

- Japan leads by a wide margin.

- The Canadian systems are close to the median and to the international mean for the 16 industrialized countries, with British Columbia slightly ahead of Ontario.

- The performance of students from the United States is mediocre.

Population B

Population B consisted of all students who were in the normally accepted terminal grade of the secondary school system and in whose academic programs mathematics formed a substantial part. "A substantial part" was interpreted by SIMS as comprising at least five hours per week of class time.

Fourteen industrialized countries participated in the SIMS Population B study. (France and the Netherlands, which took part in the A study, were not included in the B study.) At this level, international comparisons become very difficult for several reasons:

- The definition of "terminal grade of secondary education" differs from system to system. In most systems, this corresponded to Grade 12, but in England and Wales, Ontario, and parts of the Hong Kong and Swedish systems, it is Grade 13; in the Scottish system, it is partly Grade 11 and partly Grade 12.

- The results of the first group of IEA studies showed that the greater the proportion of an age cohort that completes high school, the lower its average achievement tends to be. Among the 14 industrialized systems, the proportion of students persevering

---

Table 2.1
Average National or Provincial Test Scores, Second International Mathematics Study Population A, Age 13, 1980-82

Rank	Country or Province	Average Score
1	Japan	61.9
2	Netherlands	56.7
3	Hungary	55.6
4	Belgium: Flemish region	53.2
5	France	52.6
6	**Canada: British Columbia**	**51.5**
7	Belgium: French region	51.4
8	**Canada: Ontario**	**49.2**
9	Hong Kong	49.0
10	U.K.: Scotland	48.3
11	U.K.: England and Wales	47.4
12	New Zealand	47.2
13	Finland	46.7
14	United States	45.3
15	Israel	45.1
16	Sweden	41.8
Mean		50.2

Source: Robitaille and Garden (1989); Schweitzer (1992a)

to the last year of high school ranged from 92 per cent (Japan) to 17 per cent (England and Wales, and New Zealand).

- Not all systems have five hours of compulsory mathematics in the last year of high school. It is reasonable to assume that only those students who are relatively strong in mathematics volunteer to take this subject at that level. A more selective system is likely to yield stronger achievement. Population B as a proportion of the grade group ranged from a high of 100 per cent in Hungary, where mathematics is compulsory in Grade 12, to a low of 10 per cent in Israel.

The crude achievement results are therefore misleading. We have adjusted these raw results for years of schooling (expected sign is positive) and retention rates (expected sign is negative). For the details of the methodology, see Schweitzer (1992a). The adjusted results are shown in Table 2.2; among the most notable:

- Japan and Hong Kong were the top achievers.

- The Canadian provinces registered below the medi-

Table 2.2
Average National or Provincial Test Scores, Second International Mathematics Study, Population B, End of Secondary Schooling, 1980-82

Rank	Country or Province	Adjusted[1]	Unadjusted
1	Japan	67.5	68.4
2	Hong Kong	64.7	72.7
3	Finland	59.0	58.1
4	Hungary	53.3	31.6
5	Sweden	50.5	55.0
6	New Zealand	49.6	51.1
7	Belgium: Flemish region	47.7	49.8
8	U.K.: Scotland	47.6	40.0
9	U.K.: England & Wales	47.2	58.8
10	**Canada: Ontario**	**44.9**	**48.8**
11	Belgium: French region	43.7	45.7
12	**Canada: British Columbia**	**42.9**	**33.2**
13	Israel	41.7	46.1
14	United States	34.8	35.7
	Mean		49.7

[1] Adjusted for years of schooling and retention rates.
Source: Robitaille and Garden (1989); Schweitzer (1992a).

Table 2.3
Average National or Provincial Test Scores in Mathematics, Educational Testing Service Age 13, 1988

Rank	Country or Province	Average Score (%)
1	South Korea	75.9
2	**Quebec**	**71.1**
3	**British Columbia**	**70.6**
4	**New Brunswick**	**67.1**
5	Spain	65.4
6	**Ontario**	**65.1**
7	United Kingdom	64.4
8	Ireland	62.9
9	United States	56.2
	Mean	66.5

Source: Quebec, Ministère de l'Éducation, *Education Indicators for the Elementary and Secondary Levels*, 1989

an; Ontario's mean achievement was stronger than British Columbia's, but that is entirely attributable to the fact that at the time of SIMS, calculus was not included in the B.C. curriculum. (This has been changed since then.)

- Again, the United States performed very poorly.

- In some instances, the adjustment for years of schooling and retention rates effected substantial changes — for example, a significant improvement in the case of Hungary, a remarkable deterioration in the case of England and Wales, and a substantial reduction in the difference between Ontario and British Columbia.

Educational Testing Service, 1988

In 1988, the Educational Testing Service (a private American research organization) conducted an international study of 13-year-olds, which included students from four Canadian provinces (Lapointe et al., 1989). The mathematics results are summarized in Table 2.3. One notes, in particular:

- South Korea is in first place.

- Three Canadian provinces are in second, third, and fourth places.

- Ontario is slightly below the international mean but significantly behind Quebec and British Columbia.

- The U.S. performance is, again, very poor.

Table 2.4
Average National or Provincial Test Scores in Mathematics, Educational Testing Service, Age 9, 1991

Rank	Country or Province	Average Score (%)
1	South Korea	74.8
2	Hungary	68.2
3	Taiwan	68.1
4	Soviet Union[1]	65.9
5	Israel[2]	64.4
6	Spain[3]	61.9
7	Ireland	60.0
8	**Canada**[4]	**59.9**
9	United States	58.4
10	Slovenia	55.8
	Mean	63.7
	Quebec	**64.3**
	British Columbia	**61.9**
	New Brunswick	**59.8**
	Ontario	**56.7**

[1] Russian-language schools only, in 14 republics.
[2] Hebrew-language schools only.
[3] Spanish-language schools only; excludes schools in the Catalan autonomous community.
[4] Quebec, Ontario, British Columbia, and the English-language schools of New Brunswick.

Source: Lapointe *et al.* (1992a)

Educational Testing Service, 1991

In 1991, the Educational Testing Service conducted another international assessment of mathematics and science achievement, this time for 9-year-olds as well as for 13-year-olds (Lapointe *et al.*, 1992b).

For the 9-year-old group, 14 countries participated. Canada was represented by four provinces — Quebec, Ontario, British Columbia, and the English-language schools of New Brunswick. Educational Testing Service chose to report separately on the achievements of the countries whose sampled population were regarded as "comprehensive", and those "with exclusions or low participation." Table 2.4 shows the results for the "comprehensive" populations, as well as the individual results for the Canadian provinces. The following findings emerge:

• There was a strong showing by Hungary and countries of the Far East.

• Canada is well below the mean of the 10 industrial countries included in the list.

• Among the Canadian provinces, only Quebec performed above the international mean.

• Again, there was a weak showing by the United States.

• Ontario scores even below the United States.

Twenty-one countries participated in the survey conducted for 13-year-olds, and all Canadian provinces except Prince Edward Island took part. Table 2.5 lists all countries with "comprehensive" populations, except Jordan, which does not fall among the industrialized countries. The main findings are as follows:

• There was a strong showing by South Korea and Taiwan.

• Canada is below the mean of the 14 industrialized countries.

• Again, the performance of the United States is very weak.

Table 2.5
Average National Test Scores in Mathematics, Educational Testing Service, Age 13, 1991

Rank	Country or Province	Average Score (%)
1	South Korea	73.4
2	Taiwan	72.7
3	Switzerland[1]	70.8
4	Soviet Union[2]	70.2
5	Hungary	68.4
6	France	64.2
7	Italy[3]	64.0
8	Israel	63.1
9	**Canada**	**62.0**
10	Scotland	60.6
11	Ireland	60.5
12	Slovenia	57.1
13	Spain[4]	55.4
14	United States	53.3
	Mean	64.1

[1] Students in 15 cantons only; excludes students in private and Romansch-language schools, and all students in the remaining 11 cantons.
[2] Russian-language schools only, in 14 republics.
[3] Province of Emilia-Romagna only.
[4] Spanish-language schools only; excludes schools in the Catalan autonomous community.

Source: Lapointe *et al.* (1992a)

Science

SECOND INTERNATIONAL SCIENCE STUDY, 1983-86

The Second International Science Study (SISS) was a counterpart of SIMS and was undertaken between 1983 and 1986. The study investigated the academic achievement in science of three age groups (International Association for the Evaluation of Educational Achievement, 1988; Crocker, 1990). Population 1 in this study was comprised of students approximately 10 years of age (Grade 5 in Canada), while those students in Population 2 were approximately 14 years old (Grade 9). Students in population 3 were those taking the highest level of high-school courses in biology, chemistry, or physics.

Population 1

Sixteen systems participated at this level. The "core test" of 24 items covered general science subjects appropriate for the age level of the students. Table 2.6 lists the order of achievement for 15 of the industrialized systems (the Philippines are excluded). The following results are noteworthy:

- The far-eastern systems had the highest scores (Japan, South Korea) as well as the lowest (Hong Kong, Singapore) positions.
- Canada, particularly French Canada, scored reasonably well This was due largely to Quebec's strong showing: French-language students from the other provinces did not score as well.
- At this level, the United States was very close to the mean of the 15 systems.

Population 2

The core test for this population included 30 items. Of the 17 systems that took part, the scores for the 15 industrialized nations appear in Table 2-7 (Thailand and the Philippines are omitted). The following results are noted:

Table 2.6
Average National Test Scores[1],
Second International Science Study
Population 1, Age 10, 1983-86

Rank	Country	Average Score (%)
1-2	South Korea	64.2
3	Finland	63.8
4	Sweden	61.3
5	Canada: French	60.4
6	Hungary	60.0
7	Canada: English	57.1
8	Italy	55.8
9	United States	55.0
10	Australia	53.8
11	Norway	52.9
12	Poland	49.6
13	England	48.8
14-15	Hong-Kong	46.7
14-15	Singapore	46.7
	Mean	56.0

[1] On core test of 24 items.

Source: IEA (1988); Schweitzer (1992a)

Table 2.7
Average National Test Scores[1],
Second International Science Study
Population 2, Age 14, 1983-86

Rank	Country	Average Score (%)
1	Hungary	72.3
2	Japan	67.3
3	Netherlands	66.0
4	**Canada: English**	**62.0**
5	Finland	61.7
6	Sweden	61.3
7-8	South Korea	60.3
7-8	Poland	60.3
9	**Canada: French**	**60.0**
10	Norway	59.7
11	Australia	59.3
12-13	England	55.7
12-13	Italy	55.7
14-15	Singapore	55.0
14-15	United States	55.0
16	Hong Kong	54.7
	Mean	60.6

[1] On core test of 30 items.

Source: IEA (1988); Schweitzer (1992a)

- There is a substantial dispersion among the Far Eastern systems (Japan is second; South Korea is several ranks below that; and Singapore and Hong Kong are at the bottom.
- English Canada performs well, but French Canada drops below the median. This is due to the very weak performance of Francophone students outside Quebec: Quebec's Francophone students scored 61.0, while those outside Quebec scored only 52.3.
- By age 14, the United States is well below the international mean.

Population 3

The test area for Population 3 covered biology, chemistry, and physics, although the students who took part could choose any one of these subject areas. In addition to the 30 items core test for each subject, an additional core test of 30 items was administered to each participant, irrespective of the subject tested. The results reported here are for 15 systems. South Korea did not participate at this level. Hong Kong administered the test separately to Form 6 students (attending the colony's Chinese system) and Form 7 students (attending the English system), and reported accordingly.

As with the mathematics test, the raw achievement data was adjusted for years of schooling and retention rates. The adjusted and unadjusted results for science achievement are given in Table 2.8. The most outstanding features are:

- The excellent performance of Hong Kong.
- Japan's good, but not outstanding, performance (its very good showing in the core test was offset by its relatively weak performance in biology).
- The mediocre score reported by Singapore.
- Canada's poor showing (both English and French).
- The very weak U.S. performance.
- The last place occupied by Italy (ascribed to the dominance of the humanities in that country's educational system).

EDUCATIONAL TESTING SERVICE, 1988

The science component of the 1988 ETS study of 13-year-olds is summarized in Table 2.9. Here, the outstanding points are:

- The strong performance of British Columbia, outscoring South Korea.

Table 2.8
Average National Test Scores, Second International Science Study, Population 3 End of Secondary Schooling, 1983-86

Rank	Country	Average Score (%) Adjusted[1]	Unadjusted
1	Hong Kong: Form 7	65.1	71.6
2	Hong Kong: Form 6	64.5	63.4
3	U.K.: England	59.5	68.3
4	Hungary	59.3	61.3
5	Japan	59.0	57.5
6	Norway	57.6	50.0
7	Singapore	57.4	66.2
8	Poland	55.9	55.7
9	Australia	54.9	53.1
10	Finland	52.9	47.4
11	Sweden	52.0	52.3
12	**Canada: French**	**49.8**	**36.0**
13	**Canada: English**	**49.6**	**46.7**
14	United States	45.2	40.6
15	Italy	35.0	41.6
	Mean		54.5

[1] Adjusted for years of schooling and retention rates.

Source: IEA (1988); Schweitzer (1992a)

Table 2.9
Average National or Provincial Test Scores in Science, Educational Testing Service Age 13, 1988

Rank	Country or Province	Average Score (%)
1	**British Columbia**	**69.0**
2	South Korea	68.7
3	United Kingdom	63.8
4	**Quebec**	**62.9**
5	**Ontario**	**62.6**
6	Spain	61.7
7	**New Brunswick**	**60.1**
8	United States	56.4
9	Ireland	55.4
	Mean	62.3

Source: Quebec, Ministère de l'Éducation, *Education Indicators for the Elementary and Secondary Levels*, 1989

- The weak performance of New Brunswick.
- The poor showing of the United States, confirming the SISS Population 2 results.

EDUCATIONAL TESTING SERVICE, 1991

In 1991, ETS also tested nine and 13-year-old students in science (Tables 2.10 and 2.11). As in the mathematics segment of the study, 14 countries participated. Here, again, Canada was represented by Quebec, Ontario, British Columbia, and the English-language schools of New Brunswick. As with the corresponding mathematics study reported earlier, the results of the "comprehensive" populations are reported here:

- Again, two far-eastern countries occupy the two top spots.
- The 9 and 10-year-olds from the United States performed relatively better than the older age groups.
- Canada's performance in the 9-10 age group is as good as, or slightly better than, the average for the other industrial countries listed.

Table 2.10
Average National Test Scores in Science, Educational Testing Service, Age 9, 1991

Rank	Country	Average Score (%)
1	South Korea	69.9
2	Taiwan	66.7
3	United States	64.7
4	**Canada**[1]	**62.8**
5	Hungary	62.5
6	Spain[2]	61.7
7	Soviet Union[3]	61.5
8	Israel[4]	61.2
9	Slovenia	57.7
10	Ireland	56.5
	Mean	62.3
	British Columbia	**65.9**
	Quebec	**62.8**
	Ontario	**62.1**
	New Brunswick	**61.6**

[1] Quebec, Ontario, British Columbia, and the English-language schools of New Brunswick
[2] Spanish-language schools only; also excludes schools in the Catalan autonomous community.
[3] Russian-language schools only, in 14 republics.
[4] Hebrew-language schools only.

Source: Lapointe et. al. (1992a)

Table 2.11
Average National Test Scores in Science, Educational Testing Service, Age 13, 1991

Rank	Country	Average Score (%)
1	South Korea	77.5
2	Taiwan	75.6
3	Switzerland[1]	73.7
4	Hungary	73.4
5	Soviet Union[2]	71.3
6	Slovenia	70.3
7	Italy[3]	69.9
8	Israel[4]	69.7
9	**Canada**	**68.8**
10	France	68.6
11	U.K.: Scotland	67.9
12	Spain[5]	67.5
13	United States	67.0
14	Ireland	63.3
	Mean	70.3

[1] Students in 15 cantons only; excludes students in private and Romansch-language schools, and all students in the remaining 11 cantons.
[2] Russian-language schools only, in 14 republics.
[3] Province of Emilia-Romagna only.
[4] Hebrew-language schools only.
[5] Spanish-language schools only; also excludes schools in the Catalan autonomous community.

Source Lapointe, et. al. (1992a).

Table 2.11 summarizes the results of the science tests of 13-year-old students. It is the counterpart of Table 2.5, which set out the results of the same age group tested in mathematics:

- Again, South Korea, Taiwan, and Switzerland are the top three achievers in that age group.
- Canada sinks below the international mean.
- The United States is last but one.

Geography

In 1988-89, the Gallup Organization conducted an international survey for the National Geographic Society (Gallup Organization 1988, 1989). Part of that survey consisted in identifying 16 geographical concepts (specific countries or oceans) on a map. Table 2.12 summarizes the results. Note that the sample from the U.S.S.R. was restricted to the cities of Moscow and Kursk. Among the results:

18 Education and Training in Canada

Table 2.12
Average National Test Scores, Gallup Survey of Geographical Knowledge, 1988-89

Rank	Country	Average Score (%) Total Sample	Age 18-24
1	Sweden	72.5	74.4
2	West Germany	70.0	70.0
3	Japan	60.6	59.4
4	France	58.1	57.5
5	**Canada**	**57.5**	**58.1**
6	United States	53.8	43.1
7	United Kingdom	53.1	56.2
8	Italy	47.5	58.1
9-10	Mexico	46.2	51.2
9-10	Soviet Union	46.2	58.1

Source: The Gallup Organization (1988, 1989)

- Canada's showing was mediocre, well behind that of Sweden and West Germany.

- The 18 to 24-year-old groups in the U.S.S.R. and Italy performed much better than the national averages in those two countries.

- The performance of the 18 to 24-year-olds in the United States was much worse than the national average in that country.

Summary

The fragmentary evidence provided here suggests the following:

- Canadian mathematics and science education is relatively strong at the age level of 9 or 10.

- By the age of 13 or 14, the performance of Canadian students, generally, sinks below the mean for industrialized countries.

- Canadian performance is relatively weak by the end of high school, even after adjustment for years of schooling and retention rates.

Interprovincial Comparisons

Several of the international studies mentioned above reported on the achievement of individual Canadian provinces. However, too few provinces took part in those studies to support strong conclusions. The only two exceptions are the Second International Science Study, in which all Canadian provinces participated; and the 1991 study of the Educational Testing Service, which included all provinces except Prince Edward Island. As will be demonstrated, the available data suggests that the western provinces tend to do better than the central provinces which, in turn, tend to outscore the eastern provinces. This West-to-East "tilt" is borne out by 10 of the 11 studies reported below.

Mathematics

The nine Canadian provinces that participated in the ETS study of 13-year-olds in 1991 showed a wide dispersion of achievement (Table 2.13). The West-to-East tilt is not statistically significant in that survey, thanks to the strong performance of Quebec students and the weak achievement of their Ontario counterparts. In the first ETS survey in 1988, Quebec's 13-year-olds had already recorded strong performances, whereas Ontario students were the weakest of the four participating Canadian provinces (see Table 2.3). In the 1991 ETS study, Quebec's 9-year-old students also had the highest scores among the participating Canadian provinces and were the only Canadian youngsters to exceed the mean for the 10 participating industrial countries (Table 2.4).

Table 2.13
Average Provincial Test Scores in Mathematics, Educational Testing Service, Age 13, Canada, 1991

Rank	Province	Average Score (%)
1	Quebec	68.4
2	British Columbia	66.2
3	Alberta	64.0
4	Saskatchewan	62.2
5	Nova Scotia	59.7
6	Newfoundland	58.9
7	New Brunswick	58.7
8	Manitoba	58.5
9	Ontario	58.1
	Mean of 14 industrialized countries[1]	64.1

[1] From Table 2.5. In Canada, West-to-East rank correlation = +0.35, p = n.s.

Source: Lapointe et al. (1992a)

Similarly, the poor performance in mathematics by Ontario's 13-year-old students in 1991 was foreshadowed by the 1988 study and is consistent with the weak showing of that province's 9-year-olds in the 1991 ETS study. In the latter survey, the achievement of Ontario's students was weaker than that of all other participants except students from Slovenia.

Science

Table 2.14 summarizes SISS results for 10-year-old students. The scores show a declining trend as one moves from West to East. Six provinces score above the international mean. Quebec scores higher than might be expected, given the West-to-East tilt. Table 2.15 shows the corresponding results for the 14-year-old group. Here the West-to-East rank correlation is weaker but is still significant at the 10 per cent level. Seven provinces score above the international mean.

As with the case of the international comparisons at the end of secondary schooling, here too adjustments were required for years of schooling and retention rates. The results are shown in Table 2.16. Note that British Columbia and Alberta compare well with the best of the industrialized systems (Table 2.8), but that

Table 2.14
Average Provincial Test Scores, Second International Science Study, Population 1, Age 10, Canada, 1984-85

Rank	Province	Average Score (%)
1-2	Manitoba	62.0
1-2	Saskatchewan	62.0
3	Quebec	60.5
4-5	British Columbia	60.0
4-5	Alberta	60.0
6	Prince Edward Island	57.0
7-8	Ontario	55.0
7-8	Nova Scotia	55.0
9	New Brunswick	53.0
10	Newfoundland	51.0
	Mean of 15 industrialized countries[1]	56.0

[1] From Table 2.6. In Canada, West-to-East rank correlation = +0.68, $p < 0.05$.

Source: Crocker (1990); Schweitzer (1992a)

Table 2.15
Average Provincial Test Scores, Second International Science Study, Population 2, Age 14, Canada, 1984-85

Rank	Province	Average Score (%)
1	Alberta	66.0
2	Nova Scotia	65.0
3	British Columbia	63.0
4	Manitoba	62.0
5-6-7	Saskatchewan	61.0
5-6-7	Ontario	61.0
5-6-7	Quebec	61.0
8	New Brunswick	59.0
9-10	Prince Edward Island	56.0
9-10	Newfoundland	56.0
	Mean of 16 industrialized countries[1]	60.6

[1] From Table 2.7. In Canada, West-to-East rank correlation = +0.59. $p < 0.10$.

Source: Crocker (1990); Schweitzer (1992a).

Table 2.16
Average Provincial Test Scores, Second International Science Study, Population 3 End of Secondary Schooling, Canada, 1984-85

| | | Average Score (%) | |
Rank	Province	Adjusted	Unadjusted
1	British Columbia	61.9	50.0
2	Alberta	59.5	47.0
3-4	Quebec	43.7	36.8
3-4	Ontario	43.7	48.0
5	Saskatchewan	43.5	39.0
6	Manitoba	43.4	43.75
7	Nova Scotia	36.8	39.5
8	Prince Edward Island	34.6	39.5
9	New Brunswick	30.8	41.5
10	Newfoundland	25.4	37.25
	Mean of 15 industrialized systems[1]		54.5

[1] Adjusted for years of schooling and retention rates. From Table 2.8. West-to-East rank correlation = +0.84, $p < 0.001$.

Source: Crocker (1990); Schweitzer (1992a)

all other provinces score below the mean for the 15 systems and even below the United States, whose weak performance has evoked much justified criticism in recent years. The West-to-East rank correlation is very strong.

As with the interprovincial comparisons of the mathematics study conducted by the Educational Testing Service, there is a wide variation between the nine participating provinces with respect to their students' achievement in the area of science (compare Table 2.17 with Table 2.13). Apart from the strong performance by British Columbia, Alberta and Saskatchewan, note the strong showing by Quebec and Ontario's weak performance.

As noted above, Quebec's 10-year-olds showed similarly strong results in the 1983-86 Second International Science Study, although these were not matched by the results of the 14-year-olds in that province; nor were Quebec students outperforming Ontario students at the end of their secondary education. Also, in the 1988 ETS study, Quebec and Ontario recorded similar achievement levels for their 13-year-old students (see Table 2.9). It is too early to say whether Quebec's strong showing and Ontario's weak performance in 1991 has any lasting significance. Nevertheless, it is worth noting that Ontario participated in 11 international comparisons discussed in this paper and performed below the average for the participating industrialized countries in nine of them. Quebec participated in nine comparisons and performed above the average in eight cases. This suggests that Quebec is, perhaps, more successful than Ontario at motivating students to high levels of achievement. It would be useful to investigate the causes of the differences. The Third International Mathematics and Science Studies currently under way may throw some interesting light on these matters.

Scientific and General Literacy

In 1990 Edna Einsiedel of the University of Calgary conducted a telephone survey of 2,000 adult Canadians to test their scientific literacy. The author reports that interregional differences in the literacy index are significant at the 0.05 level, using the Chi-square test (Table 2.18). Here again, there was a general tendency towards a West-to-East tilt, even though the restriction to four regions makes a rank-correlation test nonsignificant.

Table 2.18

Scientific Literacy Index of Adult Canadians, by Region, 1989

Region	(N)	Low	Moderate	High
West	572	28.5	45.5	26.0
Ontario	728	36.5	41.3	22.1
Quebec	524	55.0	34.9	10.1
Atlantic	176	46.0	39.2	14.8

Source: Einsiedel (1990)

Some of the findings of the Southam News Organization's Research Report on Literacy in Canada (1987) are contained in Table 2.19. Southam asked respondents where they received most of their elementary education (Table 2.20). The West-to-East tilt is again evident in both tables. This raises the question whether the school systems of the western provinces are more effective at instilling literacy than those of the other provinces.

The Southam study was criticized for the quality and nature of its questions, its small sample size (16,540), and the low rate of willing and usable responses (14 per cent). However, a much more thorough study conducted by Statistics Canada confirmed many of the Southam findings and also permitted a much more detailed analysis.

Table 2.17

Average Provincial Scores in Science, Educational Testing Service, Age 13, Canada, 1991

Rank	Province	Average Score (%)
1	Alberta	74.1
2	British Columbia	72.4
3	Quebec	71.2
4	Saskatchewan	69.9
5	Nova Scotia	68.7
6	Manitoba	68.4
7	Ontario	66.7
8	Newfoundland	66.1
9	New Brunswick	65.4
	Mean of 14 industrialized systems[1]	70.3

[1] From Table 2.11. West-to-East rank correlation = + 0.717; $p < 0.05$

Source: Lapointe et al. (1992b)

Table 2.19
Literacy in Canada, by Province, 1987 (%)

Rank	Province	Total Population	Canadian-born
1	British Columbia	83	85
2	Manitoba and Saskatchewan	81	83
3	Alberta	79	85
4	Ontario	76	80
5	Maritimes	75	78
6	Quebec	72	71
7	Newfoundland	56	56
West to East rank correlation		+0.93 p < 0.01	+0.96 < 0.01

Source: Southam News Literacy Survey (1987)

Table 2.20
Average Literacy Level, by Province of Elementary Education, Canada, 1987

Rank	Province	Proportion of Literate Adults[1] (%)
1	Manitoba	85.6
2-3	British Columbia	82.8
2-3	Alberta	82.8
4	Saskatchewan	80.0
5	Ontario	79.4
6	Quebec	72.3
7	Atlantic	69.4

[1] West-to-East rank correlation = +0.78; p < 0.05.
Source: Southam News Literacy Survey (1987)

In October 1989, Statistics Canada conducted a Survey of Literacy Skills Used in Daily Activities, interviewing a sample of 13,571 persons between the ages of 16 and 69, with a response rate of 70 per cent. Apart from the test questions designed to measure the "functional literacy and numeracy" of the respondents, the survey was also used to collect a large amount of additional personal information, which enabled researchers to standardize the results for:

- province of residence
- size of population in place of residence
- age
- sex
- language of interview
- country or province of birth
- year of first immigration to Canada
- years and level of schooling in Canada
- years and level of schooling outside Canada
- type of schooling (academic or vocational)
- first language of childhood
- age when first started to learn the language of the interview
- physical and learning disabilities
- parents' immigrant status
- age of parents at their immigration
- parental education

The responses to the literacy and numeracy test questions were scored by a system that yielded a mean of 250.5 and a standard deviation of 50 for the total population.

After standardization for all of the above-mentioned factors, the functional-literacy scores of respondents born in Canada were found to be significantly influenced by their province of birth, which also tended to be the province in which they received their schooling. Table 2.21 shows that even after adjustment for the factors listed above, there was a difference of approximately 30 points between the highest- and lowest-scoring provinces, which is equivalent to a standard deviation of about 0.5 or 0.6 — a substantial difference in educational achievement. Further research showed that only about one quarter of interprovincial differences in achievement could be explained by school expenditures per student (Schweitzer, 1992b). We must conclude, therefore, that some other influences caused the bulk of the differences in the "adjusted" columns of Table 2.21.

Summary

There is a recurrent West-to-East declining trend in achievement in the Canadian studies measuring science and functional literacy. This pattern is not due to the amount of schooling received, the level of spending per student, or the relative economic prosperity of the provinces. It would no doubt be worthwhile to discover the causes of this trending. If, for example, these

Table 2.21
Average Functional-Literacy Test Scores[1], Canadian-born Persons Aged Between 16 and 69, by Province of Birth, 1989

Province or Territory of Birth	Reading Unadjusted	Reading Adjusted	Numeracy Unadjusted	Numeracy Adjusted
British Columbia and Yukon	274.6	274.6	265.2	265.2
Alberta and Northwest Territories	268.0	271.5	261.7	263.8
Saskatchewan	263.4	269.8	257.6	261.0
Manitoba	266.2	272.4	260.9	264.4
Ontario	266.2	269.1	258.7	260.8
Quebec	252.1	261.7	245.4	253.5
New Brunswick	248.8	256.1	238.4	244.4
Nova Scotia	250.4	257.2	239.3	245.0
Newfoundland and Prince Edward Island	241.6	248.6	230.5	237.5

[1] Both unadjusted scores and scores adjusted for the factors enumerated in the text appear in the table.

Source: Statistics Canada, *Survey of Literacy Skills Used in Daily Activities* (1990); Schweitzer (1992b)

interprovincial differences are largely the result of differences in educational policies or practices, the lower-scoring provinces could improve their performance by emulating the high-scoring provinces.

Intertemporal Comparisons

As stated at the outset, a substantial body of public opinion believes that the quality of education has declined in recent decades. What is the available evidence on this issue?

Table 2.22
Average Functional-literacy Test Scores[1], Canadian-born Persons Aged Between 16 and 69, by Age Group, 1989

Age Group	Men Unadjusted	Men Adjusted	Women Unadjusted	Women Adjusted
16-24	267.1	264.2	251.9	249.5
25-34	272.7	267.4	262.7	257.9
35-44	268.7	268.7	261.8	261.8
45-54	251.4	259.8	250.2	259.0
55-69	226.6	245.1	226.7	247.1

[1] Both unadjusted scores and scores adjusted for the factors enumerated in the text appear in the table.

Source: Statistics Canada, *Survey of Literacy Skills Used in Daily Activities* (1990); Schweitzer (1992b)

Literacy

Statistics Canada recorded the age of the respondents in its Survey of Literacy Skills Used in Daily Activities (1990). When this information is used as a proxy in determining when the respondents entered school (Table 2.22), a pronounced age pattern emerges. The results of the unadjusted columns are misleading, however, because they do not take into account the multitude of factors that were brought to bear on the respondents after they received their formal schooling. These could have a strong influence on the functional-literacy scores. Further, the unadjusted columns do not reflect the additional years of schooling younger generations have received. The adjusted columns have been standardized for all the factors listed earlier and the results suggest that the level of skills acquired through education improved up to the 35-44 age group (that is, up to the generation that entered school between 1951 and 1960) but that there has been some deterioration, particularly in numeracy, since then.

The Canadian Test of Basic Skills (Nelson Canada, 1990, 1991) provides comparable data on achievement for Grades 4 and 8 in the years 1966, 1973, 1980, and 1991 (Table 2.23). On the whole, they indicate a deterioration between 1966 and 1973, a minor improvement between 1973 and 1980, and then another decline (to about the 1973 level) between 1980 and 1991.

The effect sizes for Grade 8 show that, in 1991, the median student of 1966 would have placed at the 56th percentile in vocabulary, the 70th percentile in reading comprehension, the 72th percentile in language skills,

Table 2.23
Average Test Scores on Basic Skills, Grades 4 and 8, Canada, 1973, 1980 and 1991

	Vocabulary	Reading Comprehension	Language Skills	Work-study Skills	Mathematics	Composite Score
			(1966 = 100)			
Grade 4						
1973	90.8	92.8	86.0	97.0	94.5	92.3
1980	95.0	97.8	89.0	98.0	93.0	94.5
1991	92.3	92.7	88.0	99.6	88.6	92.2
1966-91 Effect size[1]	-0.27	-0.27	-0.45	-0.02	-0.58	-0.35
Grade 8						
1973	91.6	90.1	88.5	96.1	95.5	92.4
1980	95.4	93.9	91.0	99.4	97.8	95.5
1991	97.5	90.8	89.5	96.3	94.1	93.7
1966-91 Effect size[1]	-0.14	-0.54	-0.58	-0.21	-0.38	-0.43

[1] The "effect size" is obtained as follows: (1966-1991)/1991 standard deviation.

Source: Nelson Canada (1991)

the 59th percentile in work-study skills, the 65th percentile in mathematics, and the 67th percentile in the composite score. The corresponding figures for Grade 4 are: 61st percentile in vocabulary; 61st percentile in reading comprehension; 67th percentile in language skills; 51st percentile in work-study skills; 72nd percentile in mathematics, and 64th percentile in the composite score. In these findings, a change that moves the "central" (median) student of 1966 up towards the 100th percentile is an unfavourable change over time, while a change that moves that student down towards the first percentile is favourable.

The finding that there was a deterioration between 1966 and 1973, and very little change thereafter, confirms the conclusions drawn from Statistics Canada's functional-literacy test. Indeed, fragmentary information obtained in connection with other research suggests that educational success in fostering cognitive achievement has stagnated, at best, over the last two or three decades and that it may, in fact, have declined.

Conclusion

International, interprovincial, and intertemporal comparisons show that there is no cause or justification for complacency about the present state and future prospects of scholarly achievement in Canada's public education systems. That achievement has been and still is respectable in the lower age groups, but it deteriorates towards the end of secondary school, particularly in mathematics and science. In addition, interprovincial differences in achievement in science are significantly large. The findings of the Canadian Test of Basic Skills over the past 24 years do not portend any sign of improvement, and there may even be some deterioration in this area as well. Functional literacy and numeracy are also significantly – disconcertingly – low.

These considerations more than justify concern about the quality of education in Canada. Such concern — and the knowledge that Canada's productivity, an important contributor to success in international competition, depends on the quality of Canadian education — warrant investigation of the most important conditions and determinants of educational achievement.

Crucial Aspects of Educational Achievement

Educational achievement is difficult to analyse because it is influenced by many factors — the characteristics of students and their families, friends, and peers; of their teachers, principals, and schools; and of school boards and provincial departments of education. All of these forces interact to form an educational system, but the system itself exists in, and is influenced by, the society that surrounds it. Indeed, it has been said that every educational system is a reflection of the particular society within which it operates. Nevertheless, certain basic features are common to all.

Students

In a system of universal and compulsory education, there is tremendous variety in the abilities, interests, inclinations, socio-economic status, and other characteristics of individual students. As a result, there are no simple answers — even to simple questions. Nevertheless, two broad observations can be made: first, education is a cumulative process; and second, motivation influences achievement, and achievement influences motivation.

The most obvious illustrations of the validity of the first observation are found in mathematics (although it is easy to find examples in other subject areas). For example, one must understand addition in order to understand multiplication. In turn, multiplication must be understood in order to understand powers, and so on. If this chain is broken in the learning process, students will encounter increasing difficulty when grappling with more complex concepts.

As for the second observation, learning takes effort, and that effort is provided by motivation ... but *achievement in learning gives satisfaction and encourages further effort* (Bloom, 1976).

The consequences of these two observations, simple and almost banal though they may seem, have very important implications. If a student fails to master a step in the curriculum, he or she is likely to face increasing difficulties mastering subsequent steps. It will require greater effort to keep up with fellow students who, in the meantime, are progressing at their own speed. At the same time, the difficulty being experienced by the slower student tends to lessen his or her motivation at precisely the moment when greater motivation and extra effort are required to catch up with the rest of the class. Such students are at serious risk of falling further behind and becoming completely discouraged. They feel that they have no control over their own fate, and their loss of self-confidence and self-esteem lessens their chances of catching up (Crocker, 1991).

The motivation —> achievement —> motivation relationship becomes a vicious circle for failing students, just as it is a virtuous circle for successful students. This shows how important it is to detect immediately any failure to master basic concepts at each step in the process of acquiring basic skills and to take remedial action. Monitoring progress regularly also helps to instill a sense of accountability in the student.

Testing is a useful tool for measuring the educational achievement of individual students. There are two kinds of standardized tests — criterion-referenced, and norm-referenced (Crocker, 1990).

Criterion-referenced tests attempt to measure achievement with respect to a clearly defined area of knowledge or skill. The scores achieved in passing such tests reflect the demonstrated degrees of mastery in the designated area of knowledge or skill. The International Mathematical and Science Studies cited earlier fall into this category.

The difference between criterion- and norm-referenced tests is illustrated by Table 2.1 in this chapter. It reports that the average score achieved by 13-year-old students from British Columbia on a particular mathematics test was 51.5 per cent: this is a criterion-referenced result. However, if we say that British Columbia students scored 1.3 percentage points higher than the mean for the students in the 16 systems reported in the table, this is a norm-referenced result.

Norm-referenced tests answer the question: how well does a particular student (or class, school, or educational system) perform relative to some norm — for example, the "average" student at the time the test was developed? Note that the "norm" in norm-referenced tests is redefined from time to time. When this occurs, raw test results cannot be used to make valid criterion-referenced, intertemporal comparisons because the achievement of the "average" student, when used as the norm, changes over time. To make valid comparisons, a new test — equating the old and the new norms of the norm-referenced test — must be performed. The results of the Canadian Test of Basic Skills reported in Table 2.23 are based on such equating (Nelson Canada, 1984, 1991).

To be useful, tests must be properly designed. If their purpose is to measure educational achievement, they should adequately cover the curriculum that the educational authorities regard as appropriate. This can cause problems when the same test is applied to different countries or provinces, as in the international and interprovincial comparisons reported in Tables 2.1 to 2.11. In such circumstances, the participating systems must agree on the appropriateness of the test problems. Obviously, every question in a given test will not be equally appropriate in every jurisdiction. In subjects such as mathematics and sciences, however, educational authorities in the participating systems tend to share a broad understanding of what could — and what should — be expected from, say, 14- or 18-year-old students in order to equip them for the next stage(s) of their lives. This was, indeed, the case in the context of the International Mathematical and Science Studies. Educational authorities found it relatively easy to agree on what constituted acceptable test material; they agreed that particular subject matter and the kind of knowledge required in mathematics and science are quite similar around the globe.

Another important requirement of a well-designed test has to do with its ability to discriminate between weak and strong students. This means that the test must be neither too easy nor too difficult. If it is too easy, all or almost all students will achieve perfect or near-perfect scores. If it is too difficult, too many respondents will fail miserably. Here, too, there is need for agreement among the representatives of the participating systems.

The interest shown by educators, policymakers, and the general public in the results of the Second International Mathematics and Science Studies — and the fact that preparatory work is currently well under way for a third survey in both disciplines — indicates that the tests are regarded as both useful and reliable. Similarly, the study of 12 systems undertaken and published by the Educational Testing Service in 1988 was followed by a study covering 28 systems. The expansion of these surveys is gratifying, especially given that the amount of money, time, and effort required to design, administer, and evaluate tests covering thousands of students around the world is considerable.

Well designed and appropriately evaluated tests have four major uses:

- As diagnostic tools, tests indicate the areas of knowledge in which students have mastery or are deficient. They can thus help to direct the efforts of students, teachers and, indeed, the entire educational system toward remedying weaknesses. This is the least controversial use of tests.
- As tools of accountability, tests and test results can, if properly handled, measure the progress of an individual or a class, as well as the achievement of a teacher and/or the educational system. It can thus serve as one indicator of whether the resources made available to the system are used effectively.
- As tools of comparison, tests have shown their usefulness through the interest demonstrated by parents, educators, businessmen, and politicians in the international surveys of skills in mathematics and science. Differences in achievement between countries, provinces, or schools serve as warning signals of possible pervasive system-wide weaknesses.
- As a type of examination, favourable test results can serve as indicators of individual qualifications for, say, promotion to a higher grade, admission to a particular course, or attestation of competence in a given field.

Some educators claim that testing creates more problems that it solves. For reasons described in detail in Appendix 2.1, however, we believe that valid and consistent interregional and intertemporal tests are both possible and desirable. They improve diagnosis and are indispensable for accountability and evaluation. The view that educational achievement is inherently nonmeasurable leads to inefficiency (Raphael, 1989).

Not only do tests make it possible to measure educational progress using objective criteria, they also motivate students by making them aware that effort and good performance have a favourable influence on their future lives. In discussing the weak average achievement of American high-school students, Bishop (1989) points out that only those few who intend to go to the most prestigious (and most selective) universities strive for the best results. The great majority of those students who go on to post-secondary education in the United States attend colleges that admit virtually all high-school graduates from the state with the requisite courses, irrespective of the marks achieved in those courses.

As for those who join the labour force after high-school graduation, Bishop quotes a National Federation of Independent Business survey revealing that high-school transcripts were used in only 14.2 per cent of cases in the hiring of high-school graduates in the United States. For most businessmen, one high-school diploma is apparently as good as another, irrespective of the marks achieved. The survey also found that only 5.2 per cent of the newly hired high-school graduates in the United States had been referred by vocational teachers, and only 2.7 per cent by someone else in the high school. Comparable information for Canada is not available, but if the U.S. findings are broadly applicable here, we must conclude that the private sector does little to motivate students who are not academically inclined (i.e., those who do not intend to go on to university) to do their best during their years in primary and secondary school.

Family and Friends

Building human capital, like all other forms of capital, involves postponement of self-gratification. Children cannot be expected to develop and be self-motivated without the guidance and support of their families and respected adult friends. Being motivated by the interest, encouragement, help, monitoring and approval of family and family friends is a vitally important contributor to a young person's educational success.

This is true throughout the period of schooling, but it is particularly relevant in the early years, during which the crucial foundations of knowledge, skills, and good working habits are laid. As Bishop (1989, p. 17) points out, "by the 9th grade, most students are already so far behind the leaders, that they know they have no chance of being perceived as academically successful". This is confirmed by the record of the Ontario eighth-graders in the Second International Science Study. A total of 3,955 students were given the same set of test questions at the beginning (pre-test) and at the end of the school year (post-test). The average score was 42.7 per cent correct in the pre-test and 51.1 per cent in the post-test. About 28 per cent (1,125) of those tested had higher scores on their pre-test than the post-test average, which means that they were capable of operating at the Grade 9 level or higher when they entered Grade 8. Also, about 36 per cent of those tested (1,411) had scores on their own post-test that were lower than the pre-test average, which means they were performing at the Grade 7 level or lower when they left Grade 8. Some educators (e.g., Bloom, 1976) even maintain that in the absence of intensive remedial effort, the die is cast for most students by the end of Grades 3 or 4, at an age when children have not yet developed sufficient judgment to discern that they lack essential tools or the maturity to make the effort required to catch up.

Unfortunately, there are many indications that strong home support is not generally available to all students. Many parents with low educational attainment themselves have low-paying jobs and low socio-economic status, and they provide little educational motivation to their children. Children from such families tend to fall behind their classmates (from families with higher levels of schooling) at a relatively early age, to become discouraged and drop out early, and then to have low-paying jobs themselves, thus perpetuating the pattern. Cheng *et al.* (1989) found that among Toronto ninth-graders in 1987, there was a strong correlation between parental socio-economic status and credit accumulation and attendance at advanced-level programs that eventually qualify students for university (Table 2.24).

Table 2.24
Credit Accumulation, Level of Study, and Parental Socio-economic Status among Toronto Ninth-graders, 1987 (%)

	0 - 7 credits	8 or more credits	Basic	General	Advanced
Professional and High-level Managerial	18	82	1	7	92
Semi-professional Technicians, Middle management, Supervisors, and Foremen	32	68	4	15	81
Skilled and Semi-skilled Craftsmen and Service workers, and Farmers	45	55	7	27	66
Unskilled Manual, Service, and Farm Labourers	45	55	14	34	52

Source: Cheng *et al.* (1989), p. 33

Table 2.25
Socio-economic Status, Credit Accumulation, and Level of Study among Chinese and Korean Ninth-graders in Toronto, 1987 (%)

	Socio-economic Status		Credit Accumulation		Level of Study		
	Professional, higher managerial	All other	0 – 7	8 or more	Basic	General	Advanced
Chinese and Korean	6	94	21	79	1	10	89
All Other	17	83	36	64	8	22	70

Source: Estimates by the Economic Council of Canada, based on data from Cheng *et al.*, 1989, p. 128

Nonetheless, socio-economic status is not the overriding factor that influences high educational achievement. Cheng *et al.* (1989) report that Chinese and Korean students demonstrate much higher educational achievement than might be expected on the basis of their socio-economic backgrounds (see Table 2.25). This suggests that awareness at home of the importance of education is the crucial factor, not socio-economic background.

The presence of parents is another important influence on a child's educational achievement. Cheng *et al.* show that the offspring of families with both parents present in the home are more likely to achieve high results than children with single parents (Table 2.26). This result suggests that societal ills (such as broken homes) are additional challenges to the educational system.

The system cannot be blamed for poor results caused by such factors, nor can it compensate for all kinds of societal ills. If parents do not have the resources or the knowledge to provide their children with an adequate and balanced diet, those children will not be able to study well. Similarly, the educational achievement of children who do not get enough sleep will suffer. Thus, parents must cooperate with the school system and make the effort to contribute to the development of good learning and working habits in their children by monitoring their homework and progress at school.

In their international study of the performance of 13-year-olds in mathematics and science, Lapointe *et al.* (1989) show that there has been a steady decline in the level of achievement, in inverse proportion to the amount of television viewing (Table 2.27). This is supported by a study of Ontario high schools (King, 1986), showing that 18 percent of the Basic-level students watch television 30 hours or more per week; the corresponding figure for General-level students is 14 percent, and for Advanced-level students, only 8 percent. Basic-level students have little or no homework and they spend much of their free time in passive activities such as television-watching rather than reading, for example, which requires more active effort.

Why is watching television associated with weak educational achievement? The results of an important study of three "typical" Canadian towns under control

Table 2.26
Credits Completed, Level of Study, and Parental Presence among Toronto Ninth-graders, 1987

	Credits Completed		Level of Study		
Parents Present at Home	0 – 7	8 or more	Basic	General	Advanced
Both	30	69	6	20	74
Mother only	41	59			
Father only	45	54			
Mother or Father only			9	21	70
Other	49	50	9	34	57

Source: Estimates by the Economic Council of Canada, based on data from Cheng *et al.*, 1989, p. 128

Table 2.27
Daily Television Viewing and Proficiency Scores in Mathematics and Science among 13-year-olds in Four Canadian Provinces and Selected Foreign Countries, 1988

	\multicolumn{6}{c}{Amounts of Daily Television Viewing (hours)}
	0–2	3–4	5 or more	0–2	3–4	5 or more
	Mathematics scores			Science scores		
British Columbia	556	537	509	569	548	519
Ireland	523	500	455	485	466	430
New Brunswick – English	549	525	508	531	505	493
New Brunswick – French	519	516	506	479	467	454
Ontario – English	537	515	486	532	514	490
Ontario – French	497	481	458	482	469	447
Quebec – English	548	535	514	531	513	491
Quebec – French	549	540	526	522	509	491
South Korea	580	561	537	562	543	518
Spain	524	508	481	515	501	478
United Kingdom	529	520	475	538	531	483
United States	494	483	443	495	486	454

Source: Lapointe *et al.*, (1989) pp. 90-91

conditions between 1973 and 1975 suggest very strong conclusions. Multitel broadcast over four television channels throughout the period; Unitel had one channel at the beginning of the period and two at the end; Notel offered no television in 1973 but had one channel at the end of the period. The researchers found that "second graders in Notel who had grown up without TV were better readers [more critical] than children who grew up in Unitel and Multitel" (Williams, 1986, p. 61).

The study also found that Grades 1 and 2 were "especially important for television's potential influence on the acquisition of fluent reading skills" and "at least in some instances, superior fluent reading skills are maintained despite the advent of TV, and catch-up by regular viewers does not occur. In addition, the grade 8-10 results indicate that the arrival of TV in Notel may have slowed the expected improvement in fluent reading over this period." Combining the results of the students' I.Q. tests with findings about television availability, the study found "that the availability of television may increase the proportion of less intelligent children who do not acquire reading skills to the point of automatic processing". The implication of this is that it "is important for parents and educators to ensure that children spend sufficient time practising reading to acquire fluency to the point of automatization. We suspect that most children find watching television a more appealing alternative, and this may be especially true of the children who are least competent" (p. 74).

The cumulative nature of education renders the mastery of reading indispensable for further progress in intellectual development. But the effect of television is restricted to its influence on reading. Williams (1986) found that it also has unfavourable effects on other educational goals — namely, creativity and problem-solving — in both children and adults. In the process of conducting the study, researchers found reduced perseverance in problem-solving tasks. "This may be due to the fact that television may develop a relatively short attention span and/or low frustration tolerance" or it may be that television provides viewers with less opportunity to gain experience in problem-solving (p. 380). This is particularly applicable to commercial television, which continuously interrupts programming with advertisements.

Given these unfavourable effects, parents must control the amount of television their children watch. Indeed, they must set an example in this respect and limit their own television viewing —especially when their children are studying or doing homework.

Another way parents can influence their children's educational achievement is by encouraging or discouraging part-time work. In 1981, almost two thirds of all high-school students earned "extra" money by working outside the home during the school year (Friesen, 1984, quoted in King, 1986). According to King *et al.* (1988), approximately 85 per cent of Ontario high-school students who work do so for reasons related to personal spending and only 13 per cent work in order to support themselves, contribute to family income, or save for future use. A moderate amount of work for pay is not harmful, but "the negative effects on students' motivation and achievement of working an excessive number of hours can easily be detected by teachers. Students taking mainly General-level courses are more likely to put in the equivalent of a regular work-week (over thirty hours) after school and on weekends. They become, in effect, part-time students" (King and Peart, 1990, p. 156).

Good schools and good teachers do their best to instill the value and priority of education into their students, but they can be successful only if they have the support of the children's families. The most important aspect of this support is convincing young people that it is not enough to "pass" courses or to be satisfied with an "average" performance, but in persuading them to exert themselves to the best of their abilities.

Teachers

The teacher's role in the educational process is crucial. Chapter 4 is entirely devoted to the teaching profession, but some aspects of teaching should be mentioned here.

As a recent OECD report (1989) points out, teaching is not only a job and a craft; it is also a profession and an art. Traditionally, teaching has been thought of as prestigious. However, among 513 occupations listed by Blishen *et al.* (1987), secondary-school teachers rank 23rd and elementary-school and kindergarten teachers ranked 42nd on the socio-economic scale.

The difference between the public perceptions of primary- and secondary-school teachers is in itself revealing when one considers the extraordinary importance of the early school years and the need for sensitivity and skill among those teachers who lay the foundations for life-long learning. More disturbing is that, despite the financial rewards and socio-economic status attached to teaching, it is not a first career choice for many who practice it. This is true even at the primary level. A study of Ontario teachers by Rees *et al.* (1989) reported that only 64 per cent of male teachers and 71 per cent of female teachers at the elementary level considered teaching as their first career choice. The situation is even worse at the secondary level, where the corresponding figures are 37 and 56 per cent, respectively. This is a very worrisome phenomenon. Teaching is a vitally important and rewarding occupation, but it is also very demanding and can lead to "burn-out". It requires a great deal of motivation, but as teachers themselves know only too well (through contact and experience with their own students), motivation and the sense of self-worth are inextricably intertwined.

In 1911, school enrolment across Canada among those aged 15 to 19 was 19 per cent. Teaching at the high-school level was still a very "select" occupation. By 1988, however, enrolments had climbed to well over 70 per cent, and the teacher/student ratio had also increased substantially. Partly as a result of larger numbers across the board, the prestige of teaching as a profession has diminished significantly, not only in Canada but in other countries as well. Nonetheless, teaching remains a prestigious occupation in some parts of the world — in Japan, for example.

The situation in Canada typifies the difficulties being confronted. A high-quality educational system is necessary to maintain and improve our economic productivity and standard of living generally. Such a system requires good and highly motivated teachers, but teachers can be motivated only if society recognizes that their contribution to the future success of the country is not only important but indispensable. Regrettably, it would take nothing less than a revolution, in terms of the perceptions of society, to provide good teachers with the prestige and respect they deserve for their contributions to Canada's material and spiritual prosperity.

Here again, there is a virtuous/vicious circle. Highly motivated teachers are needed to stimulate and guide students to high levels of academic achievement. Strong performance in this respect will generate social recognition and prestige for the profession. Prestige helps to attract the best candidates into teaching. But how can anyone expect teachers to succeed at teaching if they have to cope with students who suffer from poor diet, lack of sleep, excessive television viewing, broken homes, domestic violence, alcoholism, or other substance-abuse problems? It is absurd to expect teachers to compensate for all the ills of society. Teachers and schools must concentrate on what they are taught and designed to do: teach. If they are forced to deal with other societal problems, not only will they be unsuccessful, they necessarily jeopardize everyone's chances of success in the field of activity where they hold the comparative advantage — education.

Teachers will be highly motivated only if they are treated as professionals. Although they have considerable freedom in the classroom, they often have much less influence on policy decisions in the school and, more particularly, at the school-district level (see Table 2.28). The problem exists at all levels, beginning with the elementary level, growing at the junior high-school level and becoming most evident among teachers at the high-school level. It is becoming increasingly evident that the quality of the educational system is being impaired by the burden of the bureaucratic dimension of the system (Chubb and Moe, 1990; Migué and Marceau, 1989).

Table 2.28

Teachers' Perception of their Influence on Educational Policy Issues
Edmonton Public School District, 1985-90 (%)

| Grades | Answer[1]: "Very much or fairly much." ||
	At School Level	At District Level
Kindergarten to		
Grade 6	73.1	28.2
Grades 7 to 9	60.0	22.2
Grades 10 to 12	47.5	17.2

[1] The question asked was: "Do you feel as an individual that you have adequate influence over decisions that affect you and your job?"

Source: Edmonton Public School District Attitude Survey Results, 1990, questions 4 and 5, pp. 27, 39, 45.

Schools and School Resources

Conventional wisdom holds that devoting more resources to education will improve its quality. That, however, is a gross oversimplification.

Table 2.29 summarizes the results of 187 studies in educational research up to 1989. The column on the far left lists some of the school-related inputs believed to have an effect on student achievement (Hanushek, 1989). While that effect is commonly believed to be beneficial, the table shows that the relationship is by no means consistent.

A high ratio of teachers to students means a small class size. Other things being equal, the smaller the class size, the greater the perceived benefit to the students. At the limit, a one-on-one teaching organization, with highly motivated, sensitive, and knowledgeable teachers — i.e., a good tutorial system — can achieve excellent results even with weak students. However, of the 152 studies dealing with the teacher/student ratio, reported on in Table 2.29, only 14 recorded a statistically significant positive effect of small class size on student achievement. In a survey paper, Glass et al. (1982) reported that a reduction of the class size from, say, 30 to 20 students would result in an improvement of achievement that would move the median student to the 57th percentile. Such a policy would, however, require a 50-per-cent increase in the numbers of both teachers and classrooms.

Even if that condition were satisfied, (without pushing up salaries) and the quality of the additional teachers were no lower than that of the present teacher population, the cost of running the "new" schools would rise by at least 35 per cent. A recent large-scale study in Tennessee (Ward et al., 1990) found that by reducing the class size from 22-25 to 13-17 — by about one third — the greatest improvement in the kindergarten-to-Grade-3 group was equivalent to moving the median student to the 63rd percentile. The study also found that the effect was greatest in Grade 1 and gradually declined in Grades 2 and 3. Robitaille and Garden (1989) found no relationship between class size and achievement: some of the systems registering the highest achievements also had the largest class sizes — for example, in the last year of secondary school Hong Kong and Japan reported average class sizes of 27 and 40, respectively. Similarly, studies within systems do not show any reliable effect of class size on achievement, but this could well be the result of assigning weak students to smaller classes (Robitaille and Garden, 1989, p. 227).

In countries with strong teachers' unions, remuneration depends in part on the university diploma(s) held by teachers. Of course, there is no guarantee that a diploma means better teaching ability nor is it required that a teacher's diploma be in the subject he or she is teaching. As a result, teachers often give instruction in subjects in which their knowledge is limited or unsatisfactory. An M.A. degree in history, for example, is no indicator of the ability (or lack of it) of its holder to teach science. Small wonder, then, that Table 2.29 displays practically no relationship between teacher education and student achievement.

Teacher salaries also depend substantially on experience. However, Table 2.29 shows that teacher experience has only a limited effect on student achievement. Not surprisingly, therefore, few studies have found teacher salaries to have a statistically significant positive effect on student achievement.

Table 2.29
Estimated Expenditure Parameter Coefficients from 187 Studies of Educational Production Functions

Input:	Number of Studies	Statistically Significant +	Statistically Significant −	Total	Statistically Insignificant +	Statistically Insignificant −	Unknown Sign
Teacher/pupil Ratio	152	14	13	125	34	46	45
Teacher Education	113	8	5	100	31	32	37
Teacher Experience	140	40	10	90	44	31	15
Teacher Salary	69	11	4	54	16	14	24
Expenditures/pupil	65	13	3	49	25	13	11
Administrative Inputs	61	7	1	53	14	15	24
Facilities	74	7	5	62	17	14	31

Source: Hanushek (1989)

Among the inputs listed in Table 2.29, teacher experience has the most frequent positive influence on student achievement — a plausible finding. It is reasonable to expect that in teaching, as in other occupations, one improves through "learning by doing". Yet, even here the relationship is not clear-cut. Mediocre teachers might be expected to drop out of the profession sooner than the better ones, so the latter would gain more experience. In this case, however, causality could also go from better teaching ability to greater experience rather than the other way around, (i.e., it is not that longer experience leads to greater ability, but that more able teachers stay in the profession longer, so, it may be that ability rather than experience *per se* is captured here).

As mentioned earlier, only a few studies reported in Table 2.29 found that teacher salaries have a significant positive effect on student achievement. Since salaries form the largest single component of school expenditures it is not surprising, then, that only 20 per cent of the studies reported (13 out of 65) that expenditure per student has any statistically significant positive effect on achievement.

There is growing evidence that administrative impingement on teaching and school organization has an unfavourable effect on achievement (Chubb and Moe, 1990; Migué and Marceau, 1989). A recent study of high-school students in the United States (Anderson *et al.*, 1991) confirms this: the addition of a person to the non-teacher (administrative) staff reduces students' achievement test results and retention rates by about as much as the addition of a teacher increases them. Here again, care should be taken to note the direction of causality. (Certainly, some centres have more than the usual problems with student discipline and morale — and therefore register lower test scores and retention rates. Such centres do find it necessary to hire more administrative personnel.)

Anderson *et al.* (1991) also determined that higher capital outlays per pupil and per teacher-salary dollar have no effect on student test scores, although they do have a positive effect on retention rates. This suggests that more attractive — perhaps even luxurious — surroundings tend to attract and hold more students but surroundings do not induce improved achievement. Japanese schools are positively spartan by North American standards, yet they are very successful at training students who achieve high test scores.

There is no convincing evidence that the input variables listed in Table 2.29 have a substantial and consistent influence on student achievement — at least not within the context of the compulsory universal education systems of the industrialized nations. However, this is not to say that these inputs have no positive effects at all. Conceivably, there could be some considerably more important determinant of educational achievement that is not now captured by statistical analysis. However, the burden of proof rests clearly on those who maintain that an increase in the amount or quality of those inputs would improve educational achievement.

Opportunity to Learn and Related Questions

The studies of the International Association for the Evaluation of Educational Achievement have succeeded in quantifying a phenomenon that has long been obvious to educators and the public at large: students can be expected to know only those things which they have been taught. This is particularly so for mathematics, science, and foreign languages, but it applies to other subjects as well, As part of the process of developing each test question for the Second International Mathematical Study, the teachers of each participating student (or group of students) were asked whether their students had had an opportunity to learn how to solve the problem. The results, shown in Figure 2.3, indicate that there is a clear positive relationship between achievement (percentage of correct answers) and the opportunity to learn. Those systems (countries or provinces) that have a richer curriculum (greater opportunity to learn) tend to register higher levels of achievement (score more correct answers). Differences with respect to the opportunity to learn show up not only between countries but also within them. The IEA Classroom Environment Study (Anderson et al. 1989) found that in each country there are students in classrooms that have an opportunity to learn considerably more (measured in terms of content associated with two or three times as many test items) than students in other classrooms. The study concludes:

> *The implications of this finding for the study are straightforward. To the extent that the opportunity to learn influences student achievement, students in these different classrooms will perform differently on the post-test [i.e., after the completion of the period investigated] independent of the type and quality of instruction they receive.*

The conclusions drawn from the results of the international studies by another author are that what students

Figure 2.3
Correlation between the Opportunity to Learn and Achievement in Mathematics Among Secondary-level Students in Selected Industrialized Countries[1], early 1980s

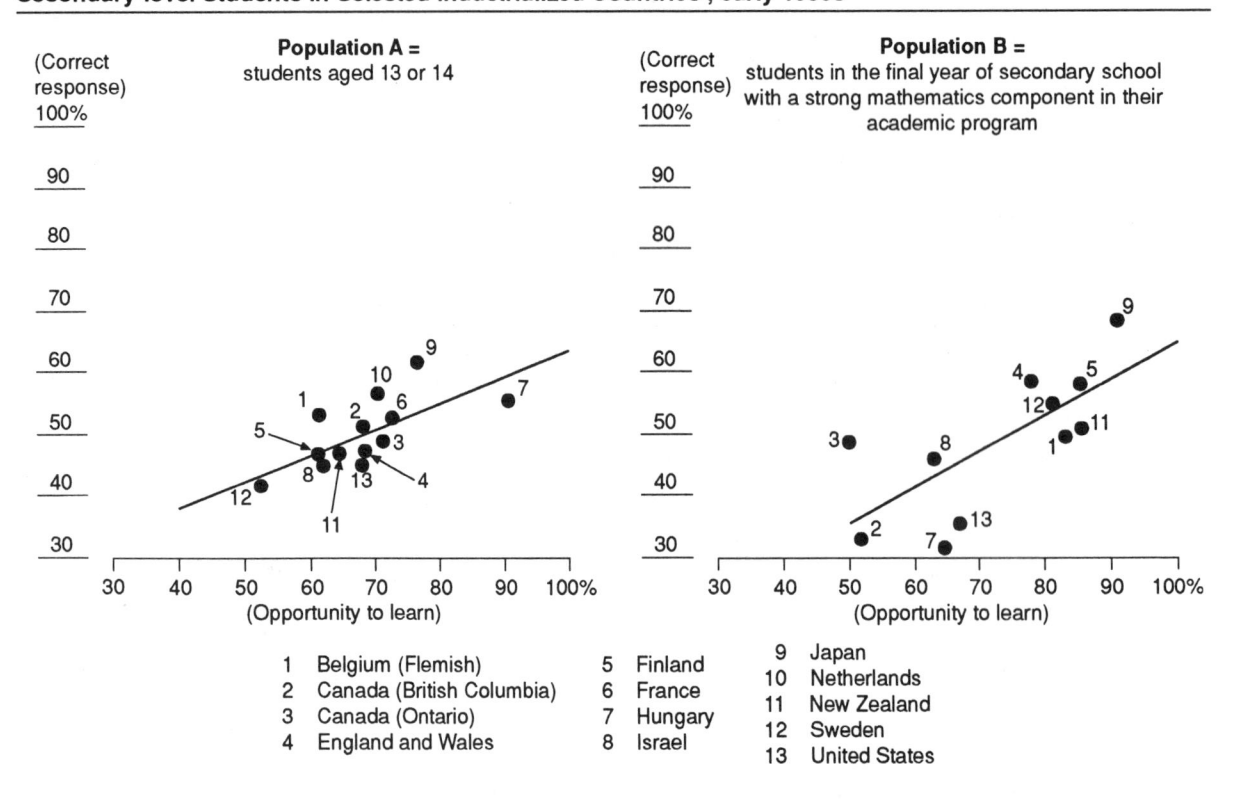

Population A = students aged 13 or 14

Population B = students in the final year of secondary school with a strong mathematics component in their academic program

1 Belgium (Flemish)
2 Canada (British Columbia)
3 Canada (Ontario)
4 England and Wales
5 Finland
6 France
7 Hungary
8 Israel
9 Japan
10 Netherlands
11 New Zealand
12 Sweden
13 United States

[1] The dots show, for each country, the correlation between the exposure of students to mathematical concepts and the level of correct responses to a test of the knowledge of mathematics.

Source: Estimates by the Economic Council of Canada based on the findings of the Second International Mathematics Study (see Robitaille and Garden)

are taught is more important than how they are taught. As Kifer points out (in Purves, 1989) "... that, of course, makes a good deal of sense. While students do not learn all they are taught, they do not learn what they have not been exposed to."

The cumulative nature of education, the importance of motivation, the feedback of achievement on motivation, and the great variations in student ability and achievement that characterize the systems of universal education pose a difficult problem. How can weak students be prevented from losing ground to their classmates, thereby losing motivation? One recommended solution is to use the technique of "mastery learning". Using this approach, the curriculum is broken down into "units" representing some skill or concept, each of which is necessary for mastering the next unit. Students are tested regularly and are given additional corrective instruction by the teacher or their fellow students until each student has mastered each unit (Slavin, 1987a).

Proponents of this method report very high positive results. However, mastery learning implies another kind of difficulty if the students in the class differ greatly in ability and knowledge, as they often do in the North American public school system. Arlin (1984a) found that in Grade 1 the average time needed for the slowest quartile of students is 2.5 times that for the fastest quartile. By Grade 4, the ratio is over 4 to 1. Due to the constraints on the time and energy of teachers that unavoidably result, (because every student must master every unit) the mastery-learning approach slows down presentation of new material and therefore the opportunity to learn, to the pace of the slower students. Arlin (1984b) calls this a Robin Hood approach because it deprives bright students of the opportunity to develop their abilities to the fullest at their own pace in favour of dragging along slower students.

Despite this, Slavin (1987a) notes that very few studies have found that group-based mastery learning has had any negative effect on the achievement of the top students. In effect, teachers using the traditional whole-class approach set the level and pace of instruction according to the knowledge and abilities of the 10th to the 25th percentile of the class (Dahloff, 1971; Arlin and Westbury, 1976) even traditional group-paced instructional models hold back high achievers for the benefit of their slower classmates.

Mastery learning has to be supplemented by substantial additional resources to pay for the time needed for corrective instruction. This does not mean that the basic idea of mastery learning is wrong. "The idea that students' specific deficits should be remediated immediately instead of being allowed to accumulate into large and general deficiencies makes a great deal of sense." (Slavin, 1987b).

The coverage-vs.-mastery dilemma highlights the difficulties implicit in declarations such as the one made by the OECD Ministers of Education in 1984 (quoted in OECD, 1989, p. 33): "The goal of educating each child to the limits of her or his ability remains paramount" (our emphasis). Such statements are meaningless, because there are unavoidable limitations to the resources available for and devoted to schooling. The reality is that there is necessarily a trade-off between the progress of the most able and the least able students. Unfortunately, all too little is known about the magnitude and nature of this trade-off and its effects on the economic growth and other benefits of social life.

One solution is to sort students according to their ability and to enable each group to progress according to the capacity of its members to absorb new material. If such an approach can be successfully translated into practice and reasonably homogeneous groups can be formed, sorting has several advantages. It enables each group — although not every individual within it — to develop to the limits of its ability. It makes the teacher's task easier by giving him or her a choice as to the level and the pace of instruction. It reduces the frustration of bright students who are forced to advance at a slower pace. It also avoids — or at least it reduces — the risk of discouragement and the consequent loss of motivation among those weak students who, in a system based on heterogenous grouping, would be left hopelessly behind.

In reality, all school systems practice sorting in one way or another. Some have several programs of differing difficulty (e.g., Advanced, General, and Basic levels in Ontario) within each high school. While students could, in principle, take some subjects at the Advanced level and others at the Basic level, depending on their knowledge, interest, and talent, in practice there is very little mixing of programs. In other systems, such as in Japan, whole schools cater to a particular level of student ability and ambition, refusing students who do not meet the criteria of the school's self-selected mandate. Still other systems (e.g., in Germany) sort students at the age of 12 into schools that lead (at the age of 15) to an academic-type school or to a very high-quality vocational apprenticeship system, combined with some additional part-time formal compulsory schooling.

The problem with this kind of sorting is that school systems, at least in North America, have not been very successful at it. In the United States, for example,

Grade 8 students are grouped homogenously for mathematics, based on their performance in arithmetic. There are four streams in Grade 8 mathematics: remedial, general, pre-algebra, and algebra. However, the Second International Mathematics Study found severe misclassifications. Some students in the remedial classes, 25 per cent of those in general classes, and about 40 per cent of those in pre-algebra classes should have been sorted into the algebra classes on the basis of their performance in arithmetic. This has serious implications because only students in algebra classes can expect eventually to be sorted into classes where they will receive the type of instruction that will qualify them for admission to university. For those wrongly excluded from algebra classes, that initial misclassification will eventually become a self-fulfilling prediction that is likely to bear heavily on them for the rest of their lives.

The same principle applies to subjects other than mathematics. Reviewing the research on grouping by ability in elementary schools, Slavin (1987b) concluded that grouping students by general ability does not enhance their achievement. Grouping them for selected subjects (particularly for reading and mathematics) can be effective if the students are not regrouped for more than one or two subjects.

It is important that the grouping reduce student heterogeneity in the specific skill taught, not in relation to I.Q. or overall achievement. Most of the time, students should remain in heterogenous classes, otherwise they may perceive themselves as stereotyped as belonging to a weak class and, as a result, may lose motivation to do better. For the same reason, individual student placement should be reassessed frequently, and the student should be reassigned as soon as she or he has caught up with the class. Heterogeneity in class is also important: Rutter *et al.* (1979) found that schools without a strong mix of students of at least average ability will not develop the degree of motivation needed for effective schooling.

Effective Schools

Although the inputs listed in Table 2.29 have no consistently positive effect on student achievement, some schools do produce consistently better results — in terms of academic achievement, retention rates, juvenile delinquency, and discipline problems —than other schools. Are there common features that characterize the efficient schools?

Such features do, indeed, exist, although not all of them are necessarily present in each of the efficient schools. What characterizes these schools is a common "ethos" consisting largely of most of the factors discussed below (Rutter, 1983; Purkey and Smith, 1983).

To understand that ethos, it is useful to consider a school as a rather complicated social organization consisting of students, teachers, administrators, and support staff devoted to the aim of transmitting knowledge and skills to the student body. As in all social organizations, success depends on the cooperation of all the participants — bearing in mind that youngsters cannot be expected to have the same degree of maturity, knowledge, and self-discipline as adults.

Effective schools emphasize academic work and succeed in conveying to their students the notion that academic success is important. They have high expectations from their students but they are careful not to set the standards so high as to render them unachievable for a high percentage of the student body. (Targets that are unrealistically high have a discouraging impact.)

Effective schools devote a high proportion of instructional time to active teaching and studying — to "time on task". The efficient use of available time is more important than the actual length of time — i.e., the number of hours in the school day or the school year. Some very effective systems — that of Hungary, for example — have relatively short school years yet show high academic achievement.

Effective schools monitor individual progress regularly. One way to do this is to set and mark homework regularly. This provides feedback from the teacher to the student, acts as a diagnostic tool, and also develops a sense of self-monitoring in the student. It is important that students know what is expected of them, that they be aware they are meeting expectations, and that they take pride in doing so. Prompt praise by the teacher for doing good work is more effective than criticism of weak performance.

Proper classroom management also contributes significantly to academic achievement. To this end, a high proportion of teaching time should be devoted to active learning, and distractions should be kept to a minimum. If teaching periods are constantly interrupted by administrative chores, discipline problems, or public announcements, academic achievement is bound to suffer.

Thus, the school must have clear and reasonable rules of order and discipline, which must be consistently enforced. Only then can the school achieve the willing cooperation of the student body and develop a proud school spirit — a veritable sense of community. This sense is strengthened by giving students responsibilities, preferably on a rotating basis, for maintaining discipline, caring for the cleanliness and decoration of the classroom, and preventing vandalism. The combination of the rules and the school spirit will induce pupils to respect the school buildings and contribute to a more pleasant working environment. More experienced teachers are better at accomplishing this than beginners but all teachers share the responsibility for building the collegial spirit that characterizes efficient schools. That spirit extends to joint planning of the curriculum, often under the leadership of the principal, and to ensuring that all teachers follow the agreed-upon program and have the same academic targets. A purposeful program of compulsory curriculum is more effective than a wide choice of electives in raising academic standards.

A healthy community spirit is difficult to create and is not easy to maintain, particularly if there is frequent staff turnover. Here, the relationship is bi-directional. The staff at effective schools, having a good collegial spirit and few discipline problems, is less likely to suffer from teacher burnout and therefore rapid turnover which, in turn, facilitates the maintenance of a collegial atmosphere and effective teaching.

As in all social organizations, much depends on the chief executive officer — the school's principal. He or she sets the tone, the aims of the school, and the direction and intensity of the effort. Ultimately, being a good leader is more an art than a craft: it cannot be taught. There is, however, one indispensable characteristic of a good principal: he or she must enjoy teaching. Unfortunately, and all too often, it is those teachers who do not like teaching who try to escape by becoming principals. Not infrequently, such persons become educational bureaucrats rather than principals of truly efficient schools.

School Choice

There is general agreement that school ethos is a crucial ingredient in high-quality schooling. But ethos is not easy to create. Students differ widely in abilities, interests, and social backgrounds. What is effective with one group may fail with another. Teaching is not only a vocation and a craft involving techniques, it is also a profession requiring self-discipline, high standards of achievement, and judgment in applying the rules of the craft. At its best teaching is an art involving sensitivity, enthusiasm, and an innovative spirit. But even a school with good teachers needs a good principal as to direct and coordinate the efforts of the staff. This calls for leadership — and other talents that cannot be taught or imposed by rules and directives.

The system of public education in most industrialized countries enjoys a near-monopolistic position. It is, however, in the nature of monopolistic institutions to develop bureaucracies inclined to deal with problems by establishing rules. Bureaucracies and the rules that emanate from them are not helpful to the development of good schooling, however.

In the United States, in particular, Catholic and other private schools fare better than public schools at achieving high scholastic standards, disciplined behaviour, and school ethos in general. This finding holds true even after adjustments for the socio-economic status of individual students and the student body as a whole, and for the intellectual quality of the school intake (Chubb and Moe, 1990; Coleman and Hoffer, 1987). Moreover, these better results are achieved at a lower cost than in the public school sector. Regulations cannot achieve what free choice accomplishes almost automatically.

There are increasingly frequent calls to allow parents more freedom of choice in schooling — a controversial issue. It will be recalled that some countries have higher scores in educational achievement than Canada, even though they do not have widespread systematic freedom of choice. At the same time, unrestricted freedom of choice implies many important features not present in our current educational system. Were it to be implemented here, parents could choose the schools their children will attend freely, without being tied to the neighbourhood public school. Parents would be free to choose any public school (and possibly any private school), not only within the limits of their school district but within the entire province. The money, perhaps in the form of "educational vouchers", would follow the child. Through their choices, parents would express their preference for each school. Currently, well-to-do-families can choose their schools by "voting with their feet" — moving to areas where schools meet their expectations.

Under the free-choice system, the parents of poorer children would enjoy the same benefit. Schools would be allowed to set their own aims within a loosely-set framework of criteria determined by the educational authorities. Some might wish to become known for their academic excellence, some for their high-quality vocational training, others for improving the achievement of slower learners, and yet others for instilling good work habits into students with discipline problems. All of these are worthy and socially useful goals, but they require different teaching talents and methods, and possibly different types of school spirit. General rules laid down by departments of education or the school boards do not favour the required flexibility.

The proponents of free choice in schooling maintain that many schools would voluntarily take advantage of the greater flexibility afforded by this system in order to improve their teaching practices and that competition would force the others to follow suit. Schools that do not meet parents' expectations would be exposed. Under such a system, unsuccessful schools would simply be allowed to go out of business; and new schools could be set up, subject only to provincial criteria of graduation, teacher certification, and health and safety requirements.

Schools would admit students on the basis of applications and could refuse any student who did not meet the school's selected "mission" standards. They would also be free to expel any student who does not cooperate in the achievement of that mission. Every school district would have to establish some sort of central office to keep track of all the school-age children in the district and their level of funding, which could vary depending on the special needs of each child and on the willingness of the district to tax itself for the education of its children. This office would also provide parents with information about various indicators of school quality and characteristics — indicators that parents need in order to make intelligent choices and to ensure that every child will have a place in a school.

Even those who favour free choice admit that such a policy is fraught with danger — at least in the short run. Conceivably, the good schools could be inundated with applications while the lesser schools would stand empty. The weaker schools would have great difficulty in raising their standards and acquiring a better reputation quickly enough to avoid being forced to shut down. Indeed, the very movement of the better students to better schools might inhibit the efforts of the weaker schools to seek such improvement, because — as the literature on effective schools shows — a nucleus of students with at least average ability is needed for the development of a learning ethos.

The proponents of school choice recommend a basic (province-wide) "scholarship" or "voucher" system for every student, but they would allow school districts to raise school taxes if they wished to do so. Not all school districts could raise taxes, however, even if they wished to do so. Low-income areas would not have the tax base required to improve their schools, even though better schools are urgently needed in those areas to provide young people with the educational tools they need to escape poverty. So, the central authorities might have to provide larger "scholarships" for the children from poor areas. Similarly, disadvantaged children might need even more school resources than those who are not at risk. Such problems could raise serious political difficulties.

Critics maintain that common schools help to create a community spirit that would be destroyed by freedom of school choice. However, defenders of choice respond by arguing that schools differ widely in quality, depending on the prosperity of the neighbourhood, and that the current lack of freedom of choice tends to perpetuate those inequalities.

Would school choice fulfill all of the promises envisioned by its proponents? A glance at the school system in the Netherlands is instructive in this respect (Louis and Van Velzen, 1991). In that country, freedom of choice has been in force for over 85 years, and over 65 per cent of all schools are private (predominantly religious). According to the Dutch constitution, "all persons shall be free to provide education"; and "private primary schools that satisfy the conditions laid down by Act of Parliament shall be financed from public funds according to the same standards of as public-authority schools". The schools can choose their own curricula, but the government sets final exams for secondary schools.

Despite the availability of choice, there is little difference in the curricula, structure, and teaching methods of the various Dutch schools. Course content and methods of instruction are determined by the teachers and their professional organizations. Parents are more interested in the religion and socio-economic level of their children's classmates and/or the distance to the school than in the method and effectiveness of teaching. While schools do advertise in order to attract students, they do not publicize the latter's achievement; to do so would be regarded as "unprofessional". Also, there is a social consensus that even with (or perhaps because of?) competition between schools there is a need to protect the students from incompetent schools. Government regulation of schools has increased significantly over the recent decades.

There are indications that choice exacerbates the problem of equity. Those parents who care for the educational achievement of their children are likely to choose good schools for them, while indifferent or ignorant parents will continue to send their children to the nearest school, regardless of its quality. This will tend to aggravate social inequalities, unless the authorities pursue a policy of strengthening the weak schools.

Subjecting schools to the "market test" is dangerous, for two reasons. The first is that, just as in medicine, the selector —in this case, the parent — is not necessarily qualified to judge the quality of the administrator of the treatment — i.e., the school and the teachers. The second reason is that, because education is a cumulative process influencing the entire life of a student, the "proof" of its quality is determined only over a long period of time. While the freedom of school choice may indeed be a useful indicator of parental satisfaction, it demonstrates only against the symptoms of the problems. It cannot be relied upon to cure the ills of the educational system.

Avenues for Future Research

Our survey of the literature on education found painful gaps in what is known about the educational systems that exist in Canada. If Canadians wish to improve the quality of their educational system — and its improvement is imperative — they must give the highest priority to closing these gaps.

Valid comparisons constitute one of the most effective ways of discovering the strengths and weaknesses of an educational system, of drawing public attention to them, and of finding ways to improve the system. The Second International Mathematics Study showed that of the 15 systems surveyed, British Columbia was the only jurisdiction that did not require calculus for university-bound students in the final year of high school. That gap has since been remedied. The Educational Testing Service showed that 13-year-old Ontario students are not doing as well in science as their counterparts in 12 other industrialized countries; their relative performance is almost as bad in mathematics — not only internationally but within Canada as well.

The Ontario Minister of Education recently announced a major overhaul of the province's school system. Interprovincial and international comparisons must become a regular and routine method for assessing provincial educational systems. While international comparisons in reading, writing, literature, geography, and social studies are more difficult to design than those in mathematics and science, such comparisons are possible on an interprovincial basis, if there is a will to make them.

Levels of achievement are useful indicators, but *levels of improvement* are the true measure of the quality of instruction. To measure properly the value added by teaching, one must keep in mind the various nonschool factors that influence scholastic achievement. The family's socio-economic status, the presence of both parents, the language spoken in the home (if different from the language of instruction), and the length of stay in Canada all come to mind as forces influencing educational achievement. An extensive study should be made to measure the influence of these forces which would enable researchers to adjust the raw data on educational achievement.

No information is currently available about the subjects in which Canadian teachers majored at university, as opposed to the subjects they are teaching today. The Second International Mathematics Study showed that only 4 per cent of Grade 8 mathematics teachers in Ontario were "fully qualified mathematics specialists" — the lowest percentage, by far, among the participating systems. Even by the end of high school, among the 13 industrialized countries for which data are available, Ontario was in ninth place for fully qualified, specialized mathematics teachers. The idea that any teacher is capable of teaching any subject well is totally wrong. We cannot hope to set the current mismatches right as long as we are ignorant of their nature and magnitude.

As shown above, Canadian secondary schools are not very good at sorting students correctly so as to ensure that they have an opportunity to develop their capacities fully. Better and more reliable sorting methods must be devised. It must be borne in mind that there is a direct relationship between sorting and the opportunity to learn, and the potential consequences of misdirecting individuals are enormous and are carried with them for the rest of their lives. Should a solution to the sorting problem prove impossible, one must ask whether it is more beneficial for society as a whole to lower the opportunity to learn of the most able students to the level of the slow learners, or to set the pace of progress to that of the top or next-to-top quarter of the typical class and leave the weakest students hopelessly behind. Either approach entails risks and consequences — not the least of which include destroying the motivation of substantial numbers of students and increasing discipline problems in class.

Individual tutoring is obviously the method that most enhances students' achievement, but it is impossible to implement such an approach in the context of compulsory mass-education. More research is needed to find the trade-off between gains in educational achievement achieved through reduced class size and the additional financial burden that such a policy would entail. Only when this knowledge is available will an informed electorate be able to decide on the appropriate size of the educational budget. It may well be true that the optimal class size depends on the subject being taught and on the learning capacity of the students — for example, small classes may be more important for weak students than for strong ones; foreign-language instruction may require smaller classes than for geography; smaller classes may be more beneficial for younger age groups. All of these possibilities require further intensive investigation.

The traditional approach to education — wherein the teacher lectures and corrects exercises; the students listen, take notes, and do exercises and homework — has proved its effectiveness over many generations. The most recent international surveys of the achievement of 13-year-old students in mathematics and science confirm this resoundingly. This does not mean that reforms in pedagogy should be discouraged or that they would not lead to improved results — but the burden of proof lies on the innovators. They must show that the changes will lead to improvements and that they are feasible in relation to the teaching and financial resources available. There would be little justification, for example, in introducing reforms requiring an adequately retrained teaching staff if they were to be implemented by people who have not mastered the new approach or do not believe in it.

A famous Swedish longitudinal study followed the total male school enrolment of the city of Malmö from Grade 3 at the age of 10 and followed them through their school education, working life, continuous and continuing education, career progress, and self-reported happiness and career satisfaction to the age of 60 in 1988 (Tuijnman, 1989). If a similar study were conducted in Canada, using a large sample of children and following them from their pre-school years through their formal education to, say, age 35, it could provide answers to many important questions. It would not be necessary to wait long before the analysis could begin and be evaluated. Soon after the beginning of the study, it would be possible to evaluate the effect of Headstart-type programs on early school achievement, and then gradually follow through its effect on late development. Similarly, various teaching techniques; the effect of the home environment and of class size; spending on various types of educational expenditures; and many other issues of interest to educators could be evaluated, provided the study were properly designed. Finally, the study could yield information on how all these factors influence one's working life, self-image, and happiness.

Appendix

Is Educational Testing a Valid Tool?

The opponents of educational testing argue that the scope and significance of education are so broad as to be beyond the scope of conventional testing and measurement and that test results are therefore irrelevant and misleading. Advocates of testing agree that test results cover few of the aims of education (listed earlier), but they in turn argue that test results can serve as very useful indicators of at least some of these goals. They also agree that no student should be assessed on the basis of a single test. No outsider knows a student as well as his or her teacher, and of course, anyone can have an atypical bad day from time to time. A judicious combination of test results and regular course work should be the basis of evaluation. Set against this, however, is the fact that teachers are not necessarily impartial judges of course work. Consciously or subconsciously, they know that their students' progress is considered to be an indicator of their performance as teachers; this is bound to influence their evaluations of those aspects of schooling which are, in practice, not measurable. Objective testing and test evaluation serve as a salutary corrective to this bias. From time to time, students must also be reminded that they will encounter situations in life when they must give account of themselves, whether the moment is convenient or not.

The opponents of testing stress the difficulties arising from the differences in curricula, different classes, schools, and school systems. They point out that students cannot be expected to know what they have not been taught and that students may have mastered other aspects of the subject not covered by a given test. This is a particularly salient argument used by those who represent educational systems that permit much local autonomy in determining curriculum, because children are supposed to be educated for the needs of the local labour market. However, this argument is fundamentally wrong.

Primary and secondary education lays the foundations for the individual's subsequent life. As pointed out by the Economic Council of Canada in 1991, about 1.3 per cent of Canada's population moves from one province to another every year. This means that over an average working life of 40 years, for example, the sheer volume of interprovincial migration is likely to affect more than half the total population of the country. The relative volume of movement within the provinces — from one area to another where the characteristics of the economic base are radically different from those where the migrant's schooling occurred — may be even larger. An educational system with a curriculum that prepares students only for the perceived needs of the local area will do a disservice to the students and to the parents. Similarly, Canadian educators and researchers can profit from studying international tests, by learning from them just where Canadian students stand in relation to their future competitors in other parts of the world. The Second International Mathematics Study revealed that British Columbia was the only system among the participating industrial countries that did not include calculus as part of the mathematics curriculum for those "who are studying mathematics as a substantial part (approximately 5 hours per week) of an academic program" during the last year of high school. This has since been remedied, partly, perhaps, because the test results drew the deficiency to attention of the public and of the relevant policymakers.

Some critics argue that some tests measure only lower-order skills, particularly the large-scale tests that rely on multiple-choice formats and use computers to analyse and assess the results. No doubt an exhaustive high-quality test should include problems that call for essay-type responses and problem solving. It is remarkable, nevertheless, that even the multiple-choice tests employed for international studies show a wide range of differences at both the national and individual levels. Interestingly, the Japanese university-entrance examinations, which are very demanding are also the multiple-choice type.

Those opposed to testing often maintain that the practice is harmful because it leads to an overemphasis of the acquisition of those skills needed to write tests, to the detriment of mastering other knowledge and the pursuit of other educational goals. This is known as "teaching to the test". However, such criticism is more justified when directed against badly designed tests than against testing as such. If a test is a sort of examination, then one of the aims of all education systems is to prove that students acquire the necessary competence. Who would be ready to undergo heart surgery under the scalpel of a surgeon who had not passed the usual and required university examinations? The same argument applies to examinations and tests in general. "Teaching to the test" is dangerous if the test material is too narrow or irrelevant. The answer is to design appropriate tests, not to abolish or avoid them altogether. As for the claim that tests put too much emphasis on lower-order skills, Canada's poor showing in international tests indicates that Canadian students are not competent even in those skills.

According to some critics, testing is dangerous because the results of even the best-designed tests will be misused or misinterpreted. For example, a recently arrived immigrant child who speaks and understands the language of instruction imperfectly cannot be expected to obtain a high score. This "lack of language" should not be interpreted as a sign of the student's lack of ability or effort, however.

Children of families with low socio-economic status frequently record lower test results than those of professional and upper-managerial parents. If the catchment area of a school has a population that consists predominantly of unskilled or semi-skilled labour and shows low test results, it should not be concluded that the school and the teachers are doing a poor job. First, parental motivation must be taken into account. It should not be beyond the skill of educational experts to devise proper appropriate adjustments for those characteristics that could potentially distort raw test scores. In any case, the proper measure of educational achievement is the gain registered by test scores over a relevant time period. This means that tests could be administered at the beginning and at the end of the school year, for example, and the difference between such pre-test and post-test scores could also be regarded as the indicator of student and teacher achievement — the "value added" in the economist's parlance (Hanushek, 1986, p. 1157; Hanushek, and Taylor, 1989, p. 198).

Some educators claim that tests promote a harmful spirit of competition between students, inevitably showing up "losers" and "winners". The losers, they argue, become less motivated, and their initial poor showing becomes a self-fulfilling prophecy over the long haul (Denis, 1971). There is some truth to this argument, but it is also easy to exaggerate.

First, the concern applies more to norm-referenced tests than to criterion-referenced tests. Second, if one accepts the view that one purpose of education is to prepare students for the next stage of their lives, one must also accept the fact that they will inevitably encounter competition in the course of their progress — when seeking admission to a university of their choice, applying for a job, or simply living in the competitive environment created by an increasingly globalized — and competitive — world economy (Holmes, 1971).

3
The Learning Continuum
Adult Education, Training and Apprenticeship in Canada

The Economic Council's Statement, *A Lot to Learn*, discusses the notion of a "learning continuum" at some length (Figure 3.1). It notes, quite rightly, that the traditional distinction between schooling and work has become blurred. Learning is a lifelong process; people move constantly between learning institutions and the labour market and many are engaged in working and in learning activities simultaneously.

In the context of the learning continuum, the concept of coherence is discussed specifically in relation to the question "how can communication among major participants in the learning process — students, teachers, employers — be enhanced?". Vocational programs at the high school and college level, and within industry are examined and major conclusions are drawn that acknowledge the need to: improve the image of vocational programs at the secondary level, improve articulation between such programs and the regular apprenticeship system, overhaul the entire apprenticeship system, improve career counselling, and encourage partnership arrangements.

This chapter reports the details of new research relating to two specific aspects of the learning continuum. First, as mentioned above, most people learn and work continuously and simultaneously; new evidence from Statistics Canada now permits us to examine the nature and determinants of this process. Second, we present a detailed analysis of apprenticeship, an important and long-standing form of learning and labour-market preparation.

Adult Education and Training in Canada

The importance of lifelong learning in Canada today is evidenced by the fact that during 1989-90 approximately 28 per cent of Canada's total labour force age 17 years and over was involved in some form of institution-based instruction or training. Much of the rest of this chapter draws on data obtained from a recent survey to examine the determinants of participation in various forms of training.

The data source, the 1990 Adult Education and Training Survey (AETS), was conducted by Statistics Canada for Employment and Immigration Canada. The survey covers all household members 17 years of age and over across Canada (excluding the Yukon and Northwest Territories), and contains information for 92,808 individuals. The information collected is specific to the period between December 1, 1989 and November 30, 1990.

Whether persons are counted as full-time or part-time trainees depends on how they are classified by the institution in which they receive their instruction. In most cases, however, the classification is determined by the number of courses in which the trainee is enrolled. A *short-term course* is a course taken on a full-time basis over a period of one month or less. These can be considered as special cases of part-time training. *Part-time training* extends over a period longer than one month and requires the trainee to take instruction on a periodic or occasional basis.

This study introduces the concept of *training participation rate* calculated from the micro data of the AETS. For example, the full-time institutional training participation rate by age and province is calculated as the ratio of the number of trainees in the designated institutions to the number of labour force members in the corresponding age group and province.

Full-time Training

Between December 1989 and November 1990, approximately 6 per cent of the total Canadian labour force over age 17 participated in full-time instructional and training programs offered by educational and training institutions, including community colleges, CEGEPs, technical institutes, universities, trade/vocational schools, commercial training schools, unions

Figure 3.1
The Learning Continuum

Source: *A Lot to Learn,* Economic Council of Canada, 1992

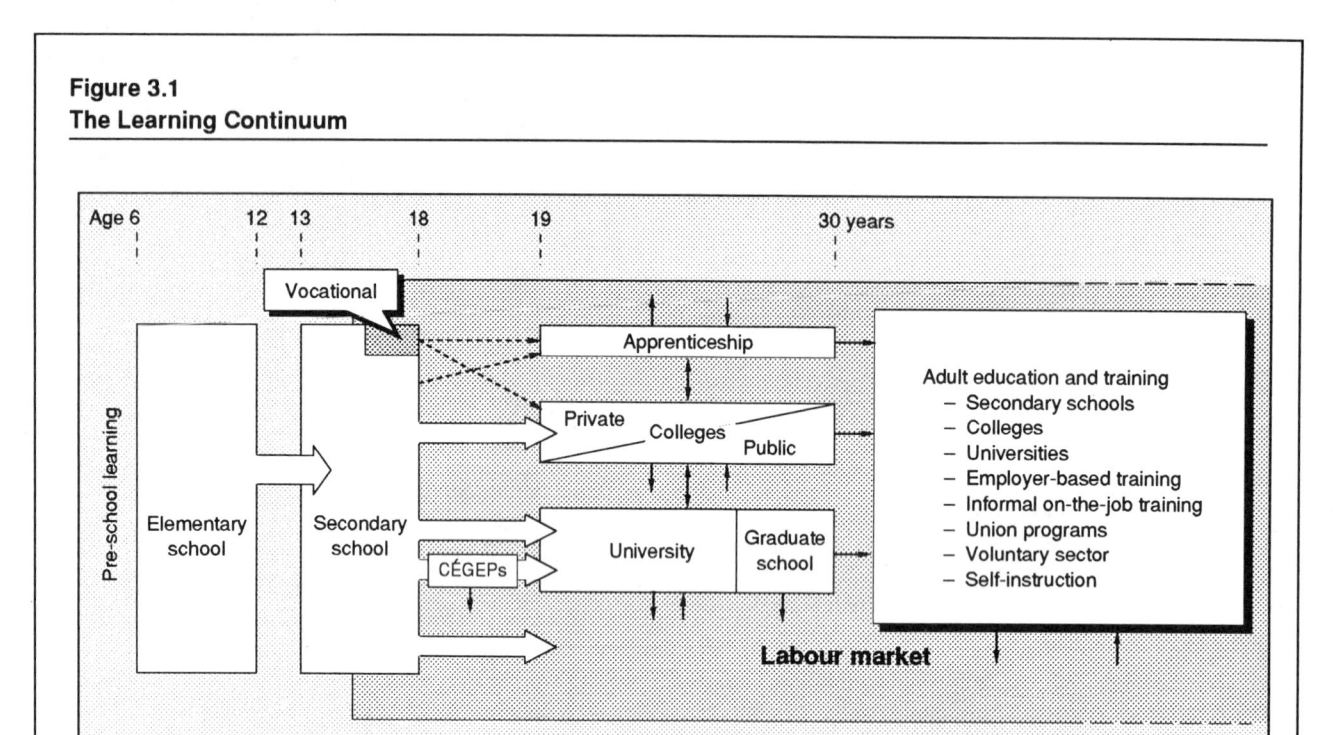

and professional organizations. This figure does not include individuals in part-time training or apprenticeship training programs. Nevertheless, the numbers support the notion that learning — in many cases, necessarily — has become a life-long endeavour for many individuals. The participation rate of full-time training programs by age group sheds further light on the pattern of life long-learning (Figure 3.2). Clearly, the younger the individual, the higher the probability that he/she participates in a full-time educational or training program. However, the Table also shows that it is almost never too late to learn: even the older age categories are involved in full-time training or education, although to a lesser extent. Although participation also varies provincially, the variation across Canada is relatively small.

Causes of Variations in Full-Time Training Participation

Figures 3.2 through 3.5 summarize the factual information on full-time participation in education and training. Although the information is interesting in itself, policy insight requires knowledge of the causes of training-participation decisions. This study attempts to shed some light on this topic by relating the training participation rate to a number of plausible explanatory variables in a multiple regression framework.

The survey provides information on full-time trainees from three different categories of institution: 1) universities, community colleges, CEGEPs, and technical institutes; 2) trade/vocational schools; and 3) commercial schools, unions and professional organizations. The aggregated training participation rate equation (i.e., the equation for all full-time trainees from all training institutions) and their disaggregated counterparts are shown at the end of this section. Since each category has a different degree of academic flavour, there is a case for estimating the training participation rate separately for each type of institution. Obviously, the participation behaviour varies from institution to institution. However, the differences are not great and for this reason, the remainder of this section is mainly a discussion of the results of the aggregated equation.

The aggregated equation for full-time training is based on the hypothesis that the full-time training participation rate (FTPARTAL) depends upon the educational attainment of the labour force (HIED), the gender mix of the labour force (LFEM), the industrial

Figure 3.2
Full-Time Training Participation Rate by Age Group, 1989-1990, Canada (%)

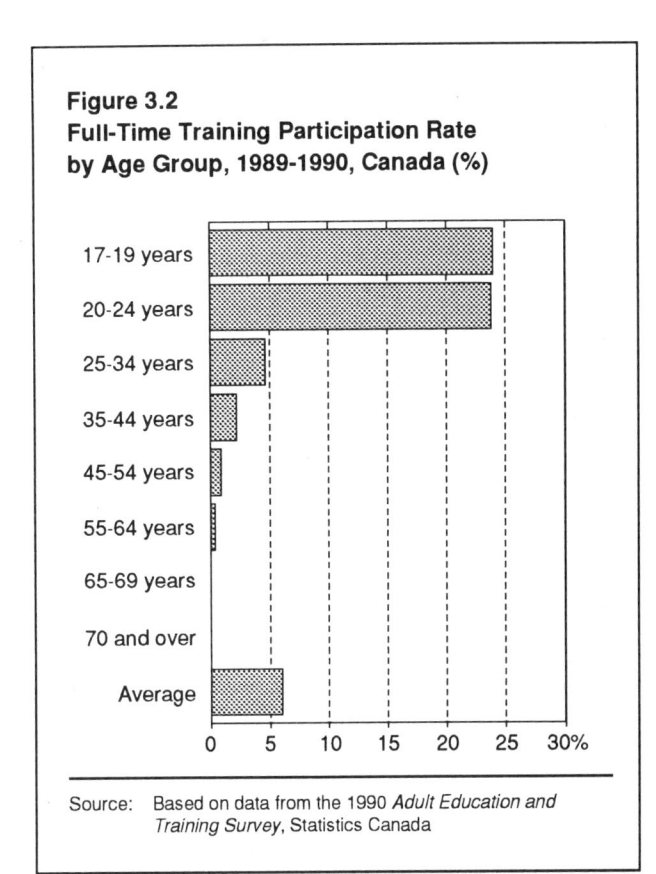

Age Group	%
17-19 years	~24
20-24 years	~24
25-34 years	~5
35-44 years	~2
45-54 years	~1
55-64 years	<1
65-69 years	0
70 and over	0
Average	~6

Source: Based on data from the 1990 *Adult Education and Training Survey*, Statistics Canada

Figure 3.3
Full-Time Training Participation Rate by Province, 1989-1990, Canada (%)

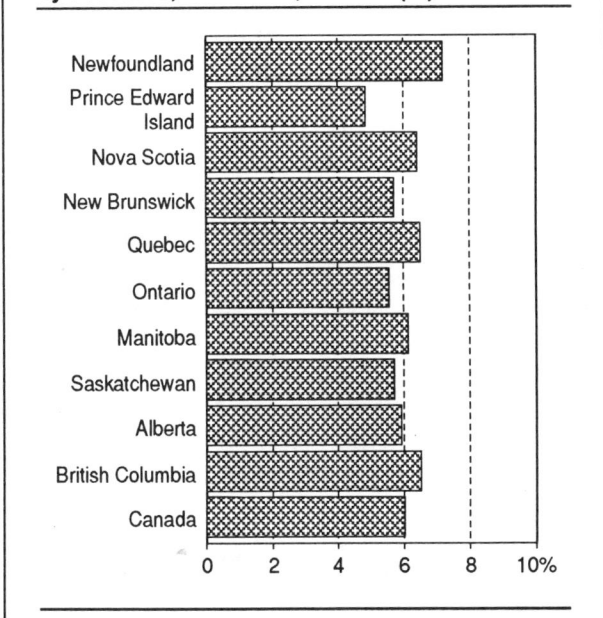

Province	%
Newfoundland	~7
Prince Edward Island	~4.5
Nova Scotia	~6
New Brunswick	~5.5
Quebec	~6.5
Ontario	~5.5
Manitoba	~6
Saskatchewan	~5.5
Alberta	~6
British Columbia	~6.5
Canada	~6

Source: Based on data from the 1990 *Adult Education and Training Survey*, Statistics Canada

Figure 3.4
Distribution of Full-time Trainees by Firm Size, 1989-1990, Canada

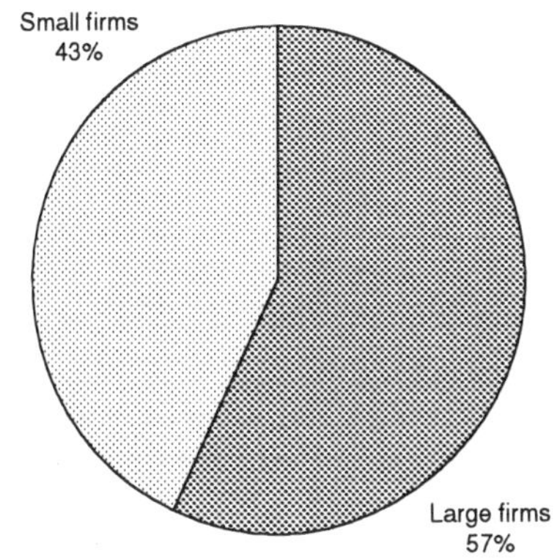

- Small firms: 43%
- Large firms: 57%

Source: Based on data from the 1990 *Adult Education and Training Survey*, Statistics Canada

Figure 3.5
Full-Time Trainees/Labour Force Ratio: Male vs Female, 1989-1990, Canada (%)

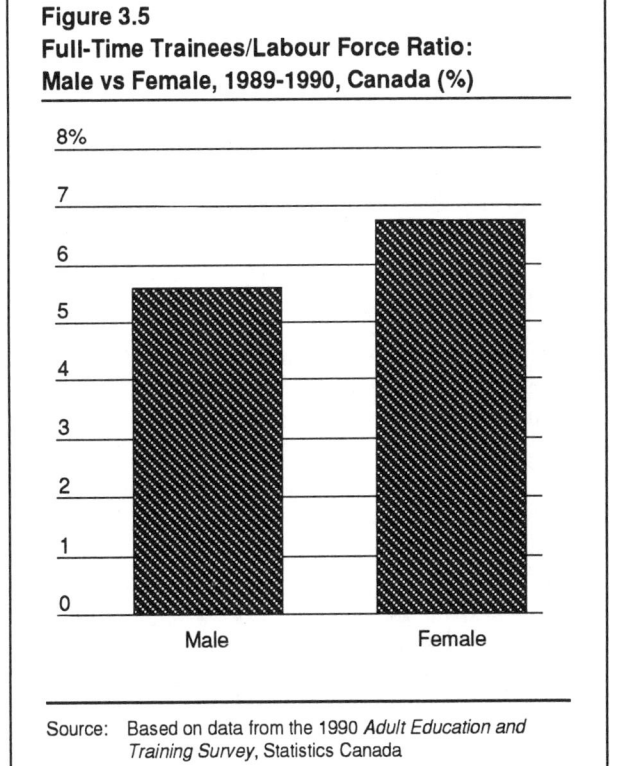

- Male: ~5.6
- Female: ~6.7

Source: Based on data from the 1990 *Adult Education and Training Survey*, Statistics Canada

composition of the economy (GOODS), the proportion of workers from large firms (LARGE), the proportion of long-tenure workers to the total number of workers (LONG), and the extent to which the training cost is borne by employers, the government, unions, professional organizations and non-profit organizations (PAIDBY) (Table 3.1). Since the survey data provide only a cross-section of the training market, the specification of the equation must be designed to take advantage of the information available. Particularly, the specification must pool the data over each age group and each province. This pooling technique requires that each observation of the dependent and independent variables be uniquely associated with the age and provincial dimensions of the variable. For this reason, the equation must also include a variable to represent the labour force by age and by province as one of its regressors (independent variables) to avoid spurious correlation between the training participation rate and other explanatory variables.

The "labour force by age and province" variable (LCOMP) serves a function essentially analogous to the seasonal dummies in a quarterly seasonally unadjusted multiple regression equation. Since the dependent variable (i.e., the training participation rate) is expressed in terms of a ratio (of the number of trainees to the total labour force of the age group and province in question), all independent variables must also be "normalized" to preserve the consistency of the specification. For example, the educational attainment variable is the ratio of the number of people with high school diplomas or higher educational attainment in group ij (age and province) to the number of labour force members in group ij; in other words, the labour force is the "normalizing factor" in this example. The precise definitions of all the variables are provided at the end of this section.

The estimated equation for total full-time trainees (including all full-time trainees from all institutions) indicates — after allowing for the effects of age-and-province differences — that the educational attainment of the labour force, the gender mix of workers, and who pays the training cost have significant impacts on the training participation rate. On the other hand, the industry mix of workers, the proportion of workers from large firms and the proportion of workers with long tenure show no systematic influence on the probability of participation in a full-time training program. These results, require further elaboration.

The estimated coefficient for the "high school or better" variable (HIED$_{ij}$) is 0.156. The proportion of workers with a high-school diploma or higher educational attainment varies from age group to age group and from province to province. The average value for this variable is 0.62. In simple terms, this means that if policy-makers could somehow increase the proportion of the work force with high-educational attainment from 62 to 63 per cent, then there is a high probability that full-time education and training participation will go up by close to 2 per cent. This finding highlights the critical importance of the drop-out phenomenon for the whole notion of life long learning (because high-school drop-outs lower the overall proportion of the labour force with high-school or better, and that in turn lowers the probability of [full-time] enrolment in education and training institutions).

The estimated coefficient for the gender mix variable (LFEM$_{ij}$) suggests that females tend to participate in full-time education and training courses more than males. As long as the rate of labour force participation by females continues to increase, the overall number of full-time female trainees will likely also increase. There is evidence that women tend to be given less workplace training than men; it is, therefore, interesting to observe that women avail themselves of institutional training to a greater extent than men.

The coefficient for the PAIDBY$_{ij}$ variable confirms that "who pays the cost of training" is an important factor in determining the full-time training participation rate. According to the survey, about 2 per cent of the labour force had their training costs paid by their employers, unions, professional organizations, voluntary organizations, or by the government. The policy implication is clear: governments and employers can directly influence the training participation decision by providing financial or funding support.

The three statistically insignificant explanatory variables may come as a surprise. However, the exact definitions of these variables have contributed greatly to the results. The simple correlation between the training participation rate (FTPARTAL$_{ij}$) and the industrial mix variable (GOODS$_{ij}$) is -0.39. This statistical relationship in its simple form is significant. It is, however, not significant in a multivariate framework that accepts the contributions of all explanatory variables simultaneously. The simple correlation between the training participation rate and the firm-size variable (LARGE$_{ij}$) is 0.097; the corresponding statistic for the tenure variable (LONG$_{ij}$) is 0.088. Even though these two explanatory variables are positively correlated with the training participation rate, the statistical associations are extremely weak.

Table 3.1
Regression Results: Full-time Eduction and Training
(Based on Pooled Cross-section Age/Province Data)

Equation	Dependent Variable[1]	LCOMP$_{ij}$	HIED$_{ij}$	LFEM$_{ij}$	GOODS$_{ij}$	LARGE$_{ij}$	LONG$_{ij}$	PAIDBY$_{ij}$	R^2	Adjusted R^2
1	FTPANTAL$_{ij}$	-0.636 (-4.780)	0.156 (2.372)	0.557 (3.339)	0.015 (0.168)	0.022 (0.355)	0.016 (0.489)	0.696 (2.971)	0.548	0.504
2	FTPARTAL$_{ij}$	-0.582 (-5.430)	0.155 (2.455)	0.570 (5.163)				0.682 (3.112)	0.544	0.520
3	FTPARTUC$_{ij}$	-0.587 (-4.917)	0.137 (2.323)	0.503 (3.360)	0.015 (0.187)	0.023 (0.400)	0.013 (0.438)	0.646 (3.076)	0.554	0.510
4	FTPARTUC$_{ij}$	-0.538 (-5.607)	0.136 (2.412)	0.511 (5.161)				0.636 (3.236)	0.550	0.526
5	FTPARTTR$_{ij}$	-0.049 (-2.833)	0.019 (2.210)	0.054 (2.489)	0.000 (0.002)	-0.000 (-0.027)	0.003 (0.736)	0.049 (1.627)	0.406	0.349
6	FTPARTTR$_{ij}$	-0.043 (-3.078)	0.018 (2.233)	0.059 (4.093)				0.046 (1.607)	0.401	0.369

[1] i = age group; j = province
[2] The t-statistics appear in brackets with each coefficient.

where

FTPARTAL$_{ij}$ = Number of full-time trainees at community colleges, CEGEPs, technical institutes, universities, trade/vocational schools, commercial training schools, unions, and professional organizations in group ij / total labour force of province j

FTPARTUC$_{ij}$ = Number of full-time trainees at community colleges, CEGEPs, technical institutes and universities in group ij / total labour force of province j

FTPARTTR$_{ij}$ = Number of full-time trainees at trade/vocational schools, commercial training schools, unions and professional organizations in group ij / total labour force of province j

LCOMP$_{ij}$ = Total labour force in group ij / total labour force of province j

HIED$_{ij}$ = Total number of people with high-school diplomas or higher educational attainment in group ij / total labour force of province j

LFEM$_{ij}$ = Total number of female labour force members in group ij / total labour force of province j

GOODS$_{ij}$ = Total number of labour force members in group ij in goods-producing industries / total number of labour force participants in group ij

LARG$_{ij}$ = Total number of trainees in group ij from large firms [100 or more workers at one location] / total number of trainees in group ij

LONG$_{ij}$ = Total number of trainees in group ij who have worked for the same employer for more than one year / total number of trainees in group ij

PAIDBY$_{ij}$ = Total number of trainees in group ij whose fees or tuition are paid by employers, unions, professional organizations, voluntary organizations or government / total number of labour force members in group ij

Source: Estimates by the Economic Council of Canada, based on the *Adult Education and Training Survey, 1989-90*, Statistics Canada

In *A Lot to Learn*, it was noted that "only 27 per cent of small firms conduct training, while fully 76 per cent of large firms do so". At first glance, therefore, the result for the firm size variable (LARGE$_{ij}$) seems to contradict that observation. However, the results are not necessarily inconsistent but, rather, non-comparable. The results in *A Lot to Learn* refer largely to company-based training, whereas the results reported here apply only to off-the-job institutional training, which may or may not be sponsored by the company.

The foregoing discussion refers to the equation for aggregated full-time training participation rate, which includes all full-time trainees in 1) universities, community colleges, CEGEPs, and technical institutes; 2) trade/vocational schools; and 3) commercial training schools, unions and professional organizations. The data are also available for the three categories of institutions separately. In order to double-check possible aggregation biases, the training participation rate equation has been re-estimated by type of training institution. The last two categories are aggregated because by themselves category 2 (trade schools) and category 3 (commercial schools) do not have a large enough sample for a valid statistical analysis. These results are also reported in Table 3.1. The estimated coefficients for the trade and commercial schools (category 2 + category 3) training participation rate equation are consistent with those from other equations with respect to *sign* and *statistical significance*, but their *sizes* are generally smaller. This stems from the fact that relatively few individuals took their training in institutions of categories 2 and 3.

Mnemonics List

In all the variables, the subscript i refers to the age group (e.g., i = 17-19 years, 20-24, 25-34, ... 55-64, 65-69, and 70 and over), and j denotes the province in question.

Dependent Variable:

FTPARTAL$_{ij}$: (number of full-time trainees at community colleges, CEGEPs, technical institutes, universities, trade-vocational schools, commercial training schools, unions, and professional organizations in group ij/total labour force of province j).

FTPARTUC$_{ij}$: (number of full-time trainees at community colleges, CEGEPs, technical institutes, and universities in group ij/total labour force of province j).

FTPARTTR$_{ij}$: (number of full-time trainees at trade-vocational schools, commercial training schools, unions, and professional organizations in group ij/total labour force of province j).

Independent Variables:

LCOMP$_{ij}$ Total labour force of group ij/total labour force of province j.

HIED$_{ij}$: Total number of people with high-school diplomas or higher educational attainment in group ij/total labour force of province j.

LFEM$_{ij}$: Total number of female labour force members in group ij/total labour force of province j.

GOODS$_{ij}$: Total number of labour force members in goods-producing industries in group ij/total number of labour force members in (goods and services) producing industries in group ij.

LARGE$_{ij}$: Total number of trainees from large firms in group ij/total number of trainees from small-and-large firms in group ij. (A firm is defined as large if it employs 100 or more workers at one location.)

LONG$_{ij}$: Total number of trainees who have worked for the same employers for more than one year in group ij/total number of trainees who have worked for the same employers (regardless of their employment duration) in group ij.

PAIDBY$_{ij}$: Total number of trainees whose fees or tuition for the programs are paid by employers, or unions, or professional organizations, or voluntary organizations, or government in group ij/total number of labour force members in group ij.

Short-term Courses and Part-time Training

Figure 3.6, shows that approximately 28 per cent of the total Canadian labour force (aged 17 and over) participated in some form of training during the survey period. The predominant form of skill-upgrading was part-time training with about 15 per cent of the work force participating in this type of instruction. Short-term courses were also quite popular: nearly 7 per cent of the labour force enrolled in short courses in the same period. Clearly, short-term and part-time training together accounted for the lion's share of total training and education. By contrast, only 6 per cent of the work force chose full-time training as the path to skill-upgrading, and less than one per cent of the labour force enrolled in apprenticeship training programs.

Nearly three out of every ten persons in the work force are likely to be enrolled in training programs at any point in time. While some individuals choose full-time instruction as their preferred way to equip themselves for the demands of the labour market, they are in the minority; more take short-term courses. However, the majority take part-time training to meet their requirements because most trainees require some income during training — full-time training usually cuts off employment income stream, which may partly explain the observation that females tend to participate in full-time training more than males. In some cases, females are the second income earners of their families but, as will be shown, this second earner explanation is not necessarily supported by the data on short-term and part-time training.

For short-term and part-time training, universities, colleges (including CEGEPs) and technical institutes are the most popular institutions (Figure 3.7). Vocational/trade schools, and private and commercial schools play a lesser role in this connection.

With respect to age, the participation rates for short-term and part-time training contrast sharply with the participation rate for full-time training reported earlier (Figures 3.2 and 3.8). Those involved in full-time training are mainly in the 17-19 and 20-24 year old age brackets, but short-term courses and part-time instruction are taken primarily by those aged 25 and over. Also, many people aged 55 and over are actively involved in taking short-term and part-time courses.

Part-time training participation rates also vary noticeably from province to province (Figure 3.9), another quite different result from that reported earlier for full-time training. Canadians from Quebec, Ontario, Alberta and British Columbia engage in part-time instruction more than their work force counterparts in the rest of the country.

Causes of Variations in Short-term/Part-time Training Participation

Specifications for the short-term/part-time equations parallel the hypotheses for the full-time training participation rate equations. The data for short-term courses and part-time training have been aggregated. However, in order to check for possible biases introduced by data aggregation, estimates have also been made for enrolment in short-term courses and part-time training separately. All of the regression results are shown at the end of this section.

The aggregated, equation for part-time training (short-term courses plus part-time programs) is entirely consistent with the equation reported earlier for full-time training. After allowing for the effects of the age-and-province differences, two factors (the educational attainment of the labour force, and "who pays the training cost") largely determine the training participation rate. The gender mix variable shows some correlation with the participation rate, but the estimated coefficient is not statistically significant at the 5 per cent level. This means, generally, that males and females are equally likely to participate in part-time instruction and training. The size of the coefficient for the "who pays for the training cost" variable is relatively large. This suggests that "who pays" plays an even more important role in determining the extent of part-time training than in the case of full-time training.

In 1989-1990, the cost of training for about 12 per cent of the labour force was borne by their employers, unions, professional organizations, voluntary organizations, or by the government. By extrapolation, if the government and employers combined their efforts to increase this figure to 20 per cent, then the participation rate of short-course/part-time training could be expected to increase from 21 per cent (the average value of the dependent variable is 0.21275) to about 29 per cent (the estimated coefficient for $PAIDBY_{ij}$ is 1.17213). Clearly, the leverage of governments and employers to influence workers' propensity to participate in short-course/part-time training is substantial.

Similar to the results for full-time training, other factors (notably the industry mix of workers, the proportion of workers from large firms and the proportion of workers with long tenure) appear to have no systematic influence on the probability of participation in short course/part-time training programs.

The age/province labour-force composition variable ($LCOMP_{ij}$), plays the same role here as in the full-time equations data. Unlike the results for full-time training, however, the estimated coefficient for this variable is statistically insignificant at the 5 per cent level. For the sake of consistency, this variable has been retained in the finalized equation.

The foregoing discussion refers to the aggregated part-time (short-term course/part-time programs) training participation rate estimates. When short-term courses are separated from part-time training programs, the results show only minor variations. For the short-term-course equation, the educational attainment variable becomes statistically insignificant. For the part-

48 *Education and Training in Canada*

Figure 3.6
Training Participation Rates, 1989-1990, Canada (%)

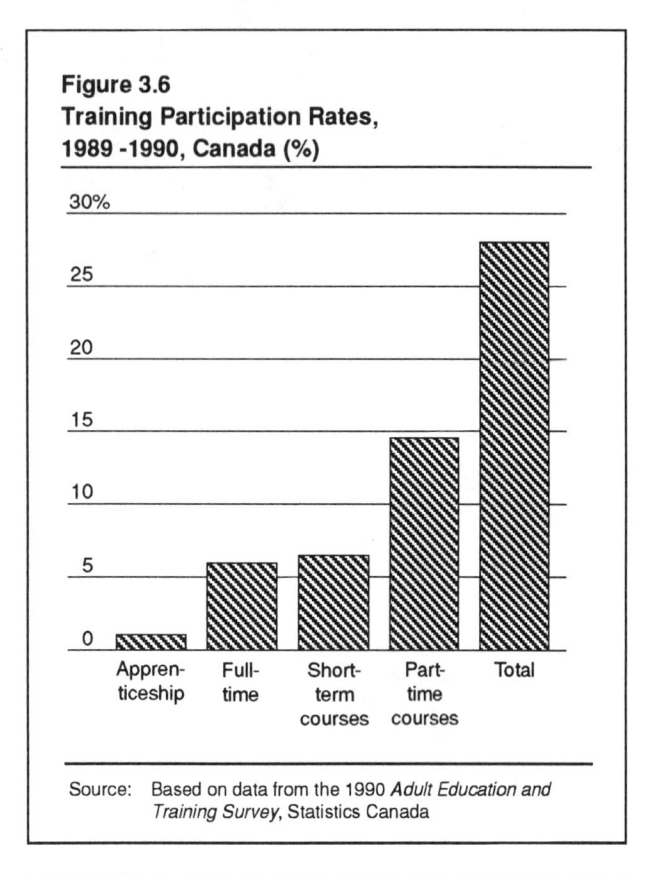

Source: Based on data from the 1990 *Adult Education and Training Survey*, Statistics Canada

Figure 3.7
Distribution of Trainees: Short-term Courses/Part-time Training, 1989-1990, Canada

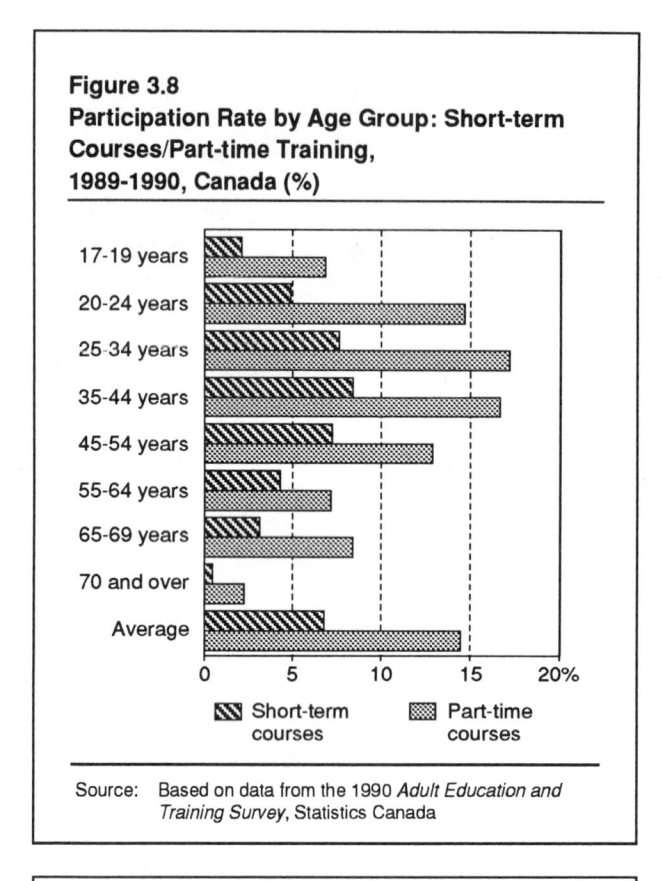

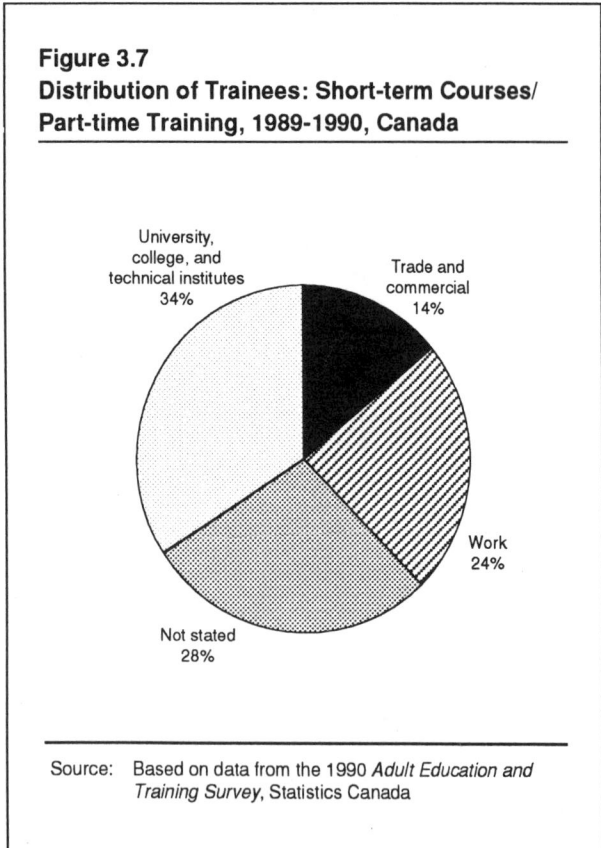

- University, college, and technical institutes: 34%
- Trade and commercial: 14%
- Work: 24%
- Not stated: 28%

Source: Based on data from the 1990 *Adult Education and Training Survey*, Statistics Canada

Figure 3.8
Participation Rate by Age Group: Short-term Courses/Part-time Training, 1989-1990, Canada (%)

Source: Based on data from the 1990 *Adult Education and Training Survey*, Statistics Canada

Figure 3.9
Participation Rate by Province: Short-term/Part-time Training, 1989-1990, Canada (%)

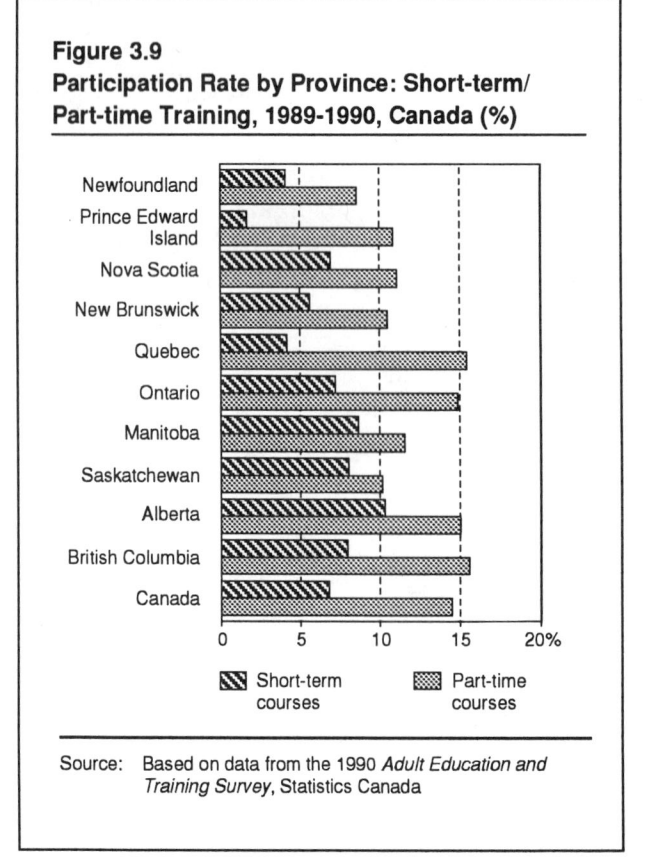

Source: Based on data from the 1990 *Adult Education and Training Survey*, Statistics Canada

time training participation rate equation, the estimated coefficients for the $HIED_{ij}$ and $PAIDBY_{ij}$ variables are both highly significant, however. A close examination of the estimated coefficients for the disaggregated and aggregated equations reveals a pattern of consistency, i.e., the sums of the coefficients of the two disaggregated equations are very close to the estimated coefficients for the aggregated equation. This is especially true for the $HIED_{ij}$ and $PAIDBY_{ij}$ variables.

In summary, the results for short-term courses/part-time programs are consistent with those reported earlier for full-time training; the underlying forces that drive the training participation rates are basically the same for both types of program. Government funding (including funding to non-profit organizations) and employers' willingness to finance training activities are the overwhelming forces in determining the participation rates of short-term courses and part-time training programs. Although the level of educational attainment of the labour force plays a lesser role, it is nonetheless important. Thus, there is much that governments can do to enhance and facilitate the process of life-long learning among Canadian workers. In addition to funding, the government might also use special tax instruments to motivate firms to train workers. Finally, the complementarity between educational attainment and further education and training is important; it underlines the urgent need to reduce the high-school drop-out rate as a means of producing a more highly-skilled workforce.

MNEMONICS LIST

In all the variables, the subscript i refers to the age group (e.g., i = 17-19 years, 20-24, 25-34, ... 55-64, 65-69, and 70 and over), and j denotes the province in question.

Dependent Variable:

$PTPARTAL_{ij}$: (number of trainees in "short-term courses + part-time training" in group ij/total labour force of province j).

$PTPARTFY_{ij}$: (number of trainees in short-term courses in group ij/total labour force of province j).

$PTPARTPY_{ij}$: (number of trainees part-time training in group ij/total labour force of province j).

Independent Variables:

$LCOMP_{ij}$: Total labour force of group ij/total labour force of province j.

$HIED_{ij}$: Total number of people with high-school diplomas or higher educational attainment in group ij/total labour force of province j.

$LFEM_{ij}$: Total number of female labour force members in group ij/total labour force of province j.

$GOODS_{ij}$: Total number of labour force members in goods-producing industries in group ij/total number of labour force members in (goods and services) producing industries in group ij.

$LARGE_{ij}$: Total number of trainees from large firms in group ij/total number of trainees from small-and-large firms in group ij. (A firm is defined as large if it employs 100 or more workers at one location.)

$LONG_{ij}$: Total number of trainees who have worked for the same employers for more than one year in group ij/total number of trainees who have worked for the same employers (regardless of their employment duration) in group ij.

$PAIDBY_{ij}$: Total number of trainees whose fees or tuition for the programs are paid by employers, unions, professional organizations, voluntary organizations, or by government in group ij/total number of labour force members in group ij.

Barriers to Training

The discussion so far has been essentially positive: the statistical analysis has focussed on the factors that encourage full-time and part-time training participation rates. There is, however, another side to the story: why do some people avoid training? Fortunately, the survey also provides some valuable information on this aspect of training. Although the data do not allow for the same type of statistical analyses as reported earlier, the information that can be tabulated from the data is nonetheless relevant to training policy.

The survey asked individuals aged 17 and over, "Was there any training or education program ... you were supposed to take for employment-related reasons but did not?" Answers to this question were as expected — close to 98 per cent of the respondents replied "no", 1.7 per cent "yes", and the rest "don't know". The "yes" answers cast further light on the issue of training participation. The individuals who answered "yes" were asked to give the reasons for not taking training or education programs. A list of 11 possible reasons was offered and respondents were asked to mark all that were applicable. Figure 3.10 summarizes the tabulated results.

Almost 30 per cent of the individuals gave "too busy" as the overwhelming reason for not taking a training or education course that they were supposed to take. "Program unavailable", "too expensive" and

Table 3.2
Regression Results: Short-term Courses / Part-time Training
(Based on Pooled Cross-section Age/Province Data)

Equation	Dependent Variable[1]	\multicolumn{7}{c}{Independent Variable[2]}	R^2	Applied R^2
		$LCOMP_{ij}$	$HIED_{ij}$	$LFEM_{ij}$	$GOODS_{ij}$	$LARGE_{ij}$	$LONG_{ij}$	$PAIDBY_{ij}$		
1	$PTPANTAL_{ij}$	-0.041 (-0.727)	0.127 (5.006)	0.101 (1.850)	0.025 (0.766)	-0.077 (-0.451)	-0.005 (-0.471)	1.172 (9.837)	0.907	0.898
2	$PTPARTAL_{ij}$	-0.037 (-0.704)	0.126 (5.086)	0.074 (1.880)				1.134 (10.796)	0.905	0.900
3	$PTPARTFY_{ij}$	-0.065 (-1.891)	0.000 (0.057)	0.007 (0.241)	0.120 (0.593)	0.188 (1.815)	0.001 (0.190)	0.771 (10.739)	0.815	0.797
4	$PTPARTFY_{ij}$	-0.078 (-2.606)						0.726 (11.997)	0.806	0.801
5	$PTPARTPY_{ij}$	-0.235 (0.394)	0.128 (4.816)	0.093 (1.628)	0.013 (0.390)	-0.110 (0.614)	-0.006 (0.560)	0.400 (3.212)	0.882	0.779
6	$PTPARTPY_{ij}$	-0.041 (-0.745)	0.125 (4.836)	0.076 (1.870)				0.408 (3.717)	0.776	0.765

[1] i = age group; j = province
[2] The t-statistics appear in brackets with each coefficient.

where

$PTPARTAL_{ij}$ = Number of trainees in short-term courses or part-time training in group ij / total labour force of province j
$PTPARTFY_{ij}$ = Number of trainees in short-term courses in group ij / total labour force of province j
$PTPARTPY_{ij}$ = Number of trainees in part-time training in group ij / total labour force of province j

The independent variables are defined as in Table 3.1.

Source: Estimates by the Economic Council of Canada, based on the Adult Education and Training Survey, 1989-90, Statistics Canada

Figure 3.10
Reasons Given for Not Taking a Training or Education Course, 1989-1990, Canada (%)

- Not aware of program
- Program unavailable
- Program not suitable
- Too old/too late
- Not interested
- Too busy
- Too expensive
- Too embarrassed
- Health reasons
- Family responsibilities
- Other

0 5 10 15 20 25 30 35%

Source: Based on data from the 1990 *Adult Education and Training Survey*, Statistics Canada

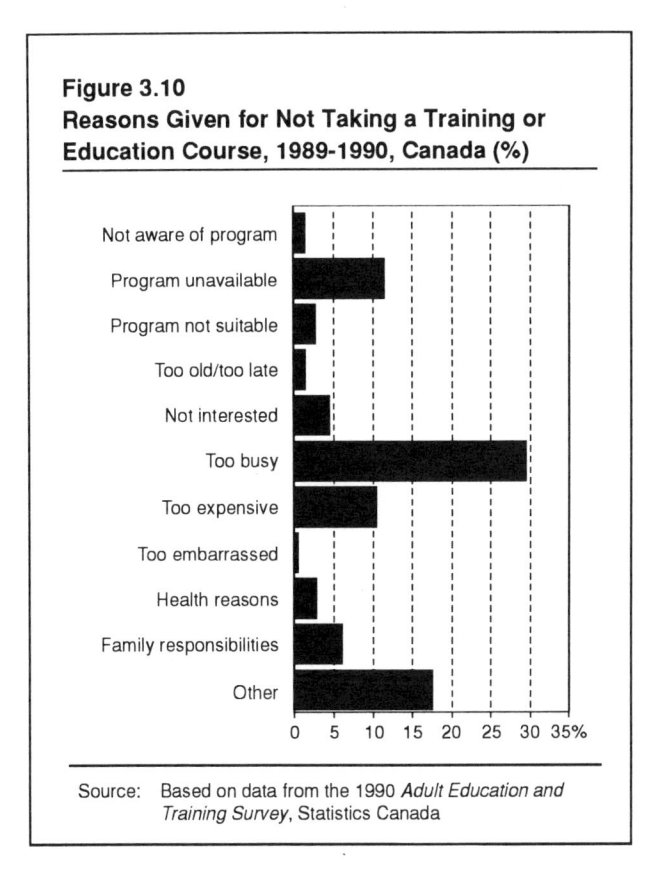

"family responsibilities" also accounted for significant proportions of the decision not to take a training or education courses. Conversely, "not aware of existing programs", "program not suitable", "too old/too late", "not interested/lack of motivation", "too embarrassed" and "health reasons" were considerably less important as barriers to training. Problems related to "program not suitable" can be solved by better planning and design. However, even if policy-makers solved these problems satisfactorily, the efficiency gains would still be negligible. Greater gains are likely to be made by concentrating efforts on solving problems concerning "too busy", "program unavailable", and "too expensive".

The empirical evidence presented here reinforces the statistical results of multiple regression analysis. The estimated equations suggest that governments and employers can encourage workers to participate in training by absorbing the training costs. In this section, "too busy" and "too expensive" together have been reported as the reasons accounting for about 40 per cent of individuals not picking up employment-related training. Clearly, one solution for "too busy" and "too expensive" is for employers to grant their workers "training leaves with pay" and for governments to channel sufficient funds to workers to finance training and instructional programs.

Apprenticeship

A Lot to Learn expressed serious doubts about the relevance, coverage and responsiveness of the Canadian apprenticeship system. Here, we offer more detailed analysis based upon two data sets: first, the National Apprenticeship Survey (NAS) conducted by Statistics Canada for Employment and Immigration Canada in 1989-90 and, second, administrative records on apprenticeships provided to Statistics Canada by the provinces and on job vacancies collected by Employment and Immigration Canada's National Job Bank.

Findings from the NAS

NON-COMPLETION OF APPRENTICESHIP PROGRAMS

Many apprentices fail to complete their training programs. During 1986-87, about 50 thousand apprentices withdrew from Canadian apprenticeship training programs either as graduates (completers), or as dropouts (non-completers). The distribution of those who left apprenticeship programs (leavers) in 1986-87 was 59.4 per cent for completers, and 40.6 per cent for non-completers.

The "non-completers/total leavers" ratio varied moderately across industries (Figure 3.11). The service sector had the lowest ratio at 37.2 per cent; "resources" had the highest rates at 43.7 per cent. If the data on individuals with either trade-related work or trade-related in-class training prior to joining the apprenticeship programs are analyzed, then the "non-completers/total leavers" ratio changes substantially (Figure 3.12). For these individuals, the proportions leaving the programs without completing all the requirements are noticeably lower for all sectors, and the resources sector registers the best performance. This suggests that the more an individual already knows about his or her trade, the more likely he or she is to complete all the program requirements successfully.

Twelve months after graduation, 96 per cent of the graduates worked in the trades in which they apprenticed, but only half the non-completers worked in their apprenticed trades within the same time-frame. Two to three years after leaving the programs, 88 per cent of the graduates were still working at their trades, but only 31 per cent of the non-completers were still doing so. The average age of apprentices at the time of leaving was 27 years; more than one thousand (of the leavers) were 45 years or over. Three years after leaving, the average hourly rate of earnings of program graduates was 17 per cent higher than that of non-completers.

Figure 3.11
Apprenticeship Programs: "Non-completers/Total Leavers" Ratio by Sector, 1986-87, Canada (%)

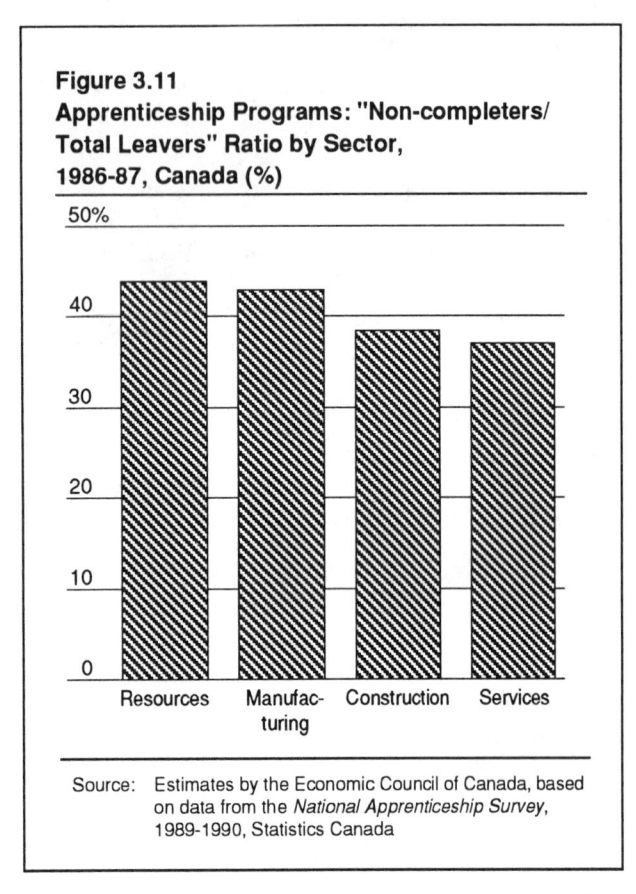

Source: Estimates by the Economic Council of Canada, based on data from the *National Apprenticeship Survey*, 1989-1990, Statistics Canada

Figure 3.12
Apprenticeship Programs: "Non-completers/Total Leavers" Ratio, Apprentices with Prior Training Only, 1986-87, Canada (%)

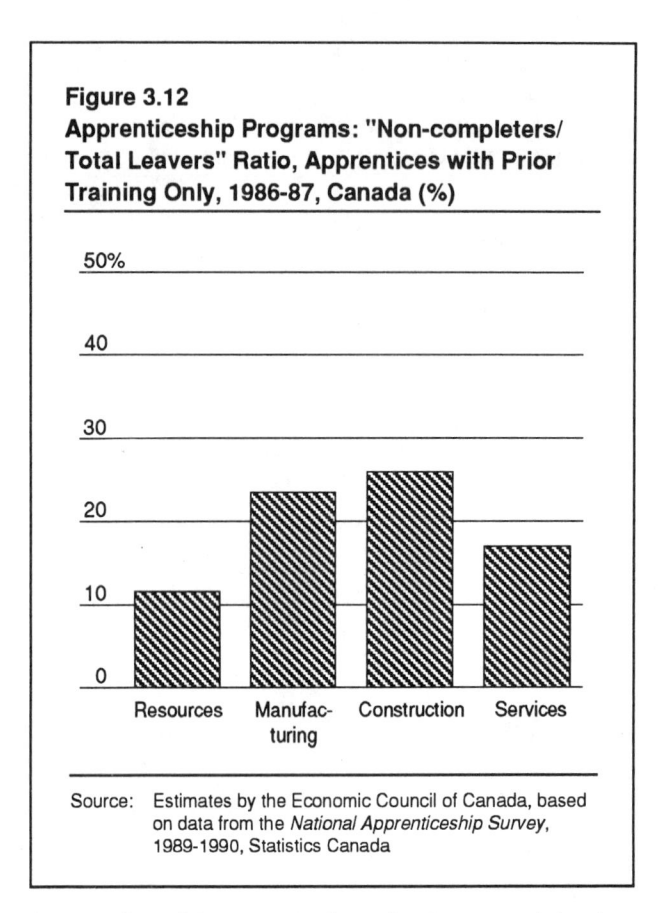

Source: Estimates by the Economic Council of Canada, based on data from the *National Apprenticeship Survey*, 1989-1990, Statistics Canada

Non-completers gave four reasons for terminating their programs. Approximately 17 per cent complained that the subjects covered in the classroom were not particularly relevant to the skills required to do the job; 16 per cent stated that not enough skills were taught to fulfill the trade requirements; 11 per cent lamented inadequate or limited equipment; and 8 per cent complained of insufficient hands-on classroom work. Out-dated equipment, field work unrelated to the trade, and excessive classroom training hours were also criticized. Many apprentices also complained of lack of money and inadequate training allowances. Some of the non-completers stated that they had acquired enough training to get a good job. Nearly 6 per cent quit simply because they no longer liked the selected trade.

Difficulty Finding Apprenticeship Employment

Apprenticeship training requires three parties to make the system work: apprentices; employers to sponsor apprenticeship training; and an authority to finance, plan, organize, and administer the programs. Apart from trainees' interests and motivations, participation by employers is of paramount importance to the success of apprenticeship programs. The NAS data shed some light on this.

About 13 per cent of the leavers in 1986-87 had difficulty finding employers to accept them as apprentices. Unemployed workers generally had the most difficulty finding employers to sponsor them.

One's first impulse might be to think that potential apprentices would have no difficulty securing the sponsorship of employers. However, the survey suggests otherwise, inasmuch as many of those included in the survey experienced difficulty in this connection, but eventually found employers to accept them. The data do not provide information on those who were sufficiently discouraged by this experience to give up the pursuit of apprenticeship training.

Integration and Efficiency

An efficient apprenticeship system would officially recognize the trade-related training or experience individuals have prior to becoming registered apprentices. In principle, all provinces allow for reductions in the length of apprenticeship terms, depending on an individual's training and work experience before becoming a registered apprentice. How well has the provincial apprenticeship credit system for prior training and experience performed?

Tables 3.3 and 3.4 provide some insight into the degree of integration between informal training and provincial apprenticeship programs. The statistics for completers are particularly revealing. Of those who completed their apprenticeship program, 33 to 42 per cent reported that they had some trade-related knowledge prior to entering their apprenticeship training, but did not receive any credit for that experience toward program requirements (Table 3.3, line 2). Except for those in service industries, non-completers had even less luck in getting such credits (Table 3.4, line 2). This lack of integration (offsetting program requirements against relevant experience gained on the job) partially explains why apprenticeship terms are so long in Canada. Compared to the German system where the term for most of the apprenticeship trades is three years, the inefficiency of the Canadian system is clear; most of the Canadian apprenticeship programs span four years.

Leavers' perceptions of the relevance of their instruction varied considerably and were dependent upon: whether the leavers were completers or non-completers; whether or not the leavers worked in trade related jobs; and in what industrial sectors the leavers worked (Tables 3.5 and 3.6). Among completers who worked in trade-related jobs, 81 per cent considered the skills learned from the training programs to be mostly or entirely relevant. There were some variations across industries, but the differences were not great. Non-completers who worked in trade-related fields also found the skills acquired from the programs to be pertinent to their jobs. In sum, the apprenticeship training programs appear to be quite successful in providing trainees with the relevant skills they require to find employment in their chosen fields.

Because the survey is limited to information on program leavers over a very narrow time horizon, the survey information does not provide any indication of the dynamic relationship between apprenticeship training and changing market conditions. The rest of this chapter is devoted to an analysis of the administrative records for some insight into this issue.

Analysis of the Administrative Records

Prior to June 1979, Statistics Canada published apprenticeship training data annually. That data was compiled from administrative records covering all provincial apprenticeship programs and was submitted to Statistics Canada by provincial directors of apprenticeship training. Since June 1979, Statistics Canada has discontinued publication but has, nonetheless, continued to compile the data. In addition, Employment

Table 3.3
Experience Prior to Apprenticeship by Industry of Employment: Completers of Apprenticeship Programs (%)

Trade-related Work Prior to Apprenticeship	Industry of Most Recent Trade-related Job			
	Resources	Manufacturing	Construction	Services
Yes, counted towards program	44.43	34.71	38.32	43.93
Yes, but not counted towards program	24.26	25.37	26.31	22.37
No trade-related work	31.30	39.92	35.37	33.70
Total	100.00	100.00	100.00	100.00
In-Class Training Prior to Apprenticeship				
Yes, counted towards program	4.17	22.29	40.21	47.97
Yes, but not counted towards program	0.00	25.48	19.23	15.38
No In-class Training	95.83	52.23	40.56	36.64
Total	100.00	100.00	100.00	100.00

Source: Estimates by the Economic Council of Canada based on data from the *National Apprenticeship Survey*, 1989-90, Statistics Canada

Table 3.4
Experience Prior to Apprenticeship by Industry of Employment: Non-Completers of Apprenticeship Programs

	Industry of Most Recent Trade-related Job			
Trade-related Work Prior to Apprenticeship	Resources	Manufacturing	Construction	Services
Yes, counted towards program	41.83	39.53	50.08	52.95
Yes, but not counted towards program	55.56	30.49	29.36	21.74
No trade-related work	2.61	29.98	20.55	25.32
Total	100.00	100.00	100.00	100.00
In-class Training Prior to Apprenticeship				
Yes, counted towards program	80.00	84.77	6.01	40.38
Yes, but not counted towards program	0.00	5.08	27.53	1.92
No In-class Training	20.00	10.16	66.46	57.69
Total	100.00	100.00	100.00	100.00

Source: Estimates by the Economic Council of Canada based on data from the *National Apprenticeship Survey*, 1989-90, Statistics Canada

Table 3.5
Relevance of Skills Learned by Sector of Employment (Completers of Apprenticeship Programs) (%)

	Industry of Most Recent Trade-related Job				Industry of Most Recent Non-trade Job 1991			
Relevance of Skills Learned	Resources	Manufacturing	Construction	Services	Resources	Manufacturing	Construction	Services
All	39.01	38.23	38.05	47.49	10.09	6.21	2.91	5.05
Most	47.35	41.33	37.61	38.22	10.52	10.21	8.72	4.28
Some	13.64	19.44	22.97	12.23	45.49	38.02	47.04	36.77
None	0.00	1.00	1.37	2.06	33.91	45.56	41.33	53.91
Total	100.00	100.00	100.00	100.00	100.00	100.00	100.00	100.00

Source: Estimates by the Economic Council of Canada based on data from the *National Apprenticeship Survey*, 1989-90, Statistics Canada

Table 3.6
Relevance of Skills Learned by Sector of Employment (Non-completers of Apprenticeship Programs) (%)

	Industry of Most Recent Trade-related Job				Industry of Most Recent Non-trade Job 1991			
Relevance of Skills Learned	Resources	Manufacturing	Construction	Services	Resources	Manufacturing	Construction	Services
All	14.47	37.77	48.79	32.54	2.81	5.58	1.60	2.77
Most	62.50	36.43	31.20	46.98	3.72	1.94	15.10	10.66
Some	13.16	24.54	12.51	15.15	45.15	28.60	37.57	27.60
None	9.87	1.26	7.50	4.34	48.32	63.88	45.74	58.96
Total	100.00	100.00	100.00	100.00	100.00	100.00	100.00	100.00

Source: Estimates by the Economic Council of Canada based on data from the *National Apprenticeship Survey*, 1989-90, Statistics Canada

and Immigration Canada's National Job Bank (NJB) collects information on job vacancies recorded by Canada Employment Centres (CECs) concerning hard-to-fill jobs reported to local CECs. These two sets of administrative records contain a wealth of information on the demand for, and supply of, apprentices at a detailed occupational level. Unfortunately, the data which are available by province and by year, lack certain details, but their occupational dimensions and time series format provide researchers with an excellent opportunity to examine the timing-and-demand issues.

The National Picture

In the broadest terms, one might ask whether fundamental shifts in the occupational and skill mix of employment wrought by technological change and the long-term shift to services have led to a corresponding change in the emphasis and direction of apprenticeship. From the existing employment data, certain incongruities may be seen. For example, in recent years, the services sector has recorded major employment growth. However, a glance at the occupations covered by apprenticeship reveals that, throughout the 1980s, more than 98 per cent of all instruction pertained to manufacturing, construction, and traditional services (Figures 3.13 and 3.14).

The conclusion is inescapable, surely, that the present system is oriented to employment in shrinking sectors and to occupational areas that, while growing, are relatively inferior in terms of remuneration and stability. This begs the question "Are knowledge-based and technology-intensive occupations unsuitable for apprenticeship?". Clearly, the present system is very highly concentrated and fails to reflect the changing structure of the labour market. In principle, 290 occupations are apprenticeable; in 1987, however, only 88 actually had registered apprentices — at a time when employers registered vacancies for nearly 400 occupational categories!

The diversity of training programs across Canada also presents a serious problem to all players on the apprentice field. A quick examination of the Ellis Figure of apprentice training programs (a table whereby the details of provincial/territorial programs for all occupational trades can be compared) is sufficient to validate this criticism. In Canada, apprenticeship training is under the jurisdiction of provincial governments and provinces have developed their own training programs independently. For this reason, consistency of program quality across the country has been impossible. Employers are never sure that graduates from the

Figure 3.13
Distribution of Registered Apprentices by Occupational Group, 1981, Canada

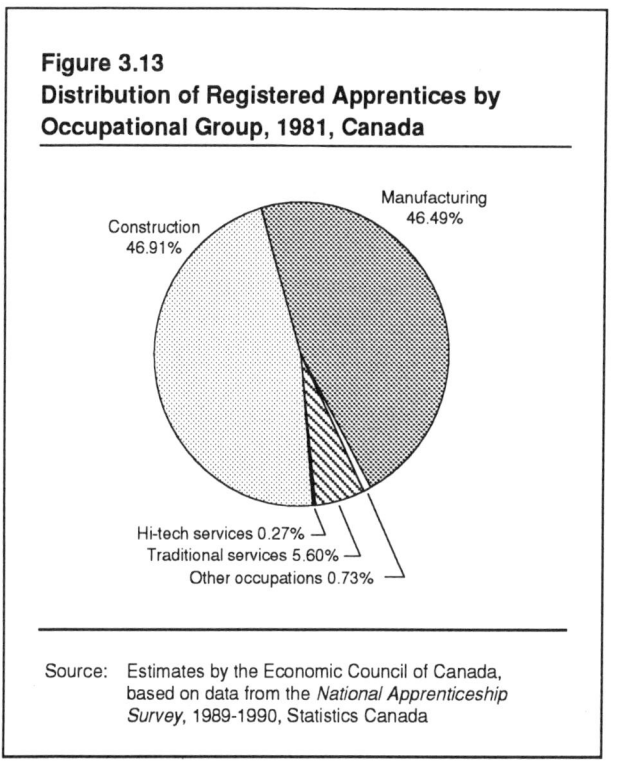

- Manufacturing 46.49%
- Construction 46.91%
- Hi-tech services 0.27%
- Traditional services 5.60%
- Other occupations 0.73%

Source: Estimates by the Economic Council of Canada, based on data from the *National Apprenticeship Survey*, 1989-1990, Statistics Canada

Figure 3.14
Distribution of Registered Apprentices by Occupational Group, 1988, Canada

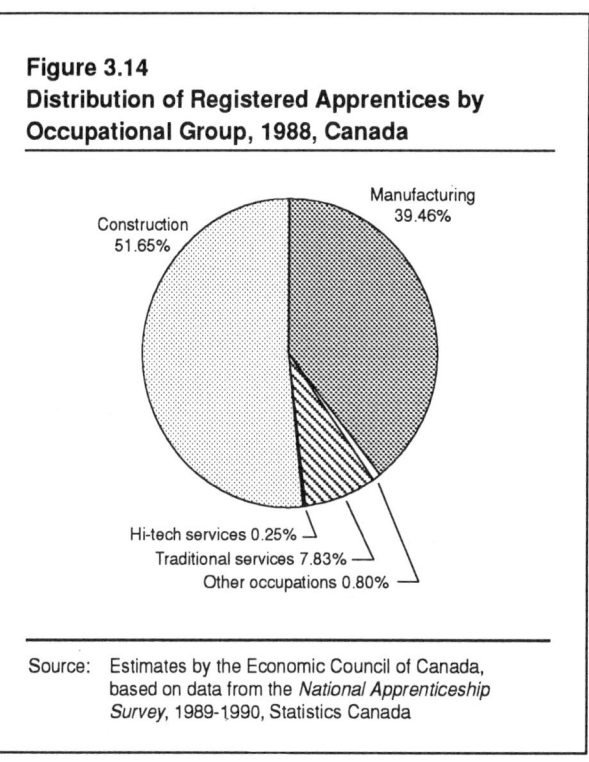

- Manufacturing 39.46%
- Construction 51.65%
- Hi-tech services 0.25%
- Traditional services 7.83%
- Other occupations 0.80%

Source: Estimates by the Economic Council of Canada, based on data from the *National Apprenticeship Survey*, 1989-1990, Statistics Canada

programs offered in one province are as well trained as those recruited from another province. For the apprenticeship graduates, this negative characteristic of the system severely and inevitably limits their mobility.

In theory, the Canadian system already has the machinery in place to ensure national standards in provincial apprenticeship training programs. The Interprovincial Standards Program (ISP, also known as the Red Seal Program) was established in 1959 for exactly that purpose. Figure 3.15 shows that the number of occupational trades that award Red Seals to more than 50 per cent of their graduates are historically few. Evidently, if apprenticeship training is to play a major role in the Canadian labour market, governments will have to make the Red Seal program mandatory for all apprenticeship trades across Canada, or establish new compulsory national standards.

Turning to the question of responsiveness to general and specific labour market conditions, the results of a correlation analysis relating graduate apprentices in various occupations to several demand indicators are reported. The basic question posed for each apprenticeable occupation is: "Does the supply of graduates positively, strongly, significantly, and contemporaneously correlate with labour market demand?". For a given occupation, if the number of graduate apprentices significantly and contemporaneously correlates with the demand variable, the program is said to be responsive. If, by contrast, the correlation involves a lag of a year or more, one may be concerned about the possibility of overshooting the demand target as market conditions change, i.e., of producing more opportunities than needed one year later. Little or no correlation also calls into question the performance of the apprenticeship system in meeting the demands of the labour market.

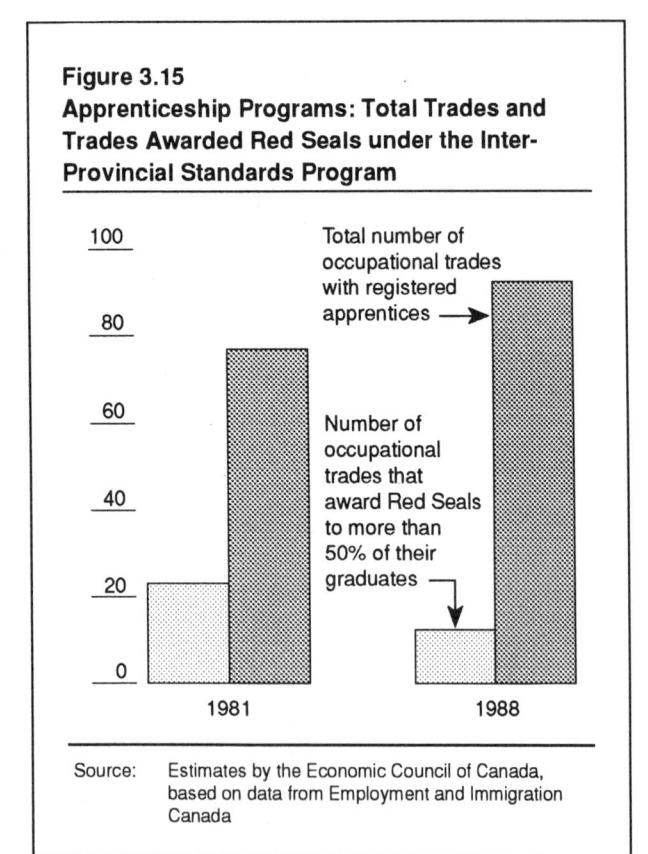

Of the 84 occupations listed in Table 3.7, correlations with general labour-market-demand conditions for the period 1974–1987 show only two occupations for which responsiveness can be regarded as "good" by our criteria. The more specific correlations between graduates and occupation-specific vacancies (on the left side of Table 3.7) show only four "good" responses. For both market demand variables, a substantial number of cases are "bad", but the overwhelming majority are "unrelated" — which may be considered to be even worse!

The Provincial Perspective

The discussion so far summarizes the analysis of the national data. However, since these data tend to mask certain province—specific details, the concerns mentioned above must also be considered from a provincial perspective.

From 1981-1988, the majority of registered apprentices in Canada were from Quebec, Ontario, Alberta and British Columbia. Regardless of their relative economic growth (or the lack of it) over time, these four provinces, together, constituted the core of the Canadian apprenticeship training programs throughout most of the '80s.

Figures 3.16 through 3.25 highlight the salient features of the provincial apprenticeship training programs, and Table 3.8 provides supporting analytical detail. The pie charts shown in Figures 3.16 to 3.25 depict the relative situations in the four major apprenticeship provinces in 1981 and 1988. The relative sizes of the pie charts show the relative change (growth or shrinkage) in the number of apprentices between 1981 and 1988 in each province. The graphs also show that the experiences of the four major apprenticeship training provinces were not similar. Between 1981 and 1988, the number of apprentices in Quebec and Ontario grew dramatically, but Alberta and British Columbia experienced declines in the same period.

The trades covered by apprenticeship training were also quite diverse. Ontario and British Columbia

Figure 3.15
Apprenticeship Programs: Total Trades and Trades Awarded Red Seals under the Inter-Provincial Standards Program

Source: Estimates by the Economic Council of Canada, based on data from Employment and Immigration Canada

offered training across a wider range of industry sectors, albeit only modestly for high-tech service occupations, but Quebec's programs concentrated entirely on manufacturing and construction trades. Alberta experienced a significant drop in registered apprentices in the construction trades, but its apprentices in low-paying traditional service occupations grew noticeably (Figures 3.22 and 3.23 and Table 3.8).

Despite the diversity across the provinces in apprenticeship training, the message is clear: apprenticeship training programs in all provinces are failing to keep pace with changes in economic activities through time. Despite individual differences, the most common factor is the rigidity — lack of noticeable change — in the composition of apprenticeship training programs in all provinces. Apprenticeship programs persistently continue to train people primarily for manufacturing and construction-related occupations. All provinces have failed to make significant in-roads into the rapidly growing high-tech service occupations.

Summary

The existing apprenticeship training system has managed — and is continuing — to product apprentices in construction- and manufacturing-dominated trades.

On the issue of employers' participation in the apprenticeship system, although the percentage of leavers who reported to having difficulty finding employers to sponsor their apprenticeship programs was comparatively low, the statistics give no indication of the number of individuals who were prevented from entering programs because of the lack of employer sponsorship initially. More employer involvement in the programs could substantially increase the efficiency of the system. In order to make apprenticeship training attractive to potential apprentices, federal and provincial authorities must formally co-ordinate apprenticeship training between provinces. Within each province apprenticeship programs must also be co-ordinated with the co-operative education/apprenticeship training programs offered by high schools and must recognize individuals' prior trade-related training and experience. The large number who drop out and the high average age of trainees are two of the most disturbing features of the Canadian system.

The data from the administrative records confirm the shortcomings of the existing system. The concen-

Figure 3.16
Provincial Distribution of Registered Apprentices, 1981

AB 25.05%
SK 4.68%
MB 2.79%
ON 23.61%
QC 15.66%
NB 3.44%
NS 3.89%
PE 0.41%
NF 2.40%
BC 18.07%

Source: Estimates by the Economic Council of Canada based on data from Statistics Canada

Figure 3.17
Provincial Distribution of Registered Apprentices, 1988

ON 30.68%
QC 29.58%
MB 2.68%
SK 2.63%
AB 16.11%
BC 9.85%
NF 1.90%
PE 0.26%
NS 3.19%
NB 3.12%

Source: Estimates by the Economic Council of Canada based on data from Statistics Canada

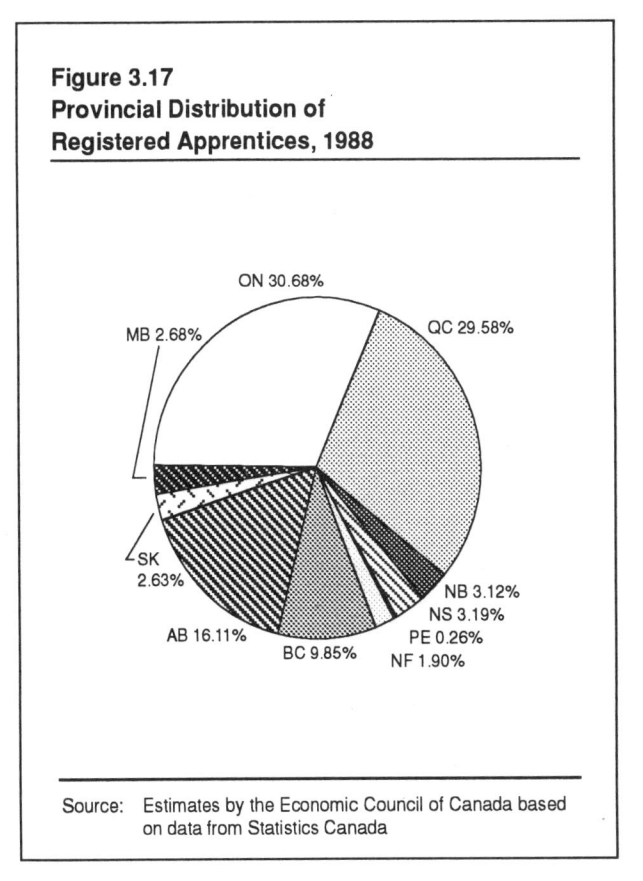

Table 3.7
Apprenticeship Graduates and Demand for Labour, Canada

Occupation Code and Description	\multicolumn{4}{c}{Graduates' Timing in Meeting the Demand for Occupational Skill}	\multicolumn{4}{c}{Graduates' Timing in Meeting the Demands of the Economy}
	Good	Fair	Bad	Unrelated	Good	Fair	Bad	Unrelated
2161122 Staker-Detailer				x				x
2163110 Draftsman		x						x
4153118 Shipping and Warehousing				x				x
4155126 Industrial Warehouseman				x				x
5135126 Vehicle Partsman				x				x
5145110 Service Station Attendant				x	x			
6121127 Cook				x			x	
6143114 Barber		x					x	
6143118 Hairdresser	x						x	
7195122 Horticulture				x				x
7195146 Landscape Gardener				x				x
7713118 Water Well Driller				x				x
8137114 Moulder				x			x	
8167122 Black-Furnace Operator				x				x
8213114 Baker				x			x	
8215110 Butcher				x			x	
8311110 Tool-Die Maker				x				x
8313114 Patternmaker				x				x
8313150 Vehicle Machinist		x				x		
8313154 Machinist			x				x	
8319150 Sawfitter		x						x
8333118 Sheet-metal Worker			x					x
8334158 Springmaker				x				x
8335126 Welder				x				x
8337110 Boilermaker				x			x	
8513138 Mechanical Fitter				x				x
8523118 Fitter-Assembler. (Misc.)				x			x	
8531296 Electric Motor Winder				x			x	
8533110 Industrial Electrician				x				x
8533118 Transport Refrigeration Mech.				x				x
8533126 Appliance Serviceman		x						x
8535114 Electronics (Industrial)				x				x
8535118 Electronics (Telecom)	x							x
8537110 Radio-TV Service Technician		x			x			
8541110 Cabinetmaker				x			x	
8549399 Woodworking & Fab. (Misc.)		x						x
8581110 Motor Vehicle Mechanic				x				x
8581122 Transmission Mechanic				x				x
8581134 Motor Vehicle Electrical Mech.		x						x
8581142 Vehicle Body Repair				x				x
8582110 Aircraft Mechanic				x				x
8583114 Streetcar-Subway Mechanic				x				x
8584112 Heavy Equipment Mechanic			x					x
8584122 Industrial Mechanic				x			x	
8584330 Farm Equipment Mechanic				x				x
8584382 Diesel Engine Mechanic				x				x
8588114 Control Mechanic				x				x
8588118 Industrial Instruments Mechanic				x			x	
8589144 Small Equipment Mechanic				x			x	
8589146 Locksmith				x				x
8589299 Machine Repairer				x				x
8591122 Jeweller-Watchmaker				x			x	
8592114 Shipwright				x			x	

Table 3.7 (Cont'd.)

Occupation Code and Description	Graduates' Timing in Meeting the Demand for Occupational Skill				Graduates' Timing in Meeting the Demands of the Economy			
	Good	Fair	Bad	Unrelated	Good	Fair	Bad	Unrelated
8592202 Marine Engine Fitter		x					x	
8595114 Vehicle Painter				x				x
8711110 Heavy Equipment Operator	x							x
8731110 Power and Operating Lineman				x				x
8731114 Industrial Plant Operator				x				x
8731118 Power Lineman		x						x
8733110 Marine Electrician				x			x	
8733117 Refrigeration/Air Cond. Mech.				x				x
8733122 Construction Electrician				x				x
8781110 Carpenter				x				x
8782110 Bricklayer				x				x
8782130 Tile Setter				x			x	
8783122 Cement Finisher		x						x
8784114 Plasterer			x					x
8784122 Lather				x				x
8785110 Painter-Decorator				x			x	
8786118 Insulator	x						x	
8787118 Roofer				x			x	
8791112 Steamfitter				x				x
8791114 Plumber				x				x
8791120 Sprinkler Installer				x				x
8791122 Gasfitter			x				x	
8793114 Ironworker				x				x
8795118 Glazier				x				x
8799130 Oil burner Mechanic		x						x
8799158 Floor-covering Installer		x						x
8799194 Housing Maintenance Service				x				x
8799399 Other Construction Trades				x				x
9318199 Truck and Transport				x				x
9512110 Printer				x			x	
9533122 Stationary Engineer				x				x

Notes: 1 Good: statistically significant at the 5 per cent level.
Fair: fair amount of positive correlation, but statistically not significant at the 5 per cent level.
Bad: (i) graduates and demand are negatively correlated, or (ii) significant, positive correlation can only be established after lagging the demand variable by one year.
Unrelated: insignificant correlation between apprenticeship graduates and demand.

2 Only occupations with graduates for at least two years and with reported unfilled jobs are included in the analysis. The sample period for the occupation-specific tests is 1983-1989; the sample period for the general economic climate test is 1974-1987.

Source: Estimates by the Economic Council of Canada based on data from Statistics Canada

60 *Education and Training in Canada*

Figure 3.18
Distribution of Registered Apprentices by Occupational Group, Quebec, 1981

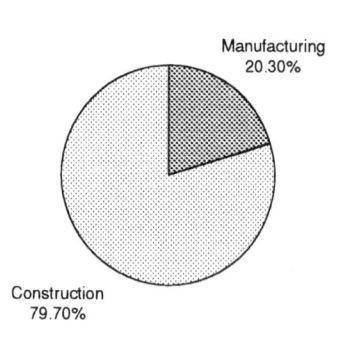

- Manufacturing 20.30%
- Construction 79.70%

Source: Estimates by the Economic Council of Canada based on data from Statistics Canada

Figure 3.20
Distribution of Registered Apprentices by Occupational Group, Ontario, 1981

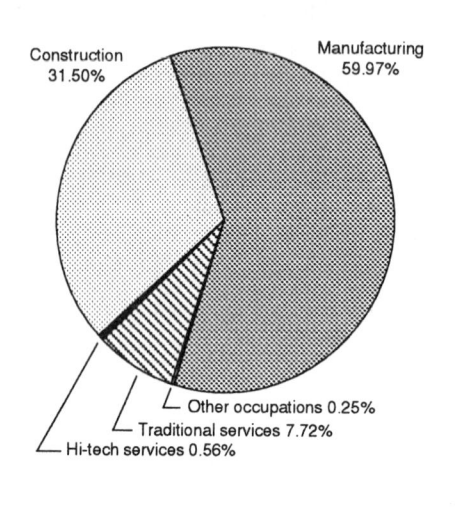

- Construction 31.50%
- Manufacturing 59.97%
- Other occupations 0.25%
- Traditional services 7.72%
- Hi-tech services 0.56%

Source: Estimates by the Economic Council of Canada based on data from Statistics Canada

Figure 3.19
Distribution of Registered Apprentices by Occupational Group, Quebec, 1988

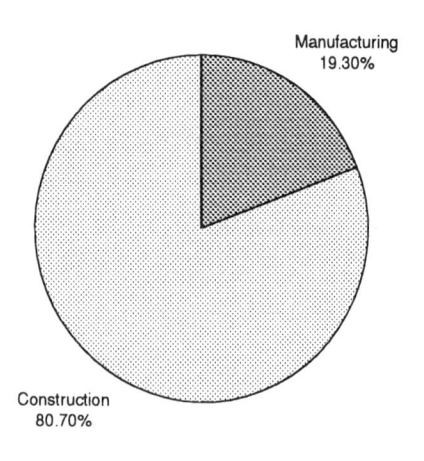

- Manufacturing 19.30%
- Construction 80.70%

Source: Estimates by the Economic Council of Canada based on data from Statistics Canada

Figure 3.21
Distribution of Registered Apprentices by Occupational Group, Ontario, 1988

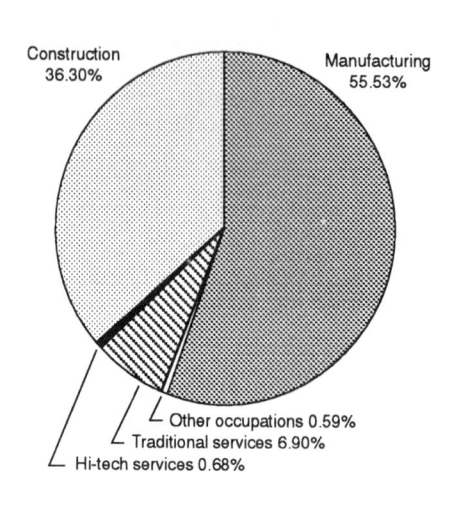

- Construction 36.30%
- Manufacturing 55.53%
- Other occupations 0.59%
- Traditional services 6.90%
- Hi-tech services 0.68%

Source: Estimates by the Economic Council of Canada based on data from Statistics Canada

Figure 3.22
Distribution of Registered Apprentices by Occupational Group, Alberta, 1981

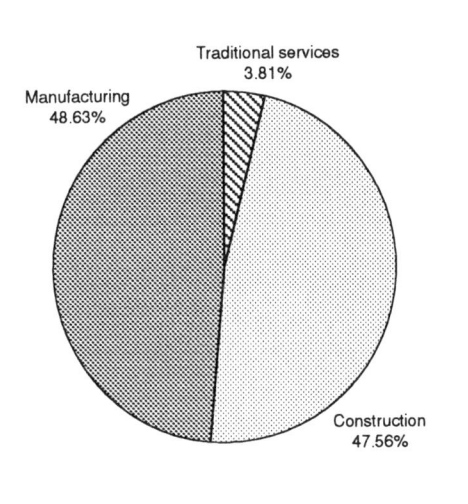

- Manufacturing 48.63%
- Traditional services 3.81%
- Construction 47.56%

Source: Estimates by the Economic Council of Canada based on data from Statistics Canada

Figure 3.24
Distribution of Registered Apprentices by Occupational Group, British Columbia, 1981

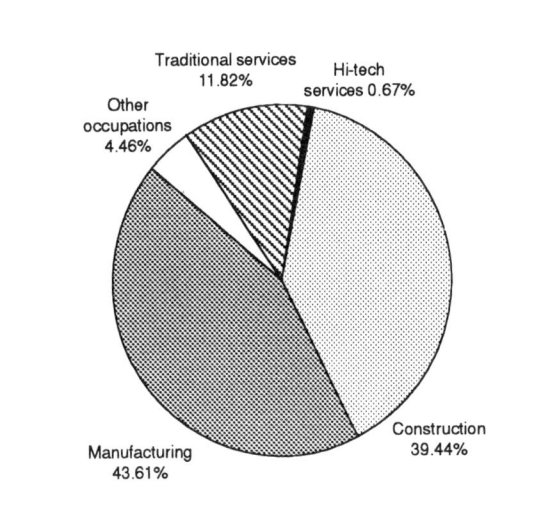

- Traditional services 11.82%
- Hi-tech services 0.67%
- Other occupations 4.46%
- Manufacturing 43.61%
- Construction 39.44%

Source: Estimates by the Economic Council of Canada based on data from Statistics Canada

Figure 3.23
Distribution of Registered Apprentices by Occupational Group, Alberta, 1988

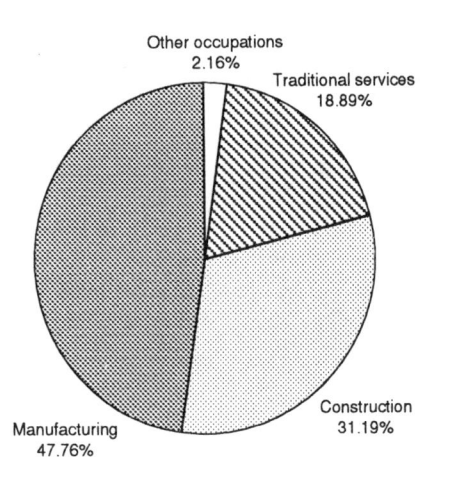

- Other occupations 2.16%
- Traditional services 18.89%
- Construction 31.19%
- Manufacturing 47.76%

Source: Estimates by the Economic Council of Canada based on data from Statistics Canada

Figure 3.25
Distribution of Registered Apprentices by Occupational Group, British Columbia, 1988

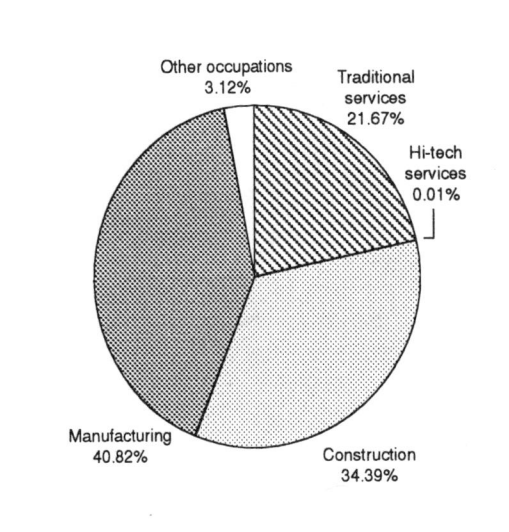

- Other occupations 3.12%
- Traditional services 21.67%
- Hi-tech services 0.01%
- Manufacturing 40.82%
- Construction 34.39%

Source: Estimates by the Economic Council of Canada based on data from Statistics Canada

Table 3.8
Apprenticeship Training by Province, 1981 and 1988

	1981		1988	
	Total No. of Registered Apprentices	"Dropouts/ Registered Apprentices" Ratio (%)	Total No. of Registered Apprentices	"Dropouts/ Registered Apprentices" Ratio (%)
Newfoundland				
Total Number Apprentices	3,324	11.88	3,065	5.77
Total in Manufacturing	1,657	11.41	1,317	6.07
% in Manufacturing	49.85		42.97	
Total in Construction	1,200	11.08	1,183	5.33
% in Construction	36.10		38.60	
Total in Hi-tech Services	0		0	
% in Hi-tech Services	0		0	
Total in Traditional Services	467	15.63	565	6.02
% in Traditional Services	14.05		18.43	
Total in Other Occupations	0		0	
% in Other Occupations	0		0	
Prince Edward Island				
Total Number of Apprentices	568	10.21	421	16.86
Total in Manufacturing	181	15.47	150	18.00
% in Manufacturing	31.87		35.63	
Total in Construction	357	7.00	220	10.91
% in Construction	62.85		52.26	
Total in Hi-tech Services	0		0	
% in Hi-tech Services	0		0	
Total in Traditional Services	30	16.67	51	39.22
% in Traditional Services	5.28		12.11	
Total in Other Occupations	0		0	
% in Other Occupations	0		0	
Nova Scotia				
Total Number of Apprentices	5,394	12.83	5,153	9.80
Total in Manufacturing	2,676	12.52	1,879	6.92
% in Manufacturing	49.61		36.46	
Total in Construction	2,265	12.76	2,432	11.55
% in Construction	41.99		47.20	
Total in Hi-tech Services	0		1	0.00
% in Hi-tech Services	0		0.02	
Total in Traditional Services	453	15.01	841	11.18
% in Traditional Services	8.40		16.32	
Total in Other Occupations	0		0	
% in Other Occupations	0		0	

Table 3.8 (Cont'd.)

	1981		1988	
	Total No. of Registered Apprentices	"Dropouts/ Registered Apprentices" Ratio (%)	Total No. of Registered Apprentices	"Dropouts/ Registered Apprentices" Ratio (%)
New Brunswick				
Total Number of Apprentices	4,773	13.58	5,049	11.73
Total in Manufacturing	2,349	12.22	1,956	11.09
% in Manufacturing	49.21		38.74	
Total in Construction	1,825	16.16	2,020	12.33
% in Construction	38.24		40.01	
Total in Hi-tech Services	14	0.00	69	20.29
% in Hi-tech Services	0.29		1.37	
Total in Traditional Services	519	11.56	993	11.28
% in Traditional Services	10.87		19.67	
Total in Other Occupations	0		11	0.00
% in Other Occupations	0		0.22	
Quebec				
Total Number of Apprentices	21,726	22.05	47,806	12.00
Total in Manufacturing	4,410	21.11	9,228	15.37
% in Manufacturing	20.30		19.30	
Total in Construction	17,316	22.29	38,578	11.20
% in Construction	79.70		80.70	
Total in Hi-tech Services	0		0	
% in Hi-tech Services	0		0	
Total in Traditional Services	0		0	
% in Traditional Services	0		0	
Total in Other Occupations	0		0	
% in Other Occupations	0		0	
Ontario				
Total Number of Apprentices	32,755	8.87	49,577	6.50
Total in Manufacturing	19,643	6.62	27,529	6.77
% in Manufacturing	59.97		55.53	
Total in Construction	10,319	12.18	17,996	4.85
% in Construction	31.50		36.30	
Total in Hi-tech Services	182	5.51	337	8.31
% in Hi-tech Services	0.56		0.68	
Total in Traditional Services	2,530	12.84	3,422	12.86
% in Traditional Services	7.72		6.90	
Total in Other Occupations	81	2.10	293	6.83
% in Other Occupations	0.25		0.59	

Table 3.8 (Cont'd.)
Apprenticeship Training by Province, 1981 and 1988

	1981		1988	
	Total No. of Registered Apprentices	"Dropouts/ Registered Apprentices" Ratio (%)	Total No. of Registered Apprentices	"Dropouts/ Registered Apprentices" Ratio (%)
Manitoba				
Total Number Apprentices	3,877	12.95	4,332	8.33
Total in Manufacturing	2,046	8.16	2,002	7.19
% in Manufacturing	52.77		46.21	
Total in Construction	1,804	18.07	2,292	9.16
% in Construction	46.53		52.91	
Total in Hi-tech Services	0		0	
% in Hi-tech Services	0		0	
Total in Traditional Services	0		38	18.42
% in Traditional Services	0		0.88	
Total in Other Occupations	27	33.33	0	
% in Other Occupations	0.70		0	
Saskatchewan				
Total Number of Apprentices	6,491	12.89	4,246	16.09
Total in Manufacturing	2,702	10.70	1.50932	16.25
% in Manufacturing	41.63		45.50	
Total in Construction	3,758	14.42	2,153	16.16
% in Construction	57.90		50.71	
Total in Hi-tech Services	0		0	
% in Hi-tech Services	0		0	
Total in Traditional Services	31	19.35	161	13.04
% in Traditional Services	0.48		3.79	
Total in Other Occupations	0		0	
% in Other Occupations	0		0	
Alberta				
Total Number of Apprentices	34,741	8.98	26,027	9.92
Total in Manufacturing	16,894	8.25	12,431	8.92
% in Manufacturing	48.63		47.76	
Total in Construction	16,522	9.43	8,119	10.41
% in Construction	47.56		31.19	
Total in Hi-tech Services	0		0	
% in Hi-tech Services	0		0	
Total in Traditional Services	1,325	12.60	4,916	11.13
% in Traditional Services	3.81		18.89	
Total in Other Occupations	0		561	14.62
% in Other Occupations	0		2.16	

Table 3.8 (Cont'd.)

	1981		1988	
	Total No. of Registered Apprentices	"Dropouts/ Registered Apprentices" Ratio (%)	Total No. of Registered Apprentices	"Dropouts/ Registered Apprentices" Ratio (%)
British Columbia				
Total Number of Apprentices	25,063	13.73	15,915	11.82
Total in Manufacturing	10,930	11.49	6,496	11.41
% in Manufacturing	43.61		40.82	
Total in Construction	9,885	15.15	5,473	10.60
% in Construction	39.44		34.39	
Total in Hi-tech Services	167	13.17	1	0.00
% in Hi-tech Services	0.67		0.01	
Total in Traditional Services	2,962	17.56	3,449	15.08
% in Traditional Services	11.82		21.67	
Total in Other Occupations	1,119	12.96	496	8.06
% in Other Occupations	4.46		3.12	

Source: Estimates by the Economic Council of Canada based on data from Statistics Canada.

tration on programs related to manufacturing and construction throughout the 1980s, when employment growth was in the information-service sector, is a clear indication of the system's failure to accommodate changing needs. The insensitivity of the system to demand conditions, the lack of proper integration with trade-related training, and the tenacity in retaining overly strict terms of apprenticeship beyond reasonable minimums are all symptoms of inflexibility.

Conclusion

The empirical evidence from the Adult Education and Training Survey confirms the importance of life-long learning for many Canadians: in 1989-1990, almost three out of every ten members of the labour force aged 17 and over were engaged in some form of educational instruction or training. The two most important factors influencing training participation rates are educational attainment, and "who pays the training costs". Clearly, governments have some policy leverage on both these variables, but employers also play a critical role determining decisions to participate in training programs.

Apprenticeship is an important component of the "learning continuum", but it has serious problems. In many respects it is an anachronism, geared more to the industrial needs of the '50s than to those of the '90s. Nowhere in Canada has the occupational structure of the apprenticeship system evolved to match a labour market that is being transformed by new technologies and by new ways of organizing work. In the apprenticeable trades themselves, labour supply and demand are mismatched. To complicate matters still further, differences in national standards detract from the mobility requirements of a pan-Canadian labour market. This situation should not be allowed to continue. Policy-makers now have an opportunity to make much needed changes and to "put things right". All Canadians would benefit from such a worthwhile investment in Canada's future.

4
The Economics of the Teaching Profession

Teachers are an essential component of the educational system. They are ultimately responsible for educating children and young people and for transmitting the knowledge, skills, and — to a large extent — the values of society. Teaching has never been a simple task. Today, however, teachers face challenges not encountered in earlier times. The expansion of knowledge, the rapid pace of technological change, the changing nature of Canadian society (as reflected in growing numbers of immigrants who speak neither official language and the growing incidence of single-parent families, for example), make the task of teaching increasingly complex. Also, given teachers' day-to-day contact with students, it is only through their co-operation, understanding, and continuing support that truly effective reforms will be implemented.

Teaching also merits attention by virtue of its sheer size as an occupational group. Education is a big business in Canada: in 1990-91, full-time teachers numbered 293,000 at the elementary and secondary levels, and 62,500 at the post-secondary level.

Calls for educational reform grew steadily in many OECD countries during the 1980s. That was nowhere more the evident than in the United States where many of the educational reform policy proposals have focussed on the teaching profession. On the basis of the available evidence, it appears that when Canada is compared to the U.S., Canadian concerns about teacher quality differ only in degree — with Canada comparing more favourably —but not in kind.

The structure of teaching as a profession is an important problem common to both countries. Pay-scales, responsibilities, and status do not differentiate between good and poor teachers. As a result, poor teachers are shielded from having to account for their performance and, given tenure and seniority, are also protected from censorship. There is, moreover, little incentive for good teachers to produce outstanding performances year after year beyond their personal commitments to high performance standards and their recognition that educating children and young people is important. What may be even more serious is that the present educational system depends equally on the services of both good and poor teachers.

This chapter provides an overview of the teaching profession in Canada. Section I profiles teachers in terms of age, years of experience, educational attainment, and sex.

Section II considers anticipated changes in the demand for teachers in the 1990s. Demand for teachers is expected to increase over the years ahead in response to growing numbers of retirements and projected increases in student enrolments. This increased demand poses both an opportunity and a threat. It is an opportunity because it attracts bright, highly motivated, and deeply committed individuals to teaching; it is a threat because in terms of sheer numbers the requirement to fill teaching positions may erode standards and lead to the staffing of classrooms with less-than-the-best teachers for the next two or three decades.

Section III deals with teacher training. A review of the literature suggests that the Canadian educational system has not given enough attention to teacher training. Instead, the system has developed extensive bureaucratic controls designed to standardize the treatment of both students and teachers.

Section IV is an analysis of teachers' incomes. The analysis focusses on how teachers' salaries compare to salaries in other occupations requiring similar levels of education and training —occupational alternatives for teachers considering a career change or for individuals considering teaching as a career. The key questions here are whether salaries for junior teachers are adequate to attract bright and able people into teaching and, equally important, are salaries high enough at mid- and late-career points to retain the best teachers and provide them with incentives that promote commitment to teaching and good performance in the classroom.

Section V draws upon the analyses of occupational incomes in relation to teacher supply and demand as discussed in the previous two sections. The discussion integrates what is known about the characteristics that distinguish an occupation from a profession and a job from a career, and develops a set of recommendations as to what steps might be taken to improve: the supply and the quality of new teachers; the quality, motivation, and job satisfaction of mid-career teachers; and to allow the educational system as a whole to draw upon the qualities of our best teachers and to utilize the capabilities of average teachers effectively.

Concluding comments are presented in Section VI.

I A Profile of Teachers in Canada

The average age of teachers increased steadily throughout the 1970s and the 1980s. In 1972-73, 44 per cent of elementary and secondary school teachers were younger than 30 years of age; 43 per cent were aged 30 – 49 (Figure 4.1). By 1989-90, the proportion of the youngest teachers had dropped to 11 per cent while the proportion of teachers aged 30 – 49 grew to 73 per cent.

The changing composition of the age component for the teaching profession in Canada reflects the fact that, perhaps more than for any other occupational group, the timing and magnitude of additions to the teaching force are determined by the demographic structure of the Canadian population. During the late-60s and early-70s, the school-aged population grew dramatically as children born during the baby-boom entered school. This precipitated a sharp increase in the demand for teachers. With the ensuing "baby bust", enrolments declined and adjustments to the demand for teachers took the form of sharply reduced hiring rates, although proportionately the changes in the number of teachers relative to the number of students were quite small. Some attrition occurred due to retirements and other reasons but, overall, turnover in teaching was relatively low. The result is that today a majority of teachers is middle-aged and it can therefore be expected that the number of retirements will increase throughout the 1990s.

The rising average age of teachers is also reflected in their increasing average number of years of experience. In the case of elementary-secondary school teachers, the average number of years of experience increased from 9.5 years in 1977-78 to close to 15 years by the late 1980s.[1]

Another marked change in teaching as a profession is discernable in the shift in the proportion of teachers with university degrees. In 1968-69, the percentage of teachers holding a university degree in eight provinces (excluding Ontario and Quebec for which no data were available) was 40 per cent; by 1985-86, that figure had risen to 82 per cent.[2] These higher educational qualifications reflect rising certification standards required by provincial education ministries. By the mid-1980s, most provinces required a minimum of 4 years of post-secondary education and completion of a university degree to qualify for elementary and secondary school teaching certificates.[3]

Declining enrolments in the late-1970s and 1980s translated into weak demand for new teachers but the supply of new teacher recruits remained high — as evidenced by the number of applications to faculties of education which far surpassed the numbers of available spaces and new teaching positions. Thus, higher certification requirements were easier to implement and, presumably, the diminishing number of positions increased competition among prospective teachers and provided them with an incentive to complete a university degree.

Teaching is characterized by some distinctive gender patterns. When all educators are taken into account, over half of them are women. However, that statistic masks a number of notable imbalances. For example, at the elementary level in 1975-76, close to 75 per cent of all teachers were women; by 1985-86 that proportion had decreased only slightly to 72 per cent (Table 4.1).

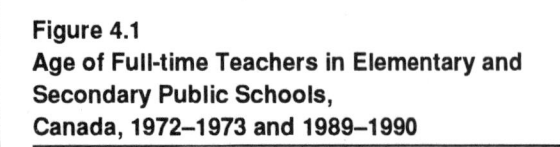

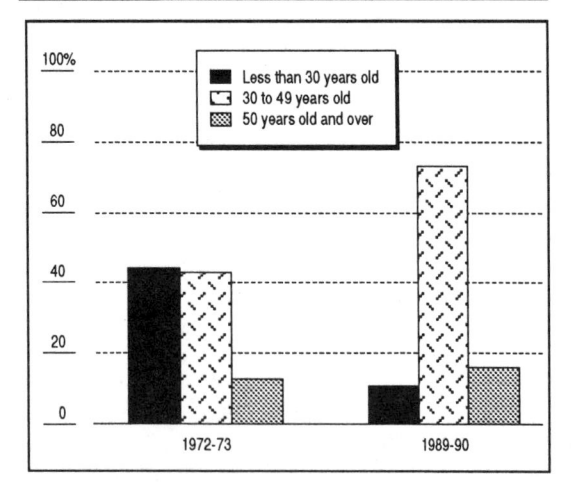

Figure 4.1
Age of Full-time Teachers in Elementary and Secondary Public Schools,
Canada, 1972–1973 and 1989–1990

Source: Estimates by the Economic Council of Canada, based on data from Statistics Canada

In contrast, between 1975-76 and 1985-86 just under two-thirds of all teachers at the secondary level were men. However, during the same period, men held 83 per cent of the principal positions at the elementary school level; only 17 per cent were women. At the secondary level, only 3 per cent of principals were women in 1975-76; that proportion increased to only 6 per cent in 1985-86. Similar patterns are apparent for positions of vice-principal and department head, where the percentage shares held by women were much smaller than the overall share of educators' positions (54.2 per cent) and where women's shares at the secondary level were considerably smaller than at the elementary level.

If the structure of the educational system is regarded as a pyramid (with authority increasing in accordance with rising school and staff levels), then it is clear that at present women form the base of that pyramid while men occupy the higher levels of the decision-making and authority structure. Lockhart observes that such a hierarchical structure reveals "... a retention of 'traditional' patriarchal social attitudes with respect to who 'nurtures' and who 'commands'".[4] He goes on to explore whether weaker attachment to the labour force and women's attitudes explain the low representation of women in positions of authority and he concludes that "... it would appear that deeply entrenched institutional norms and practices, not self-deprecating attitudes on the part of female teachers, are responsible for the extraordinarily low proportion of women teachers who occupied administrative positions through to at least the mid-1980s".[5]

The average school-teacher today, then, is middle-aged, has several years of teaching experience, and holds a university degree. Most teachers at the elementary level are women, most at the secondary level are men, and the overwhelming proportion of those in administrative positions — principals, vice-principals, and department heads — are men. Knowing these characteristics is useful, not simply because they identify who is teaching school today but, more importantly, because they are central to the patterns of teacher supply and demand and teacher earnings and career structures.

II Teacher Supply and Demand

Perhaps more than any other occupation, the number of elementary-and secondary-school teachers required at any time is determined largely by demographic factors — particularly by the number of students in each age-cohort enrolled in the school system. Other factors play smaller, but nonetheless important roles; one of the most notable is the pupil-teacher ratio.

Enrolments at the elementary and secondary levels in Canada have shown marked swings since 1960. The driving forces behind those swings were the baby boom of the 1960s and the baby bust of the 1980s. The baby boom was precipitated by the rise in the birth rate during the '50s and '60s; the baby-bust was what followed during the '70s and early '80s when the birth rate dropped sharply. Beginning in the mid 1980s there was a second, although less marked, increase in the number of births — the baby-boom echo — as the baby-boomers began having children of their own. Such swings in birth rates ripple through the school system as age-cohorts progress from one grade to the next, thereby stimulating variable demand for teachers at different levels.

Table 4.1
Women as a Proportion of All Educators, by Staff Position, Elementary and Secondary Schools Canada, 1975-76, 1980-81 and 1985-86

	Elementary			Secondary			Total		
	1975-76	1980-81	1985-86	1975-76	1980-81	1985-86	1975-76	1980-81	1985-86
Teacher	74.3	71.7	72.3	35.5	33.8	35.4	61.1	59.2	59.9
Principal	16.7	14.8	17.0	3.3	3.9	6.0	14.3	13.1	14.8
Vice-Principal	20.0	21.1	25.9	6.7	7.5	11.7	14.9	16.1	20.1
Department Head	34.3	33.5	38.3	19.3	20.7	23.2	20.3	21.7	24.3
Total	68.5	65.9	66.9	31.5	30.3	32.0	55.0	53.3	54.2

Source: Statistics Canada, *Characteristics of Teachers in Public Elementary and Secondary Schools*, Cat. no. 81-202, 1974-75/1975-76; 1980-81; 1985-86.

The number of students at the elementary-secondary level grew steadily from 4.2 million in 1960 to a peak of 5.84 million in 1970 (Table 4.2). Enrolment dropped thereafter to 4.93 million in 1985 — a level last recorded in the mid-'60s. Since 1986, however, enrolment has shown an upward trend. These enrolment swings were reflected in similar shifts in the total number of teachers at the elementary-secondary level, although it is interesting to note that the shifts in the numbers of teachers lagged behind the enrolment shifts, with the total peaking at 285,000 in 1976. Thereafter, the number of teachers decreased to 267,598 in 1984; it has been increasing since then, however.

It is also notable that during periods when enrolments were increasing, the annual rate of growth in the number of teachers was greater than the rate of growth in the number of students. However, when enrolments were declining, the rate of decrease exceeded the rate at which the number of teachers decreased. As a result, the measured overall ratio of students to teachers decreased from 25:1 in 1960 to 17:1 in 1988. It should be pointed out, however, that Statistics Canada reports data on teachers under a very broad heading which includes classroom teachers, principals and vice-principals, and non-teaching academic staff. Furthermore, class size varies from school to school, and even from subject to subject; the reality of most classrooms, therefore, is that the actual pupil teacher ratio varies from as low as 15:1 to 30:1 or more in some cases. Nevertheless, as a general rule, both shifts in educational philosophies and teachers' unions have worked toward a reduction in class sizes.

The issue of teacher supply and demand is complex and is influenced by a number of factors. The demand for teachers can be defined as: the number of teachers required in relation to determinants such as pupil numbers, the curriculum to be delivered, the organization of schools, budget levels, and the cost of teacher remuneration. The supply of teachers is determined by: the number of individuals able and willing to undertake training and to take up and remain in teaching positions, study requirements, and working conditions and salaries. Further, teacher surpluses or shortages rarely characterize an entire system; rather, they reflect the needs of specific locations or specific subject areas. To complicate the issue further, most factors (with the exception of the size of the mandatory-school-age population) can be influenced by policy.

The volatile nature of the Canadian labour market for teachers during the '60s, '70s and '80s had a number of long-term effects. Large numbers of young recruits entered the profession in the '60s, but the hiring rate dropped significantly in the 1970s and 1980s. As a result, the teaching profession has aged. However, these hiring swings also had other effects that help shed light on educational recruitment. Examination of these other effects helps to shed light on the backgrounds of those teaching today and also provides insights into the challenges that faced teacher recruiters in the 1980s.

Perhaps more than any other activity, education imposes one over-riding constraint (at least for the compulsory-school-aged population) — the requirement to have a teacher at the front of the class. In other areas, health for example, adjustments can be made when there is a staff shortage to accommodate the problem; staff can double-up or treatments can be modified or eliminated altogether. The patient-doctor ratio must grow or service will be reduced.

Corresponding adjustments are simply not possible in education. The commitment to provide educational services to all Canadians of compulsory school age means that school services must be provided and schools must be staffed. There is very little flexibility in the system. Some increase(s) in class size is possible, as is combining grades in a single classroom. Occasionally, not offering a course of studies is an option, but the fact remains that any significant increase in the number of school-children necessarily involves an increase in the number of teachers required, as well.

Throughout the 1960s the demand for teachers was very high. At the same time, the rate of participation in university education — enrolments — also increased, and the supply of university graduates grew rapidly. Lockhart, in a recent study of Canadian teachers, observes that the coincidence of the growth in the demand for teachers and the supply of university graduates after 1960 had two major effects. First, an oversupply of university graduates with general Arts degrees occurred in relation to the demand for new recruits in most managerial and semi-professional occupations. This meant that employment prospects for some Arts graduates at least, were limited. Lockhart observes that "The exception was teaching which, during the baby-boom period, was not only expanding at unprecedented rates but, unlike most other formally licensed occupations, did not then require either high levels of academic achievement or

Table 4.2
Number of Students and Teachers[1], and Ratio of Students to Teachers
Elementary-Secondary Level, Canada, 1960-88

	Number of students	Year over year Change in number of students (%)	Number of teachers	Year over year Change in number of teachers (%)	Ratio of students to teachers
1960	4,204,520		163,978		25.6
1961	4,412,828	5.0	174,271	6.3	25.3
1962	4,612,579	4.5	185,639	6.5	24.8
1963	4,805,329	4.2	194,197	4.6	24.7
1964	4,997,105	4.0	206,266	6.2	24.2
1965	5,163,192	3.3	211,172	2.4	24.4
1966	5,316,035	3.0	225,578	6.8	23.6
1967	5,474,741	3.0	243,900	8.1	22.4
1968	5,650,547	3.2	256,756	5.3	21.8
1969	5,775,028	2.2	269,284	4.9	21.4
1970	5,836,193	1.1	272,291	1.1	21.4
1971	5,805,823	-0.5	271,995	-0.1	21.3
1972	5,759,882	-0.8	273,834	0.7	21.0
1973	5,690,216	-1.2	272,649	-0.4	20.9
1974	5,632,847	-1.0	277,255	1.7	20.3
1975	5,594,684	-0.7	280,975	1.3	19.9
1976	5,513,615	-1.4	284,925	1.4	19.4
1977	5,410,495	-1.9	284,666	-0.1	19.0
1978	5,294,010	-2.2	280,808	-1.4	18.8
1979	5,184,697	-2.1	278,301	-0.9	18.6
1980	5,106,288	-1.5	275,035	-1.2	18.6
1981	5,024,201	-1.6	277,566	0.9	18.1
1982	4,994,033	-0.6	272,566	-1.8	18.3
1983	4,974,920	-0.4	270,992	-0.6	18.4
1984	4,946,142	-0.6	267,598	-1.3	18.5
1985	4,927,806	-0.4	267,620	0.0	18.4
1986	4,937,991	0.2	269,899	0.9	18.3
1987	4,972,883	0.7	276,447	2.4	18.0
1988	5,024,117	1.0	282,201	2.1	17.8

[1] Full-time.

Source: Statistics Canada, *Education in Canada*, Cat. no. 81-229.

carefully pre-planned undergraduate programs."[6] According to a Statistics Canada study of 1969 university graduates, fully half of those who were employed in 1971 held jobs in the education industry. Forty-two per cent of the graduates with a bachelor's degree had become teachers. These proportions decreased by 1978 but remained significant nevertheless. Forty-one per cent of the university graduates in 1976 were employed in the education industry; 37 per cent of those with a bachelor's degree had become teachers.[7]

Who were the newly-recruited teachers in the late '60s and early '70s? Lockhart finds that most were recent University graduates holding degrees in the fine arts and humanities. However, there were also significant numbers of graduates from the biological sciences, agriculture, mathematics, and the physical sciences. He contends that most of these new recruits entered teaching because they could not find jobs in other occupations — basing his argument on the fact that less than half of those who entered teaching had declared early majors in pedagogy. Indeed, a recent study of Ontario teachers found that about two-thirds of both male and female elementary-school teachers reported teaching as their first occupational choice; at the secondary-school level 56 per cent of female teachers but only 37 per cent of male teachers reported teaching as their first choice.[8]

Between 1950 and 1960, all employment sectors except teaching and university and college employment showed a decline in the proportion of newly-hired graduates. Schoolteaching, however,

> ...doubled its proportional recruitment of new graduates... *This absorption of occupationally displaced graduates into the teaching-ranks was facilitated not only by the easy convertibility arrangements of teacher-training institutions, but also by the teacher-training philosophy which elevated pedagogic 'methodology' above substantive subject knowledge as the principal ingredient in the professional preparation of teachers. Given this philosophy, it didn't much matter what the academic background of those who came to the teacher-training faculties might be.*[9]

From about 1970 to the mid-1980s, declining enrolments had the opposite effect on the labour market for teachers; each year, fewer teachers were required, resulting in an over-supply of newly trained teachers. In the United States, an alarming trend was noted during this period, prompting the release of a number of major reports on an observed deterioration in the quality of education overall, and the quality of teachers in particular.[10] The Carnegie Forum, for example, reported that while average Scholastic Aptitude Test (SAT) scores of U.S. high school seniors intending to major in education rose slightly during the mid-1980s, that small gain followed a period of over 10 years during which the scores of prospective teachers deteriorated more quickly than the scores of all college students.[11] Also during the '70s, teachers in the United States experienced a 15 percent real wage decrease which helped reduce the over-supply of teachers.[12] One might expect such a development to work against teaching as an occupation and to make it less attractive to the most able candidates and, this is precisely what happened. The mediocrity of those entering teaching and the real reduction in wages worked in combination to lower the status of teaching as a profession. Recognition of this alarming development and the fact that teachers' salaries in the United States were not competitive with other occupations prompted efforts on the parts of governments to reverse this trend and, as a result, teachers' salaries did increase between 1981 and 1986.

What of the Canadian experience? Unfortunately, Canada has no simple yard-stick comparable to the SAT scores in the United States which can be used to obtain an overall sense of the academic ability of newly-recruited teachers. Consequently, researchers must rely on a variety of indirect evidence.

First, Canadian teachers are paid more than teachers in the United States, by a wide margin. Furthermore, salaries at the lower end of the earnings scale and into the middle of that scale tend to be higher for Canadian teachers than for those in other occupations. Therefore, if only salaries are considered, teaching should be attractive to potential entrants.

Second, Canadian teachers are better-qualified than most of their counterparts in the United States. In an analysis of teacher supply and demand in Ontario for the period 1988 – 2008, Smith considered the qualifications of the pool of prospective applicants to teacher education programs. She found that "... in contrast with the U.S. experience ... Ontario institutions report that the strength of the applicant pool, and standards generally required for admission (e.g., minimum grade point average of B+) are extremely high and have never been higher".[13] Another study reports on the academic achievement of education students compared to other undergraduates between 1973 and 1984 at the University of Calgary.[14] That study concluded that, at the junior course-level, Education students enrolled in courses outside the Faculty of Education did not perform as well as other comparable undergraduates; the opposite was true, however, at the senior course-level where Education students generally outperformed their counterparts from other faculties. Overall, students who entered Education faculties after earning a B.A. or equivalent degree performed as well academically as their peers who did not go on to seek a degree in Education.

Although not comprehensive, the available evidence suggests that the quality of Canadian teachers has not deteriorated to anywhere near the same extent as it has in the United States. Especially in their early years, Canadian teachers' salaries, have remained relatively high. Also, because there has been an over-supply of people who have wanted to pursue a career in teaching there has been increased competition for teaching positions. It would appear that, if anything, the calibre of new entrants to teacher education programs has increased in Canada over the last decade.

The labour-market for teachers in Canada is again in a state of flux, however. Enrolments are beginning to increase and, over the course of the next decade, the number of retirements can also be expected to increase as many of the teachers hired during the 1960s reach retirement age. This raises the question as to whether admission standards to faculties of education will be lowered because of the growing need to staff schools. Even more to the point — considering the urgent calls to improve the quality of the educational system generally, in light of increasingly intense global competition — can Canada simultaneously improve the quality of its teachers while increasing the number to meet rising demand?

Individual provinces have been engaged in their own analyses of the problem of teacher demand and supply. In her study of the Ontario situation, Smith notes that "(Ontario's) ... teacher shortage (is) in its infancy"[15] and that that shortage will be "full blown" by the mid-1990s. Furthermore, "... in a number of instances, boards are also reporting that they are now having difficulty in hiring the calibre of teachers to which they have become accustomed and in several areas, such as French programs, they cannot find a sufficient number of qualified teachers."[16] On a more positive note, Smith also observes that there has been a growing interest in teaching as a profession.

Adding support to this claim, there has been a steady rise in the (provincial) total number of applications to consecutive[17] teacher education programs — from approximately 8,000 in 1985, to 13,500 in 1988. Of the latter, only about 4,300 were admitted to Ontario teacher education institutions.[18] According to Smith, Ontario "... is in the fortunate position of being able to meet the need for an increased supply of new teachers without lowering the standards for admission or reducing the program requirements as an incentive to attract more people into the profession."[19]

Recent developments suggest that earlier predictions of a teacher shortage in the mid-1990s may have overestimated the demand for new teachers. Although enrolments are increasing as expected, fiscal constraints imposed by governments and heavily burdened taxpayers are forcing school boards and provincial ministries of education to try to reduce the number of teachers. The result, of course, is rising pressure to increase the pupil-teacher ratio — a development that is being vigorously opposed by the teachers' unions. While the outcome of this struggle is not entirely predictable, it is evident that some trade-offs will be necessary, making it not altogether clear whether an overall teacher shortage will develop or not. One thing is certain, however; there will be a substantial demand for new teachers by the end of this decade when large numbers of older teachers are expected to reach retirement age.

National and provincial estimates of teacher demand and supply mask serious shortages that have been apparent for some time and which continue even during periods of teacher over-supply. Such shortages exist in particular locations, including remote areas in Northern Ontario and northern Alberta and some major metropolitan areas (notably the City of Toronto) where housing costs and occasionally difficult school environments combine to discourage some teachers from locating there.

Another concern has to do with shortages of teachers in specific subject areas. Most provinces are short of teachers in mathematics, the sciences, technical disciplines, and all disciplines in French-language school boards outside Quebec.[20] These shortages are serious and often result in teachers teaching out-of-field (that is, teaching subjects for which they have had little or no training.) These shortages are not unique to Canada and, indeed, are reported by most major OECD countries.[21]

Shortages of French teachers — for French-language training and French-immersion programs — reflect what is, in many respects, a uniquely Canadian problem. Across Canada, the demand for French immersion courses has grown quickly. Many French-language teachers come from Quebec, often for short terms of a year or two. Turnover among them is high and the shortage is compounded in light of the fact that French-speaking teachers of mathematics, the sciences, and technical subjects are in even shorter supply.

Shortages of teachers of mathematics, the sciences, and technical subjects are part of a complex web of trends that are affecting most developed countries. More and more, governments are urging industry to move to technology-based production in order to meet the demands of global competition. However, that requires a technologically and scientifically literate population from which to draw managers and workers alike. Increasingly, a technologically literate and well-educated population is needed to provide a good market base and to make responsible decisions regarding the direction of technological change. It is reasonably certain, therefore, that demands will be placed on the educational system to provide children and young people with the knowledge and skills they need to support themselves, and an economy and society based on science and changing technologies. Despite this, the number of students enrolled in mathematics, science, and engineering programs at the post-secondary level remains stagnant. This is especially disturbing because graduates from these programs constitute not only the pool of new scientists and engineers for the labour market, but also the source of most of the new science and technology teachers who are desperately needed in the schools.

This raises the question of signals. Are the status and pay accorded scientists, engineers, and technologists in our society sufficiently high to attract people into these occupations? Is the quality of the scientific and technological education provided to students sufficiently high to attract their interest? And why are women not attracted to these fields (although it should be noted that male enrolments in these post-secondary fields are beginning to show signs of weakness)? Some observers who have noted the declining interest in science and technology among students question whether, in teaching science and technology, the social relevance of these fields is being made clear. They argue that it is not, and that too often these subjects are taught within rigid boundaries with little attempt to create interdisciplinary linkages.[22]

Clearly, the combined forces that shape the supply and demand of teachers raise a number of policy issues. While the evidence does not suggest there is a shortage of people who are interested in teaching as a career, there is serious concern about the ability of the faculties of education to produce the required number of teachers, and to provide teachers with the right skills and subject specialties. However, Canadian Faculties of Education are also under additional pressure. Ensuring an adequate supply of properly-trained new teachers is one thing; attending to the needs of teachers who are already employed is another. Technological developments, changing social and economic needs, and the sheer growth in the quantity of information and knowledge across all educational disciplines mean that in-service teacher training (training provided to practising teachers) is also likely to become more important over the years ahead.

III Teacher Training

Several recent U.S. studies have called for a massive overhaul of the American educational system, beginning with pre-service and in-service teacher training. Concern has also been expressed in Canada that teacher training is not receiving the attention it deserves. Increasingly, teacher training is being seen as a continuum. It is also being recognized that having the qualifications to become a teacher does not in itself provide all the knowledge needed over the course of a teaching career. Training must be on-going and carefully shaped to meet changing needs. That is not to say that Canadian teachers are not now involved in in-service training. On the contrary, in Ontario in 1984-85, for example, there were more full-time-equivalent teachers (4,689) taking "additional qualification" (AQ) courses than full-time students taking pre-service courses (3,883).

There is also a substantial investment in teacher training courses by the universities. The sum invested is estimated at $30 million annually.[23] Nonetheless, AQ courses are often seen to be "superficial".[24] Also, many school boards do not encourage their teaching staffs to upgrade their professional skills, i.e., they do not provide programs or offer financial support for such upgrading. And although teachers' collective agreements provide for several days per year of "professional development", those days are generally spread throughout the year and cannot possibly provide teachers with the time needed for in-depth training. It would seem, given the scope of the challenge, that a much more systematic approach to in-service training is required — especially in view of existing teacher shortages in specific subject areas.

How did this situation develop? Some critics argue that it is partly a result of the way the educational system is organized. Fullan and Connelly note that "schools are primarily bureaucratic rather than professional".[25] Darling-Hammond, in her analysis of the U.S. system, claims that the purpose of bureaucratic controls has been to make the system 'teacher-proof' by prescribing,

> ... the content and conduct of teaching by specifying tests, texts, curricular guidelines, and management procedures. These were accompanied by rules for grouping, grading, and labelling students in ways that would determine the treatment they were to receive... The goal of such policies was to reduce the apparent need for knowledge and decision-making on the part of teachers and school administrators. By standardizing "treatments", the policymakers hoped to worry less about whether teachers knew what to do.[26]

Fullan and Connelly reach similar conclusions regarding the Canadian school system, explaining that:

> *... the schools were designed for an age when the status of women was low; when the teaching workforce was mostly drawn from middle-class women and lower-class men; and when the prevailing cultural view was that the purpose of the schools was to produce a subservient workforce literate in the basic skills to support an economy run by a creative elite educated in the private schools. Evolving notions of industrial success, in the form of bureaucratically-run organizations, were transferred to the evolution of schools as places of learning and work.*[27]

In essence, these authors contend that teachers have not been treated as professionals. Admittedly, Canadian teachers' post-secondary qualifications have risen dramatically since 1960, but, if the argument is accepted — that bureaucratic controls have been used to shape and regulate the tasks and performance of teachers — then it is equally reasonable to accept the argument that teacher training has not always been highly focussed and that training subsequent to certification has also not been given a very high priority. Fullan and Connelly claim that "we simply do not understand the process of learning to teach"[28] and that the faculties of education themselves must become more professional in their research on teaching and learning.

The paternalistic approach to teacher management is also manifest in other ways. Promotion within the teaching ranks occurs in a fairly lock-step manner with annual increases tied to and dependent upon educational background and years of experience. By returning to school to earn a more advanced degree, a teacher may progress to a higher professional category or earning-scale, or may transfer into the administrative ranks. Otherwise, personal initiative and motivation have little to do with advancement. It is not surprising, therefore, that teaching is often referred to as a "...strangely 'careerless' career".[29]

The analysis that follows in the next section shows that in terms of earnings, the teaching profession is typified by a fairly flat career structure. Beginning teachers' salaries are high compared with salaries of more experienced teachers but little, if any, distinction is made between good teachers and poor ones. Most people choose to become teachers because they like to work with children or they hope to play a socially-supportive role. However, outstanding effort that is not rewarded, acknowledged or even recognized, year after year, will necessarily take its toll on motivation, job satisfaction, and commitment.

The unusual professional career structure of the teaching profession is not unique to Canada. It has also been criticized in major U.S. studies undertaken during the mid-'80s and has been noted by the OECD.[30] In all cases, the authors have concluded that the system must change. Teachers should be given the autonomy to perform as professionals and rated (if not categorized) on the basis of how — and how well — they perform.

Giving teachers genuine autonomy and responsibility in their roles as educators of children is a delicate issue. It requires confidence in the system of new teacher training and the ability of principals and administrators to help teachers manage schools. Before considering the question of professionalization however, the structure of teachers' earnings must be examined.

IV Teachers' Earnings

Earnings and career patterns are important aspects of any occupation. It is also important to know how these compare with alternative occupations. Presumably, higher levels of earnings and potential for advancement in an occupation have some bearing on the quality (and number) of people who enter that occupation and remain in it. Earnings also affect job satisfaction and motivation.

Of course, other factors also have an important influence on individuals' decisions to enter an occupation and the "return" they derive from their work. The major attractions to teaching are:

- interpersonal — a desire to work with young people or people in general
- service — worthy social and moral contribution to the community and society
- familiarity — a fondness for the job and the school setting -material — job security and good salaries
- working conditions and schedule — a preference for the regular (daily) hours and school vacation schedule.[31]

Other occupations also have similar attractions. Medicine, for example, has interpersonal and service aspects. Ultimately, of course, how and why an individual makes an occupational choice is highly personal, and depends on that individual's perceptions, the influence of others, and chance. Frequently, too, an individual must settle for a second or third career choice. In other words, occupational choices are highly subjective (and variable over time) and there is little reliable information upon which to base comparisons between occupations. Earning power, however, is common to all occupations and is an objective, differentiating indicator. That being the case, comparisons based on a variety of earnings indicators were made for the teaching occupations and for a number of comparable occupations.

The selected sample of "comparable" occupations is based on two specific ratings coded in the Canadian Classification and Dictionary of Occupations, which provides definitions for more than 6000 occupations in Canada. These ratings are: the "general educational development" (GED) rating of occupations, and the "specific vocational preparation" (SVP) rating. The GED is a code assigned on the basis of education contributing to reasoning development and the acquisition of "tool" knowledge. Using mathematical and language skills, for example, the code ranges from 1 (denoting the ability to carry out specific tasks) to 6 (denoting the ability to understand and work with complex concepts). The SVP is a code assigned on the basis of the amount of time needed to acquire the information, techniques, and skills required for average work performance in a specific occupation. The code ranges from 1 (a task that can be learned from a brief demonstration) to 9 (a task requiring over 10 years of training). Based on the GED and SVP requirements for various teaching occupations, a sample of comparable occupations was selected. An effort was made to select occupations that, in a sense, are similar in kind to teaching, that is, that involve professional working arrangements and allow scope for the use of similar sorts of skills. The medical profession was included, for example, because it involves working with people and working in scientific and technical fields. Also included were samplings of social workers and librarians for women and lawyers and dentists for men — all of which are occupations that have, at least in the past, been common alternatives for one gender or the other.

Data on earnings by occupation were obtained from Statistics Canada for Canada, the 10 provinces, and the Yukon and Northwest Territories. Two indicators were based on decile information. To calculate earnings deciles, earnings for each occupation were listed in ascending order of magnitude, then grouped into ten classes, each representing 10 per cent of earners. Statistics Canada provided two indicators based on these earnings deciles: 1) the upper dollar limit of the bottom 10 per cent of earners (the bottom decile), and 2) the lower dollar limit of the top 10 per cent of earners (the top decile). These measures provide a rough estimate of starting salaries, on the one hand, and salaries that are paid to individuals who are "established" in their careers, on the other.

Both dimensions are important in considering the relative attractiveness of different occupations to potential entrants, and the factors that are likely to influence a person entering an occupation and remaining in it throughout his or her working career. One can argue, for example, that a high starting salary in one occupation will attract higher quality entrants. However, it can also be argued that a lower starting salary will also attract high quality entrants because the occupation holds out the prospect of attaining very high earnings later in one's career. It might also be assumed that the earnings' potential of different occupations have an effect on motivation, commitment, and job satisfaction.

Four other indicators are also shown:

- earnings at the upper dollar limit of the bottom 25 per cent of earners (the bottom quartile)
- earnings at the lower dollar limit of the top 25 per cent of earners (the top quartile)
- average earnings
- median earnings

Table 4.3 shows earnings of the various teaching occupations for Canada and the provinces for 1986. The dollar values represent 1) earnings at the upper bound of the bottom 10 per cent of earners and 2) earnings at the lower bound of the top 10 per cent of earners. Near the bottom of the earnings scale, inter-provincial variations in the earnings of secondary-school teachers, elementary and kindergarten teachers, and teaching administrators were moderate in 1986. Marked differences are apparent, however, in the case of community college teachers, where earnings near the bottom of the scale ranged from a low of $15,205 in Saskatchewan to a high of $26,655 in Quebec.

The Quebec system includes collèges d'enseignement général et professionnel (CÉGEPS) which offer courses ranging from the high-school level, to technical training, to courses equivalent to first-year university. This may partially account for the relatively high starting salaries of college teachers in Quebec in 1986.

In general, provincial earnings variations were greater at the upper end of the income scale than at the lower end. This was particularly the case for university teachers, for whom earnings in 1986 ranged from $53,146 in Newfoundland to $70,018 in Alberta in 1986, and for secondary-school teachers for whom earnings ranged from $36,756 in Prince Edward Island to $50,456 in Ontario.

The earnings of selected comparable occupations relative to the earnings of the teaching occupations for Canada in 1986 are shown in Table 4.4. The information in Table 4.4 consists of indexes of occupational earnings relative to the earnings of university teachers, secondary-school teachers, and teaching administrators. Four sets of indexes were calculated for each group of occupations: earnings at the upper limit of the bottom 10 per cent of earners; earnings at the lower limit of the top 10 per cent of earners; earnings at the upper limit of the bottom 25 per cent of earners; and earnings at the lower limit of the top 25 per cent of earners. By comparing teachers' earnings at each of these points on the earnings scale, it is possible to determine how well teachers are paid as they progress through their careers.

Consider university teachers first. The comparisons here are with 17 other occupations, including doctors, lawyers, dentists, scientists and engineers, and public sector employees. All other occupations earn less than university teachers near the bottom of the earnings scale, which, for most individuals, represents an early point in their careers. Thus, lawyers still at the articling stage are included in the group 'lawyers and notaries'. At the top of the earnings scale, however, university teachers fall from 1st to 6th place, lagging behind doctors, lawyers, dentists, and some engineers, but they still rank higher than most other occupations in that group.

The second group of occupations includes teachers at the secondary-school, elementary-school and kindergarten, and community college levels, and special education teachers. Again, compared to the 14 other occupations in this category, secondary-school teachers compared quite well near the bottom of the earnings distribution in 1986, where their earnings ranked first. The position of secondary-school teachers erodes considerably, however, near the top of the earnings scale where they fall to 7th place. While the ranking of elementary and kindergarten teachers changed from 7th place near the bottom of the earning scale to 9th near the top, their position relative to secondary school teachers improves considerably, increasing from 68 per cent of secondary school teachers' earnings at the lower end of the earnings scale to 92 per cent near the top.

A similar pattern is shown by community college teachers, whose ranking changed from 2nd place near the bottom of the earnings scale to 5th place near the top, when compared to all other occupations in this group. However, community college teachers improve their position relative to secondary-school teachers, increasing from 96 per cent of the earnings of secondary school teachers near the bottom of the scale to 102 per cent at the top of the scale.

On the basis of the data shown in Table 4.4, it appears that, relative to other comparable occupations, secondary-school teachers are relatively high earners at the lower end of the earnings scale, but their position deteriorates in relative terms at the high end of the earnings scale. Elementary and kindergarten teachers do not compare as favourably at lower income levels, but they "catch up" substantially at higher earnings levels. Finally, community college teachers begin nearly as well as secondary school teachers and show an improvement relative to them, but their position relative to other occupations shows some deterioration.

The discussion so far has been based on earnings deciles and has therefore focussed on the low and high extremes of the earnings distribution. Other information contained in Table 4.4 allows an even broader look at the question of the earnings of teachers relative to comparable occupations, however. Columns 3 and 4 show the earnings levels that mark the upper limit of the bottom 25 per cent of earners and the lower boundary of the top 25 per cent of earners. This information captures a broader range of earners and allows a comparison of earnings that approximate the levels typical of earners in the middle-income range of the various occupations. What is apparent from this is that university teachers compare quite well to other occupations at both the bottom and the top earnings quartiles, ranking first at the bottom quartile and third at the top, where they fall behind only doctors and dentists. Similarly strong performances are shown by secondary school and community college teachers; and while elementary and kindergarten teachers rank lower compared to non-teaching occupations, their position

Table 4.3
Earnings at Upper Limit of Bottom 10 Per Cent of Earners and at Lower Limit of Top 10 Per Cent of Earners Teaching Occupations, Canada and Provinces, 1986

	NF	PE	NS	NB	QC	ON	MB	SK	AB	BC	Canada
Upper Limit of Bottom 10 per cent of Earners											
University teachers	27,492	—	29,227	30,489	27,709	29,721	29,982	30,383	31,663	28,895	29,425
Community college teachers	21,826	—	23,031	25,560	26,655	21,763	24,078	15,206	24,143	21,987	24,955
Secondary school teachers	24,143	23,077	25,417	24,110	25,353	27,330	26,578	25,077	25,297	27,095	26,013
Elementary and Kindergarten teachers	21,508	18,967	19,324	19,748	17,122	16,759	18,476	20,415	18,519	17,014	17,705
Administrators, Teaching and Related	27,849	26,388	24,772	26,659	27,022	25,285	24,985	27,644	24,864	25,056	25,689
Lower Limit of Top 10 per cent of Earners											
University teachers	53,146	—	59,795	58,868	62,665	66,778	70,788	68,086	70,018	64,557	65,117
Community college teachers	41,932	—	43,322	41,482	43,986	50,456	41,550	42,067	47,609	46,522	47,321
Secondary school teachers	39,037	36,756	43,477	38,604	41,159	49,034	43,269	42,871	43,626	43,576	46,518
Elementary and Kindergarten Teachers	35,448	35,374	41,728	36,845	37,527	45,164	40,897	40,939	42,116	41,297	42,875
Administrators, Teaching and Related	53,338	58,392	58,842	52,249	55,748	63,210	59,415	59,390	59,661	61,672	60,645

Source: CEIC, COPS Information Manager (CIM) Data Base

Table 4.4
Index of Earnings of Selected Comparable Occupations Relative to Teaching Occupations, Canada, 1986

	Upper limit of bottom 10 % of earners		Lower limit of top 10 % of earners		Upper limit of bottom 25 % of earners		Lower limit of top 25 % of earners	
		(Rank)		(Rank)		(Rank)		(Rank)
University Teachers	**100**	**(1)**	**100**	**(6)**	**100**	**(1)**	**100**	**(3)**
Physicians and Surgeons	50	(16)	1191	(1)	75	(11)	137	(1)
Dentists	19	(18)	1091	(2)	56	(18)	125	(2)
Lawyers and Notaries	49	(17)	109	(3)	66	(16)	94	(5)
Economists	74	(10)	90	(11)	77	(10)	83	(12)
Sociologists/Anthropologists	65	(13)	72	(18)	68	(15)	71	(18)
Chemists	68	(12)	78	(17)	68	(14)	71	(17)
Physicists	80	(7)	93	(7)	84	(5)	91	(7)
Biologists	64	(14)	80	(13)	69	(13)	75	(14)
Architects	59	(15)	79	(16)	64	(17)	73	(16)
Chemical Engineers	96	(2)	105	(5)	93	(2)	96	(4)
Civil Engineers	85	(6)	93	(8)	83	(6)	88	(8)
Electrical Engineers	90	(4)	89	(12)	86	(4)	87	(9)
Industrial Engineers	80	8)	80	(15)	77	(9)	77	(13)
Mechanical Engineers	86	(5)	90	(10)	83	(7)	87	(10)
Mining Engineers	95	(3)	106	(4)	91	(3)	92	(6)
Government Administrators	79	(9)	91	(9)	79	(8)	86	(11)
Officials and Administrators (unique to government, NEC)	74	(11)	80	(14)	72	(12)	74	(15)
Secondary School Teachers	**100**	**(1)**	**100**	**(7)**	**100**	**(2)**	**100**	**(4)**
Elementary and Kindergarten Teachers	**68**	**(7)**	**92**	**(9)**	**85**	**(5)**	**92**	**(8)**
Community College Teachers	**96**	**(2)**	**102**	**(5)**	**102**	**(1)**	**102**	**(2)**
Special Education Teachers	**52**	**(14)**	**89**	**(11)**	**66**	**(13)**	**83**	**(10)**
Nurses, (graduate and non-supervisory)	66	(9)	72	(14)	71	(9)	74	(13)
Librarians and Archivists	63	(11)	89	(10)	66	(11)	82	(11)
Writers and Editors	54	(13)	107	(4)	65	(14)	96	(6)
Social Workers	65	(10)	80	(13)	70	(10)	77	(12)
Physical Sciences Technologists/Technicians	69	(6)	92	(8)	76	(8)	85	(9)
Life Sciences Technologists/Technicians	57	(12)	84	(12)	66	(12)	74	(14)
Systems Analysts	74	(5)	100	(6)	81	(7)	95	(7)
Pharmacists	67	(8)	108	(3)	83	(6)	98	(98)
Government Administrators	90	(3)	128	(1)	96	(3)	116	(1)
Officials and Administrators (unique to Government, NEC)	84	(4)	112	(2)	87	(4)	100	(3)
Administrators in Teaching	100	(2)	100	(3)	100	(2)	100	(3)
General Managers	81	(6)	159	(1)	82	(3)	121	(1)
Financial Officers	68	(7)	82	(7)	58	(7)	73	(7)
Managers - natural sciences	120	(1)	121	(2)	103	(1)	112	(2)
Managers - financial	81	(5)	100	(4)	71	(6)	88	(5)
Government Administrators	91	(3)	98	(5)	79	(4)	92	(4)
Officials and Administrators (unique to Government, NEC)	85	(4)	86	(6)	71	(5)	79	(6)

[1] Earnings at the lower limit of the bottom 25 per cent of earners because no data are given for earners at the top decile.

Source: Based on Data from COPs Information Manager (CIM) Data-Base.

improves from 85 per cent of secondary school teachers' earnings at the bottom 25 per cent of earnings, to 92 per cent at the top.

Considering all of the information on teachers' earnings presented thus far, the following conclusions can be drawn:

- University, secondary-school, and community-college teachers all compare very well to other occupations when measured against the line drawn by the upper limit of earnings of the bottom 10 per cent of earners. Also, while the position of elementary and kindergarten teachers is not as strong, their earnings at this lower level, nonetheless, are higher than seven of the 14 occupations compared.

- Teachers' earnings diverge at the top of the earnings scale. There is some slippage in the earnings rankings of both university and community-college teachers, relative to comparable occupations; some slippage is also evident with respect to earnings of elementary and kindergarten teachers. The most notable deterioration in performance, however, is apparent for secondary school teachers.

- In fact, weaknesses with respect to teachers' earnings only appear near the top of the earnings scale. In the middle of the scale, the data on earnings quartiles show that university teachers, secondary-school teachers and community college teachers rank high compared to other occupational groups. Furthermore, while the earnings of elementary and kindergarten teachers (shown in the far right columns of Table 4.4) rank around the middle of the occupations being compared, the gap between their earnings and those of secondary-school teachers narrows considerably.

Additional insights into teachers' earnings are provided by Table 4.5 which shows "earnings potential" for the teaching occupations in 1986 — that is, the percentage increase in earnings from the bottom 10 per cent of earners to the top 10 per cent, and from the bottom 25 per cent to the top 25 per cent. These ratios give a sense of what teachers can hope to gain over the course of their careers. Considering first earnings for the bottom and top 10 per cent of earners, it can be seen from Table 4.5 that secondary school and community college teachers have the most limited (smallest) earnings potential. The Canadian average for secondary school teachers, for example, is 179 per cent which means that, on average, teachers at the top of the earning scale earn roughly 79 per cent more than teachers near the bottom of the earnings distribution.

The Canadian average, of course, masks considerable inter-provincial variation. In 1986, the earnings potential (based on deciles) of community college teachers in Saskatchewan was very high (277) compared to their earnings potential in other provinces; this can partly be explained because earnings for this group at the bottom decile were extremely low. In British Columbia, Alberta, Nova Scotia, and especially Ontario, the earnings potential of elementary school teachers was extremely high compared to the experiences of the other teaching occupations and to other provinces. In contrast, in Newfoundland and New Brunswick, no teaching occupation performed strongly, so late-career teachers in these provinces could, on average, expect to earn less than double the earnings of teachers near the bottom of the earnings distribution.

When the earnings potential of each teaching occupation group is compared to that of its comparable occupational groups, university teachers rank near the bottom, although they compare more favourably in Manitoba and Saskatchewan; elementary school teachers rank near the middle; without exception, however, the earnings potential of secondary school teachers in 1986 ranked last in all provinces when compared to the earnings potential of comparable occupations.

The conclusions to be drawn from this comparative analysis of salaries are:

- First, as a group, teachers are relatively well-paid, on average.[32]

- Second, teachers appear to be very well-paid compared to other occupational groups at the bottom end of the income scale — that is, near the beginning of their careers.

- Third, however, signs of weakness are apparent at the top end of the scale for secondary-school and community college teachers and, in some provinces — notably Newfoundland, Nova Scotia, and New Brunswick — for university teachers.

What these results tend to confirm is that some teachers, notably secondary-school and community college teachers, can expect flat career structures. While they may enjoy the benefits of comparatively high earnings levels relative to other occupations early in their careers, the increases they can expect over the course of their careers are low in relative terms. Undoubtedly, there are many non-pecuniary reasons why people choose to become teachers and why they stay in teaching. Nonetheless, the common wisdom underlying rising pay structures is that as an individual progresses in a career, pay increases and higher salaries act both as a means of recognizing ability, effort, and experience and as an incentive for continued strong performance. It might be expected, therefore, that steeper (rising) earnings curves will have a stronger impact on motivation and job satisfaction than shallow (rising) curves. Indeed, the analysis reported above found that for the teaching occupations, earnings compared quite favourably to other occupations up to the middle of the earnings

Table 4.5
Earnings Potential, Teaching Occupations, Canada and Provinces, 1986

	NF	PE	NS	NB	QC	ON	MB	SK	AB	BC	Canada
Percentage Growth from Top of Bottom 10 Per Cent of Earners to Bottom of Top 10 Per Cent of Earners											
University Teachers	193	—	205	193	226	225	236	224	221	223	221
Community College Teachers	192	—	188	162	165	232	173	277	197	212	190
Secondary School Teachers	162	159	171	160	162	179	163	171	172	161	179
Elementary and Kindergarten Teachers	165	187	216	187	219	269	221	201	227	243	242
Administrators, (teaching and related)	192	221	238	196	206	250	238	215	240	246	236
Percentage Growth from Top of Bottom 25 Per Cent of Earners to Bottom of Top 25 Per Cent of Earners											
University Teachers	130	151	142	136	149	150	157	154	153	142	149
Community College Teachers	128	126	135	127	130	135	125	130	130	130	135
Secondary School Teachers	127	121	129	121	129	130	128	133	132	126	135
Elementary and Kindergarten Teachers	123	128	142	137	126	155	150	148	150	141	145
Administrators, (teaching and related)	134	137	132	122	134	139	140	134	133	159	140

Source: Calculations based on COPS Information Manager (CIN) Data Base

V The Professionalization of Teaching

The notion of the professionalization of teaching is closely linked to questions of teacher performance, teacher status, and school ethos. The broad outlines of a professionalized career structure are outlined in Tomorrow's Teachers: A Report of the Holmes Group, but similar ideas are expressed in other studies, including the recent report (1991) of the National Advisory Board on Science and Technology to the Prime Minister, and Learning to Win: Education, Training and National Prosperity. Essentially, these reports call for a classification system for teachers based on ability and motivation, not merely on the number of years of experience. Distinctions would be made between instructors, career teachers, and career professionals — or what is often referred to as master or lead teachers. These categories would recognize and otherwise accommodate different levels of ability and effort, professional training, and status within the profession. Such differentiation would have several benefits. It would give ambitious teachers something to work toward; it would allow the educational system to draw upon the special talents of outstanding teachers and would raise the status of the teaching profession in society and so help to attract highly capable people.

At present, the educational system draws upon the talents of teachers indiscriminantly — poor teachers teach as many hours and as many students as good ones. Most adults can look back and identify one or two good teachers who had positive life-long effects on them. Others can identify one or two bad teachers who, for some, turned them off school altogether. By having categories of teachers or a rating capability, the system could make more productive use of the available human resources.

Teachers who are merely capable could be restricted to basic teaching tasks. Lead teachers, on the other hand, could play an important role in teacher training, in coaching new teachers and assisting those experiencing difficulties, in illustrating innovative and effective teaching styles — while still involved in the classroom.

The question of how to recognize and reward outstanding teachers is not a new one. Traditionally, career advancement for teachers has been along the path of administrative promotion. Promoting good teachers to administrative positions, of course, takes them out of the classroom, where they are needed. Another approach suggested recently is to use 'merit pay'. Several experiments with merit pay have been undertaken in the U.S., less so in Canada. Critics of the practice argue that principals are not up to the task, that it is too time-consuming for principals and supervisors, and that it is too open to personal manipulation. Considering the number of schools and boards across Canada, standardization of the process would, indeed, seem to be difficult, if not impossible. Alternatively, there is a strong case for supporting the more formalized instructor/professional teacher/master teacher approach, wherein different steps to accreditation would be set out.

Finally, the professionalization of teaching is linked to the entire body of literature on school ethos and effective schools. That literature argues that effective schools are those run by committed professionals who have the freedom to make choices and decisions, and where differences (among schools) as to how things are done are encouraged rather than stifled by bureaucratic standardization. Under such a system, the role of the principal would change from that of administrator to one of facilitator and group leader. This would, undoubtedly, require fairly large-scale retraining of principals.

It is increasingly being argued that our most capable people will not be drawn into teaching, nor will we make maximum use of teachers' talents, until teachers are treated as professionals and given greater freedom and authority to make decisions. At the same time, however, it is unlikely that parents will be willing to give teachers greater authority until they are convinced that teachers are, indeed, capable professionals. The key, then, is to find a point of entry into this circle.

Summary

Canadian teachers are caught between two overwhelming bureaucracies: the large administrative systems of school boards and provincial ministries of education and the network of teachers' unions. Although for different reasons, both bureaucracies have worked to ensure that all teachers are treated alike — regardless of their performance. Motivated by the need to provide more or less standardized educational programs to millions of pupils, the educational bureaucracy has placed its faith in standardized curricula, statements of teachers qualifications, and other common procedures rather than in individual teacher performance. Teachers' unions, in pursuing fair and equitable treatment of their members have, in the end, ensured that "all teachers are equal".

The result is that the educational system draws upon the talents of teachers indiscriminately — poor teachers teach as many hours and as many students as good ones — and given current pension regulations, there is no incentive for poor or burned-out teachers to leave the profession. The problem is compounded by the fact that most teachers have little employment experience outside the educational system — most graduated from high school, then from university, then proceeded directly to teaching positions in the school system — and so have little flexibility in terms of finding alternative employment. As a result, relatively few positions have opened in recent years for new teachers and these are usually the first to be cut when fiscal constraints require reductions.

In considering the educational system and the place of teachers in it, there appears to be a paradox. Today's teachers are highly educated, well-paid and experienced. They have also been involved in the processes that have seen the pupil/teacher ratio drop substantially in recent years. Yet, within the same time-frame, there has not been any significant improvement in student achievement. On the contrary, most Canadians consider the performance of the educational system in Canada to be inadequate; it is simply not good enough to ensure an improving standard of living in coming decades.

Identifying the role of teachers — whether on the basis of intuition or on highly-aggregated descriptive statistics — is very difficult. Having earned a university degree, there is no guarantee that the individual who earned it can teach. Age and experience may improve the performance of some individuals but they can also lead to disillusionment and "burn-out" in others. Moreover, shrinking pupil/teacher ratios tell us little about the changing character of students in the classroom and the problems that teachers face. It would be dishonest — or at least misleading — to suggest that all, or even most, teachers in Canada are either good or bad. All of us, whether former or current students, parents, or simple observers of the education scene, know that the school system is made up of both. They cannot be identified by their looks or their degrees; only by their performance in the classroom. Students and parents usually know who they are, so it would be surprising, indeed, if principals do not know who they are as well. However, the bureaucracy, including the unions, has been very successful in protecting the jobs of teachers who are just not good enough while at the same time unwittingly penalizing excellent teachers.

What can be done to help the teaching profession contribute to a better educational system in Canada? A useful first step would be to screen teachers-in-training more carefully. Conventional training methods give novice teachers too little classroom exposure. They need more time to discover whether they can actually work with children and young people before committing themselves to a teaching career. Another useful step would be to recognize explicitly that not all teachers are equal in terms of ability and performance. Some teachers are simply better than others, and the system should make more effective use of its best teachers. At the same time, there must be an acceptable route out of the classroom to facilitate if not promote the departure of inadequate teachers. Recommendations on how the system could move in these directions are contained in the concluding chapter.

Endnotes

1. Statistics Canada, *Salaries and Qualifications of Teachers in Public Elementary and Secondary Schools*, CAT. 81-202, 1977-78 and 1985-86.

2. Statistics Canada, *Salaries and Qualifications of Teachers*, Cat. 81-202, 1968-69 and 1985-86.

3. See Canadian Teachers' Federation, *Teaching in Canada*, March 1988.

4. Lockhart, Alexander, *Schoolteaching in Canada*, (Toronto: University of Toronto Press, 1991), p. 31.

5. ———, *Schoolteaching in Canada*, p. 32.

6. ———, *Schoolteaching in Canada*, p. 43.

7. Picot, W. G., *University Graduates and Jobs: Changes During the 1970s*, Statistics Canada Catalogue 89-501, 1983.

8. Rees, R., et al., "A Study of the Recruitment of Ontario Teachers", Social Program Evaluation Group, Queen's University, Kingston, Ontario, March 1989.

9. Lockhart, *Schoolteaching in Canada*, p. 45.

10. See, for example, *Tomorrow's Teachers: A Report of the Holmes Group* (East Lansing, Michigan: The Holmes Group, Inc., 1986) and *A Nation Prepared: Teachers for the 21st Century: The Report of the Task Force on Teaching as a Profession* (New York: Carnegie Forum on Education and the Economy, 1986).

11. See also, Linda Darling-Hammond, *Beyond the Commission Reports: The Coming Crisis in Teaching* (Santa Monica, California: Rand, 1984).

12. Darling-Hammond, Linda, "Teaching Supply, Demand, and Standards", *Educational Policy*, Vol. 3, No. 1, 1989, p. 1-17.

13. Smith, Laverne, *Perspectives on Teacher Supply and Demand. In Ontario, 1988-2008*, Ontario Ministry of Education (Toronto: Queen's Printer for Ontario) 1989, p. 32.

14. Violato, Claudio, "A Longitudinal Comparative Study of the Academic Achievement of Education and Other Undergraduate Students", *Canadian Journal of Education*, Vol. 15, No. 3, 1990, p. 264-76.

15. Smith, *Perspectives on Teacher Supply and Demand*, p. 43.

16. ———, *Perspectives on Teacher Supply and Demand*, p. 43.

17. There are two routes to obtaining a bachelor of education degree — either by successfully completing the required number of university courses in the faculty of education, or by first successfully meeting the requirements for a degree in another faculty (e.g., arts or science) followed by a one- or two-year program in the faculty of education. The latter is referred to as a consecutive or after-degree bachelor of education degree.

18. Smith, *Perspectives on Teacher Supply and Demand*, p. 26. These figures are an over-estimate of the total number of applications because many prospective students apply to several universities simultaneously.

19. ———, *Perspectives on Teacher Supply and Demand*, p. 26-27.

20. See for example, Smith, *Perspectives on Teachers Supply and Demand*, 1989; Alberta Education, A Snapshot of Teacher Supply and Demand in Alberta, 1989/90, *Alberta Education*, 1990; Guy Léveillé et Christian Arsenault, "Les besoins in personnel enseignant de 1990 à 2010 : Une étude de Nouveau-Brunswick", *Education Canada*, Vol. 31, No. 2, Summer 1991; A. McDermott and S. McKitrick, *Final Report on Supply and Demand Survey of Teachers of Technological Studies Projected for September 1990*, Sponsored by the Ontario Secondary School Teachers' Federation, September 1990.

21. See OECD, Education Committee, "Teacher Demand and Supply: The Labour Market for Teachers", March 1990.

22. For an interesting analysis of why students drop out of the sciences and maths at the undergraduate level, see Sheila Tobias, *They're Not Dumb, They're Different: Stalking the Second Tier*, (Tucson, Arizona: Research Corporation, 1990).

23. Fullan, M. and F. M. Connelly, *Teacher Education in Ontario: Current Practice and Options for the Future* (Toronto: Ontario Ministry of Education, 1987), p. 24.

24 ——, *Teacher Education in Ontario*, p. 28.

25 ——, *Teacher Education in Ontario*, p. 44.

26 Darling-Hammond Linda, "Teacher Supply, Demand, and Standards", *Educational Policy*, Vol 3, No. 1, 1989, p. 1-17.

27 Fullan and Connelly, *Teacher Education in Ontario*, p. 56.

28 ——, *Teacher Education in Ontario*, p. 47.

29 ——, *Teacher Education in Ontario*, p. 42.

30 OECD, *Schools and Quality: An International Report*, (Paris: OECD, 1989).

31 Joseph, P. B. and N. Green, "Perspectives on reasons for becoming teachers", *Journal of Teacher Education*, November-December 1987, p. 28-33.

32 Average teachers' earnings not only compare favourably to average earnings of other occupations in Canada, but also to average earnings of teachers in other countries, including the U.S., Japan, and Germany. See S. M. Barro and L. Suter, *International Comparison of Teachers' Salaries: An Exploratory Study*, National Center for Education Statistics (Washington, D.C.: U.S. Department of Education, 1988). Barro and Suter's findings are summarized in Economic Council of Canada, *A Lot to Learn* (Ottawa: Supply and Services Canada, 1992).

5
The Cost and Funding of Education

Canada spends large amounts of money on its educational system. Nonetheless, many critics allege that the performance of the Canadian school system does not reflect the level of spending it receives, compared to other countries. This chapter assesses Canada's position relative to other countries with respect to total spending on education using a number of indicators of national financial commitment to education.

The first and most familiar is the proportion of gross domestic product (GDP) spent on education, but this measurement, though simple, does not take any country-specific explanatory factors into account.

Table 5.1 shows public spending on education (all levels) as a percentage of GDP for each OECD country. In 1989, Canada spent 6.2 per cent of its GDP on education[1], ranking fifth among OECD countries behind Norway, Sweden, Denmark, and the Netherlands. That share was higher than the average of 5.6 per cent for all OECD countries.

The proportion of the total population participating in a country's educational system (i. e., the ratio of educational spending per student to GDP per capita – also known as the national participation rate) is one of the major influences on the ratio of educational spending to GDP. In other words, the higher the percentage

Table 5.1
Indicators of Public-sector Spending on Education Relative to Gross Domestic Product, Selected OECD Countries, 1989 (%)

	Public-sector Spending on Education Relative to GDP	Proportion of the Population Enrolled in Education	Spending per Student Relative to GDP Per Capita	Rank
Norway	7.2	22.9	31.4	3
Sweden	7.1	16.8	42.3	1
Denmark	7.0	20.6	34.0	2
The Netherlands	6.5[1]	22.9	28.4	4
Canada	**6.2**	**24.5**	**25.3**	**7**
New Zealand	5.6[1]	27.1	20.6	13
Austria	5.5	20.3	27.1	5
France	5.3	25.6	20.7	12
Australia	5.3[3]	22.3	23.8	9
United Kingdom	5.0[2]	24.3	20.5	14
Switzerland	5.0	19.7	25.4	6
Italy	5.0[3]	20.1	24.9	8
Belgium	4.9[1]	23.5	20.9	11
United States	4.8[3]	24.9	19.3	16
Japan	4.7[1]	22.0	21.4	10
Germany	4.1[1]	20.6	19.9	15
Average	5.6	22.4	25.4	

1 1988
2 1987
3 1986

Source: OECD, Education in OECD Countries, 1989-90 (forthcoming) and 1986-87

of the population participating in the system, the larger the share of GDP that is ordinarily devoted to education. In a sense, the relationship is an index of a country's commitment to education. Hence, it is interesting to see how countries rank based on a measurement of their financial commitment to education, adjusted for the rate of participation in education in each country. In this connection, the ratio of educational spending per student to GDP per capita can also be seen as a way to compare the resources allocated to each student by the educational system, and the resources allocated to each inhabitant by the economy as a whole (see column 3 of Table 5.1).

Canada's relatively high rate of participation in education is one of the factors that account for the high level of spending on education relative to GDP. Canada, in fact, ranks seventh among OECD countries in terms of spending per student as a proportion of GDP per capita. Understandably, countries such as Switzerland and Austria which have fairly low rates of participation in education, are higher than Canada in the OECD ranking. The most highly industrialized countries, including France, Japan, the United States and Germany rank below Canada. Using this measurement, however, Canada falls slightly below the average for OECD countries and is closer to the group of countries with the lowest figures. Figure 5.1 shows this clearly.

How do spending levels in different countries compare with respect to the various levels of schooling? Have these countries different rankings for spending at the primary and secondary levels as distinguished from to total expenditures on education? As Table 5.2 shows, Canada (only after Australia) devotes the largest proportion of its resources to post-secondary studies. In part, this reflects the high concentration of student population at this level. Considering only the ratio of spending per student to GDP per capita at the primary and secondary levels, Canada drops from seventh to eighth place among OECD countries.

Although Canada spends more on education than most countries, its level of spending is not substantially different from that of other countries. However, certain factors artificially inflate education spending in this country. As noted above, Canada's rank among OECD countries falls when such factors as the high rate of participation in education and the relatively large post-secondary sector are taken into account.

Other characteristics specific to the Canadian educational system also have an effect on costs. One such characteristic is provincial jurisdiction over education, resulting in a relatively large number of different (provincial) school systems. Each provincial system is further subdivided into school boards and, in some large urban areas, it is not unusual to find school

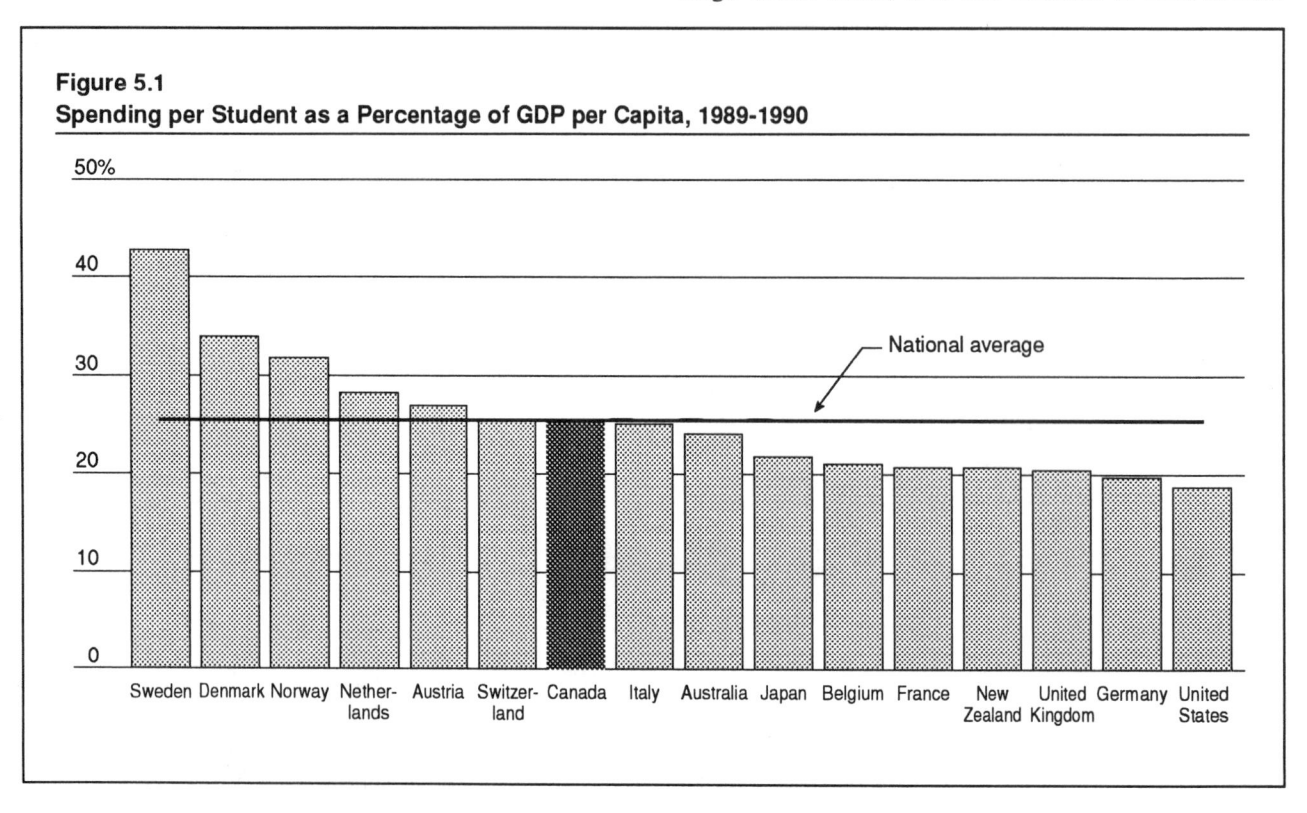

Figure 5.1
Spending per Student as a Percentage of GDP per Capita, 1989-1990

Table 5.2
Public-sector Spending on Education, by Level of Education, 1986-1987, as a Percentage of Total Spending

	Pre-school	Level 1	Level 2	Level 3
Denmark	–	61	21	18
Sweden	–	60	24	16
The Netherlands	–	27	41	31
Norway	53	30	17	–
Canada	–	**67***	–	**33**
Austria	7	19	52	22
France	13	24	48	16
New Zealand	2	38	43	18
Australia	1	62**	–	37
Belgium	–	28	52	20
Switzerland	3	76**	–	21
Japan	1	41	44	14
United Kingdom	3	26	50	21
Italy[1]	9	29	45	17
United States	47***	–	32	22
Germany	3	17	56	25

[1] 1984
* Includes spending at pre-school level and levels 1 and 2.
** Includes spending at levels 1 and 2.
*** Includes spending at pre-school level and level 1.

Source: OECD data

boards subdivided even further, along religious and linguistic lines. This proliferation is explained and defended primarily on the grounds of protecting religious and linguistic rights.

A second factor that sets Canada apart is the vastness of its territory and the low population density of many of its regions. Another distinguishing feature of the Canadian educational system is the diversity of cultural backgrounds within its school population. In 1988, 16 per cent of Canadian residents were born in other countries — one of the highest proportions among OECD countries. This rich linguistic and cultural diversity poses special problems for Canadian educators and efforts to meet these challenges entail costs that are not incurred by less heterogeneous societies.

Canada's Situation

Trends in Spending

In 1989-90, total public spending on education in Canada was just over $44 billion (Table 5.3), representing more than 6 per cent of Canada's GDP. Approximately 64 per cent of this expenditure was devoted to elementary and secondary schooling. The rest was divided among universities (20.4 per cent), vocational training schools (18 per cent), and colleges (8 per cent).[2]

Some broad patterns can be discerned from an estimation of provincial spending by level of education. For example, the proportion of funding allocated to elementary and secondary schooling by the Atlantic provinces is similar, on average, to that of Canada as a whole. On the other hand, these provinces spend a higher-than-average proportion on vocational training. Quebec allocates a substantial share of its spending to the college sector. This partly reflects the fact that in Quebec's educational system, the college sector is an an intermediate stage between secondary school and university, as well as the provider of vocational training, fulfilling a function very different from that of community colleges. In fact, a much higher proportion of students is enrolled in this system than in community colleges. In British Columbia and Alberta relatively more emphasis is placed on vocational training relative to Ontario (where the primary emphasis is placed on elementary and secondary education) with the result that the proportion allocated to vocational education in the two Western provinces is relatively higher than in Ontario.

Table 5.4 illustrates expenditure patterns in the elementary and secondary sectors over the past three decades. Between 1961 and 1991, total spending in current dollars in the two sectors rose, on average, by 10.9 per cent, with the strongest growth pattern recorded during the 1960s. A slowdown was observed during the following two decades. Spending in constant dollars also grew steadily during the 1960s, but slowed abruptly thereafter.

The trend in spending in the elementary and secondary sectors was linked to enrolment. As Figure 5.2 shows, enrolments increased during the 1960s, but declined during the following decade. Figure 5.2 also shows that periods of strong growth in total real spending are associated with periods of strong growth in elementary and secondary enrolment. Table 5.4 shows that real expenditures per student rose more slowly than total spending during the 1960s, and there was a continuous deceleration from 1961 to 1991 (see lines two and three in the table).

Figure 5.3 shows the relative change in the components of total real spending in the form of an index, with 1961 as the base year. Administrative expenditures recorded the largest increases over each decade. However, it must by noted that although this component clearly affects total costs, its share of total expenditures is so small that its overall effect is negligible.

Table 5.3
Total Public-sector Spending on Education, by Level of Education and by Province, Canada, 1989-1990

	Total Spending ($ Millions)	Elementary Secondary	Community College	Training University	Vocational
Canada[2]	44,170	63.6	8.0	20.4	8.0
Newfoundland	980	60.2	4.0	19.9	15.9
Prince Edward Island	180	59.5	6.6	21.4	12.5
Nova Scotia	1,390	59.1	2.7	28.4	9.2
New Brunswick	1,110	62.7	3.7	21.0	12.6
Quebec[1]	10,760	58.4	13.0	21.8	6.8
Ontario	16,640	69.1	6.6	19.3	5.0
Manitoba	1,840	68.8	4.0	19.7	7.5
Saskatchewan	1,700	63.7	4.7	20.9	10.7
Alberta	4,440	60.5	9.1	19.7	10.7
British Columbia	4,500	63.2	7.0	19.6	10.3

Proportion of Total Spending (%)

[1] In Quebec, students attend a CÉGEP (general and vocational college) after completion of secondary V (equivalent to grade 11 in the other provinces). CÉGEP instruction includes elements of education and training that are given in part at higher levels of secondary school and in part at the community college and early university levels in the other provinces; the CÉGEPs also provide some vocational training.

[2] Includes the Yukon and Northwest Territories.

[3] Includes vocational training provided by trade and vocational schools, community colleges, institutes of technology, etc., as well as on-the-job training and apprenticeship programs. However, it does not include vocational training given in secondary schools.

Source: Statistics Canada, *Education Statistics, Estimates*, Catalogue No. 81-220

The growth in real spending on salaries also exceeded the growth in total real spending. This factor can be broken into two components: increases in real average salaries and increases in the teacher/student ratio. As Table 5.4 shows, the contribution of average salaries to total growth in spending is far greater than that of the teacher/student ratio. At the same time, the increase in real salaries does not seem out of line, as it closely parallels the growth in real personal income in the economy as a whole during this period. The steady rise in the teacher/student ratio (or the decrease in average class size), combined with the normal increase in salaries, therefore account for the increase in salary expenditures.

In contrast to the salary and administrative components, which rose faster than total spending, outlays for capital formation, equipment, transportation, health, sports facilities and staff training all exhibited relatively low growth rates.

Spending per Student

Any attempt to rank the provinces by level of total spending on education produces a misleading picture of each province's actual financial commitment to education, since it does not take relative size into account. Thus spending per student is a more appropriate measurement, since the number of students is a reasonable proxy for the size of the provincial population. As Figure 5.4 and Table 5.5 show, Ontario and Manitoba are nearly tied for first place with respect to spending per student, followed closely by Quebec and Alberta, while the Atlantic provinces rank last.

Historically, Quebec has spent most on its elementary and secondary students. In 1983, for example, Quebec ranked first among the provinces by this criterion while Ontario placed slightly below the national average and very close to the Western provinces taken as a whole (Figure 5.5). The Atlantic provinces, however, ranked last.

Interprovincial differences in student/teacher ratios are one of the factors that explain the ranking of the provinces in terms of spending per student. Manitoba, Ontario and Quebec have the lowest student/teacher ratios in Canada (Table 5.5). This inevitably creates upward pressures on salary spending per student. Conversely, the Atlantic provinces have the highest

The Cost and Funding of Education 91

Figure 5.2
Rate of Increase in Real Total Spending and Number of Students, Elementary and Secondary Levels, 1962-1991

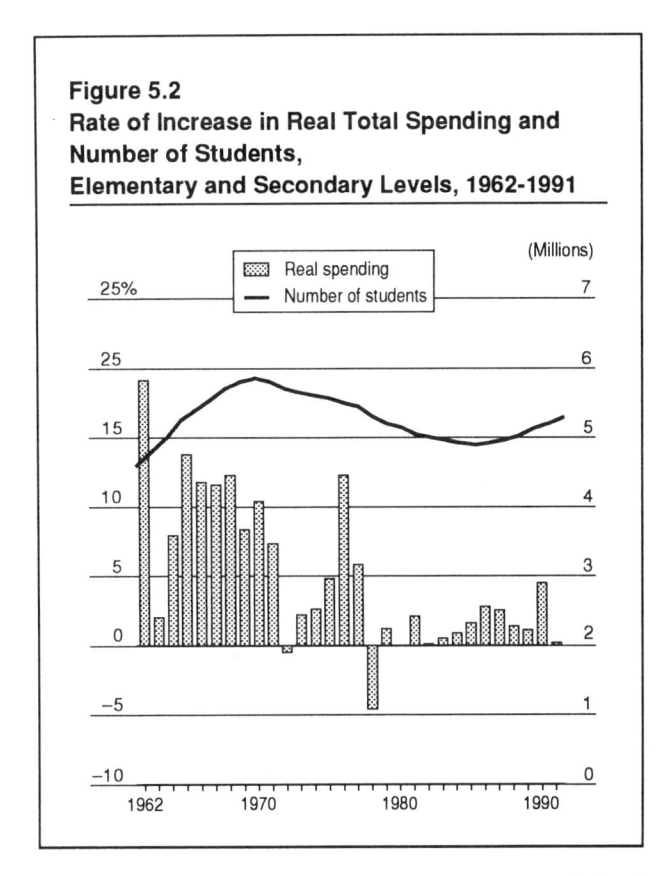

Figure 5.3
Index of Real Spending per Student, by Expenditure Categories, Elementary and Secondary Levels, 1971, 1981, 1991, Canada

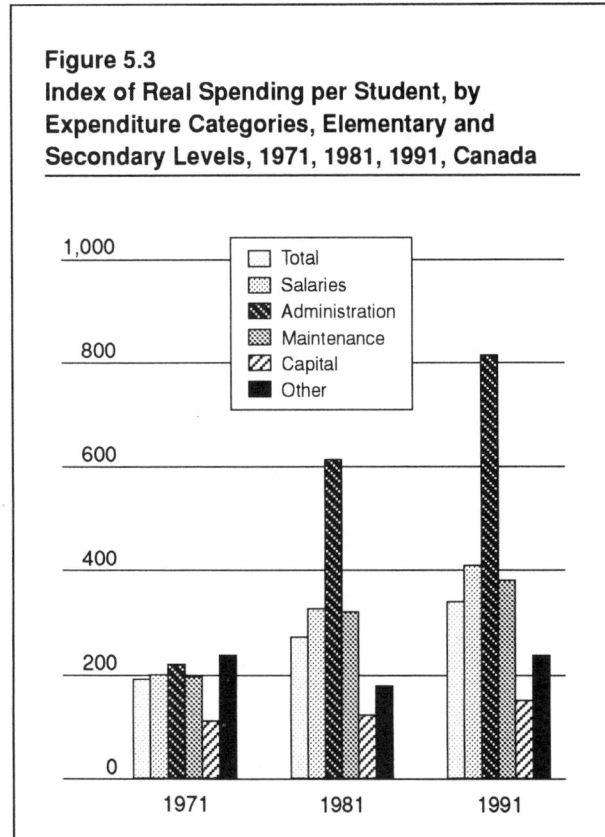

Figure 5.4
Spending per Student, 1989-1990, Elementary and Secondary Levels ($ 000)

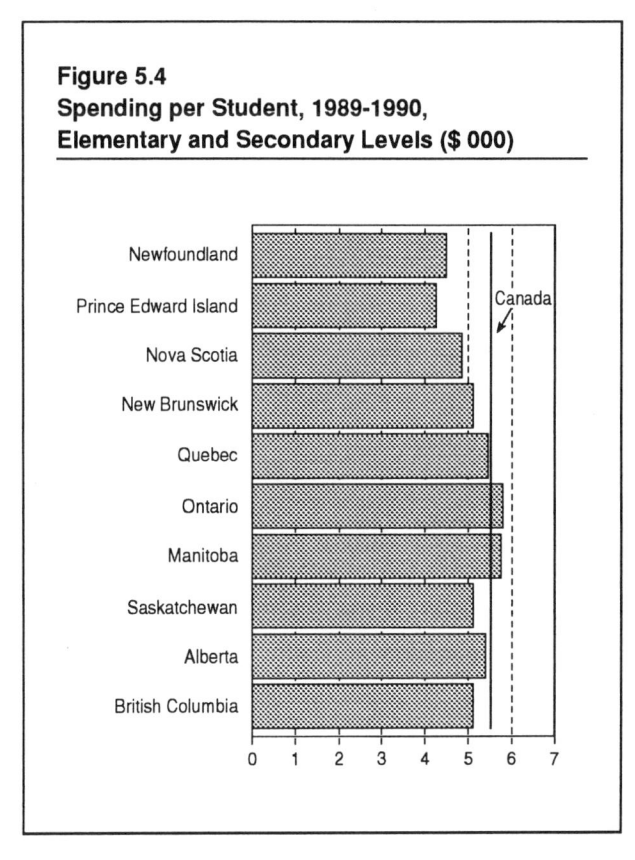

Figure 5.5
Spending per Student, 1983, Elementary and Secondary Levels ($ 000)

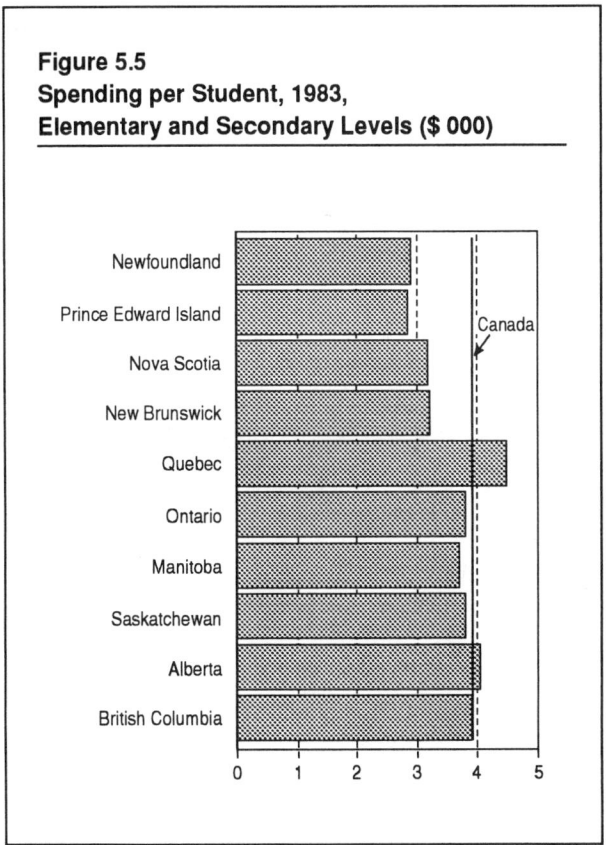

Table 5.4
Average Annual Rate of Increase in Education Spending, 1961-1991 (%)

	1961–1971	1971–1981	1981–1991
Total Nominal Spending	13.7	10.7	8.3
Total Real Spending	10.5	1.6	2.9
Total Real Spending / Student	6.7	3.5	2.3
Real Salary Expenditures / Student	7.2	5.0	2.3
Real Average Salary	5.1	3.1	2.1
Per-capita Annual Income	4.5	3.8	1.9
Pupil Teacher Ratio	2.0	1.8	0.2
Real Administrative Expenditures / Student	8.4	10.6	2.9
Real Capital Expenditures / Student	0.9	1.1	2.2
Other Real Expenditures / Student	9.1	-2.5	2.4

Source: Estimates by the Economic Council of Canada, based on data from Statistics Canada

Table 5.5
Spending per Student and School Enrolment Indicators, 1989-1990

	Spending/ Student	Enrolment Rate[1]	Student/ Teacher Ratio
Canada[2]	5,790	60.2	15.9
Newfoundland	4,440	63.7	15.6
Prince Edward Island	4,270	60.8	17.3
Nova Scotia	5,080	63.7	16.0
Quebec	5,740	44.5	15.7
Ontario	6,170	70.9	15.3
Manitoba	6,050	62.0	14.8
Saskatchewan	5,320	61.9	16.7
Alberta	5,671	56.7	17.2
British Columbia	5,330	57.9	16.7

[1] The enrolment rate at the elementary and secondary level corresponds to the proportion of students out of the total 15 - 19-year-old population. The student/teacher ratio corresponds to the total number of full-time equivalent students divided by the number of full time equivalent teachers.

[2] Includes Yukon and Northwest Territories.

Source: Statistics Canada, Education Statistics, Estimates, Catalogue No. 81-220

Figure 5.6
Ratio of Education Spending to GDP, Elementary and Secondary Levels, 1989-1990

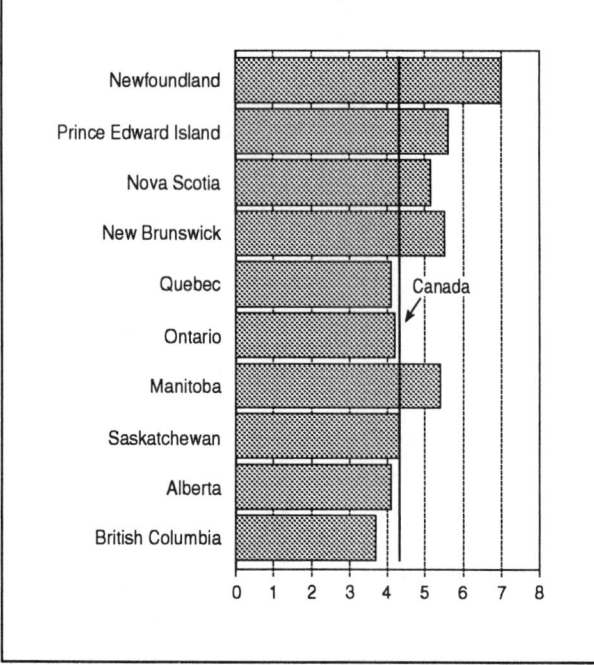

student/teacher ratios, which partly explains their relatively low levels of spending per student.

Ratio of Educational Spending to GDP

The ratio of total spending on education to provincial GDP is one measure of the (financial) importance that a province places on its educational sector. In 1989, more than 4 per cent of Canada's GDP was allocated to primary and secondary education (Table 5.6 and Figure 5.6). The Atlantic provinces spent the highest percentage of their respective GDPs on education. This finding contrasts with that in the previous section, where it was noted that the Atlantic provinces' per student spending at the primary and secondary levels was particularly low. This suggests that, low as it is, per student spending in these provinces, low as it is, represents a major financial commitment relative to provincial GDP.

Of the three provinces with the highest levels of spending per student — Ontario, Manitoba, and Quebec — Ontario and Quebec both fall below the Canadian average when educational spending is measured as a percentage of provincial GDP. Thus, the financial commitment made to education by Ontario and Quebec does not appear to be a great burden — at least in relative terms. Manitoba's ratio of educational spending to GDP, however, is very high.

Finally, the three Western provinces — Alberta, British Columbia, and Saskatchewan — whose levels of spending per student are also below the Canadian average, also have below-average educational expenditure/GDP ratios.

Ratio of Spending per Student to GDP per Capita

Table 5.6 and Figure 5.7 show the ratios of educational spending to provincial GDP, adjusted for the participation rate. According to this indicator, the ranking of the Atlantic provinces relative to the rest of Canada remains unchanged. Since the education participation rates in the Atlantic region are near or above the Canadian average, the adjusted financial commitment of these four provinces remains considerable. Because the rate of participation in education is relatively low in Quebec, per-student spending as a percentage of per capita GNP is higher than in Ontario, where the participation rate is relatively higher.

Table 5.6
Total Education Spending and Enrolment Rates, Elementary and Secondary Levels, 1989

	As % of GDP	Enrolment Rate[1]	Per Student as % of GDP Per Capita
Canada[2]	4.3	18.5	23.3
Newfoundland	7.0	22.7	31.5
Prince Edward Island	5.7	19.1	29.8
Nova Scotia	5.2	18.1	28.8
New Brunswick	5.5	18.8	29.2
Quebec	4.1	16.4	25.0
Ontario	4.2	19.2	21.9
Manitoba	5.5	19.3	28.5
Saskatchewan	5.4	20.2	26.7
Alberta	4.0	19.7	20.3
British Columbia	3.7	17.5	21.7

Note The average for Canada includes, in addition to the ten provinces, the Yukon, the Northwest Territories and overseas territories and undistributed expenditures. That is why the Canadian average seems low compared to the provincial values..

Source: Estimates by the Economic Council of Canada based on data from Statistics Canada

Figure 5.7
Ratio of Spending per Student to GDP per Capita, Elementary and Secondary Levels, 1989-1990

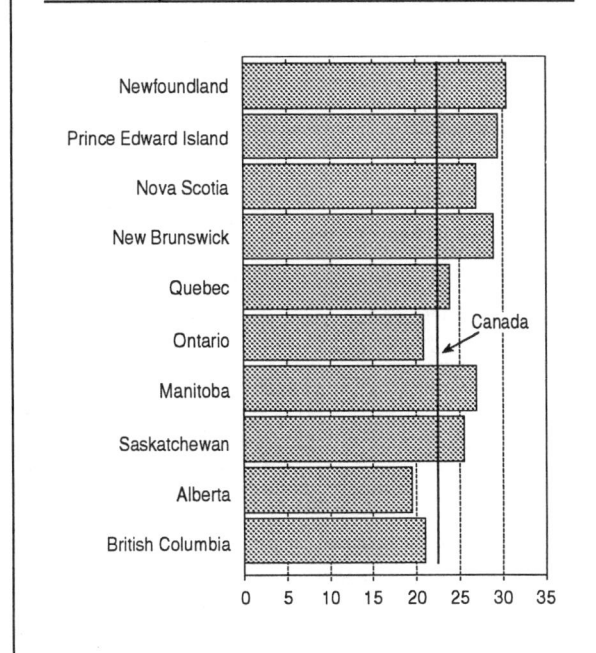

94 Education and Training in Canada

A more detailed analysis of the ratio of spending per student to GDP per capita suggests a fairly strong cyclical component. Indeed, there is a significant positive correlation between provincial unemployment rates and spending levels per student as a percentage of GDP per capita. In all likelihood, the higher a province's unemployment rate, the higher the enrolment of regular and adult students at the secondary level. When this cyclical component is removed from the ratio of per-student spending to GDP per capita, Manitoba and Saskatchewan take first place, replacing the Atlantic provinces. Ontario also moves up by several positions, while Alberta and British Columbia remain at the bottom of the ranking.

Figure 5.8 illustrates the relative ranking of the provinces. For each province the first (top) bar (black) represents the *difference* between the provincial per-student expenditure/per-capita GDP ratio and the average ratio for the 10 provinces. Using this criterion, the Atlantic provinces stand at the top of the ranking, while Alberta and Ontario are at the bottom. The second (middle) bar (striped) represents the residuals of the estimated equation with an unemployment-rate variable. The residuals in this instance are, in a sense, net of the cyclical component. The Atlantic provinces then drop from the top of the ranking. The cyclical component also appears to be an important element in explaining the weakness of the per-student spending/per-capita GDP ratio in Ontario. The financial commitment of this province would be similar to that of the other provinces if its unemployment rate were equal to the Canadian average.

Two other variables were then considered in estimating provincial cost equations: an output variable — the graduation rate — and an input variable — the number of schools per capita. The net effect of these variables is represented by the third (bottom) bar (denser stripe). The introduction of these variables reduced the residuals, especially in the Western provinces and Quebec. In Alberta and British Columbia, the relatively low expenditure levels can be explained by relatively low graduation rates. In Quebec, however, the low level of financial commitment is explained primarily by the relatively low number of schools per capita.

Nearly 75 per cent of the variance in the provincial per-student spending/per-capita GDP ratios can be explained by the variables mentioned above — unemployment rate, graduation rate, and number of schools per capita. Certain variables that were thought *a priori*, to be important proved not to be significant. One of those was the population-density variable, which was used to approximate transportation costs; another was the variable for the number of immigrants as a percentage of the total population. Our research determined that, on average, the presence of a large number of immigrants does not result in significantly higher costs of education at the aggregate provincial level.

In short, the ratio of spending per student to GDP per capita is strongly influenced by a cyclical component. Graduation rates and the number of schools are also important variables in explaining interprovincial differences.

Spending by Category

Specific categories of educational expenditure also affect the expenditure/GDP ratio. In 1986-87, teachers' salaries accounted on average for 60 per cent of total educational spending (Table 5.7). Administration and maintenance together made up just over 18 per cent, while capital outlays accounted for another 8 per cent. All instructional materials — although essential to teaching — accounted for only 2.5 per cent of the total.

Figure 5.8
Residuals of the Estimated Equations of Financial Commitment

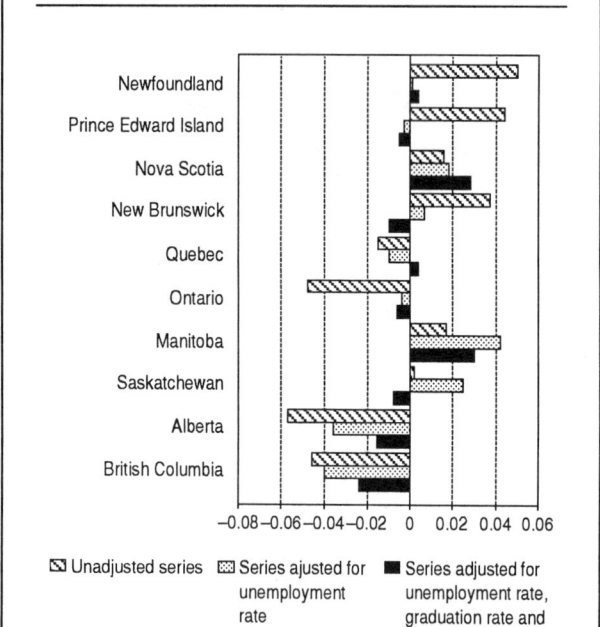

[Bar chart showing residuals by province: Newfoundland, Prince Edward Island, Nova Scotia, New Brunswick, Quebec, Ontario, Manitoba, Saskatchewan, Alberta, British Columbia. X-axis range: -0.08 to 0.06.

Legend:
- Unadjusted series
- Series adjusted for unemployment rate
- Series adjusted for unemployment rate, graduation rate and number of schools]

Table 5.7
School-board Expenditures, by Component and by Province, 1986-1987

	Teachers' Salaries	Instructional Supplies	Administration	Transportation	Fixed Maintenance	Assets	Other
Canada	60.5	2.5	7.0	5.4	11.2	8.1	5.3
Newfoundland	69.1	1.5	6.1	5.2	9.1	8.0	1.0
Prince Edward Island	61.1	0.9	6.3	8.4	10.5	12.3	0.0.
Nova Scotia	68.0	1.3	4.6	4.9	9.9	7.6	3.7
New Brunswick[1]	70.3	1.5	5.5	7.9	13.1	0.7[1]	1.0
Quebec	55.8	2.1	8.1	6.5	9.6	8.3	9.6
Ontario	63.4	2.8	7.5	5.2	11.7	6.2	3.2
Manitoba	56.8	3.3	8.0	4.4	10.9	11.5	5.1
Saskatchewan	56.9	3.8	4.6	7.6	11.4	8.4	7.3
Alberta	59.9	2.6	5.6	5.3	11.7	12.2	2..7
British Columbia	58.5	2.4	5.0	2.5	14.1	10.5	7.0

[1] In New Brunswick, most of these expenditures fall under the responsibility of th Department of Education. An estimate based on data from the department suggest that approximately 10 per cent of total expenditures is devoted to fixed assets.

Source: Statistics Canada, *Financial Statistics on Education, 1986-87*, Catalogue No. 81-208

Interprovincial differences in the share of total spending devoted to teachers' salaries are fairly significant. In 1986-87 the highest shares were found in the Atlantic provinces, with New Brunswick recording the highest share of 70 per cent. Quebec spent the smallest proportion of its funding on teachers: less than 56 per cent. In part, this was a carry-over from the early 1980s when the Quebec government determined to control educational costs. In the Western provinces, the share of teachers' salaries in terms of total educational spending remained relatively low — below the Canadian average.

Student/teacher ratios in primary and secondary public schools during the same period did little to explain the differences in the proportion of total spending devoted to teachers' salaries. The Atlantic provinces, for example, which allot a large share of their total spending to teachers' salaries, had relatively high student/teacher ratios. Conversely, Quebec and Manitoba had fairly low student/teacher ratios and proportions of spending devoted to salaries. Only the three most westerly provinces had low proportions of spending allotted to teachers' salaries and high student/teacher ratios.

Average teachers salaries also vary considerably from province to province. They are generally below the Canadian average in the Atlantic provinces and Quebec. The average salary is higher than the Canadian average in Ontario and about equal to the average in the Western provinces.

On average, capital spending accounts for 8 per cent of total educational spending in Canada and there are indications that this is generally too high in Canada. An econometric analysis of the relationship between some inputs and outputs of primary and secondary education suggest that the capital stock is above its optimum level. In fact, the cost of acquiring an additional unit of capital now appears to be higher than is warranted by the resulting increases in efficiency. This may appear to contravene common sense because more and better facilities and equipment are generally assumed to be a good thing.

It is a fact, nonetheless, that primary and secondary schools appear to be underutilized. School facilities are used constantly for non-educational activities during the evenings and weekends, and often, whether their use involves social activities or municipal recreational programs, these activities are offered at rates considerably below actual cost. In Quebec, for example, the Ministry of Education allows school boards to rent their facilities to municipalities for the symbolic sum of one dollar plus operating costs. Although discussions are under way to consider changing the rules (to reflect the actual costs of using these facilities) the present school system continues to subsidize community activities.

A second indicator of the high level of capital spending in the public sector is that private schools devote a lower proportion of their expenditures to capital purchases. In 1984-85, private schools in Canada spent less than 5 per cent of their budgets on capital outlays compared to approximately 8 per cent in the public sector. Their capital outlays per student are also much lower than those of public schools. In 1986-87, for example, capital spending per student in Canada totalled $340 for public school boards and $220 for private primary and secondary schools. Interprovincial differences in the share of capital outlays are fairly large. The highest proportions are in the Western provinces. Ontario devotes the lowest proportion of its total spending — 6.2 per cent — to capital outlays.

The data for the share(s) of school-board spending on administration as a percentage of the total educational expenditure, show that Quebec's education system is the most expensive to administer, followed closely by those of Ontario and Manitoba; the systems in Saskatchewan, Nova Scotia, and British Columbia operate at the lowest costs. The data produce the same result for administrative spending per student (Table 5.8). The average spending per student for Canada as a whole in 1986-87 was $304; that for Quebec was $398, and for Ontario $336. The Atlantic provinces spent little on administration — $161 in New Brunswick and $166 in Nova Scotia, for example — as did British Columbia, which spent $194.

Administrative costs considered above include only costs incurred by school boards. To these must be added the administrative costs incurred by the various provincial Ministries of Education. The middle column of Table 5.8 shows the combined administrative expenditures per student by school boards and the provincial ministries. The ranking picture does not change substantially, however. Quebec's ranking remains above that of the other provinces, while the Western provinces, particularly British Columbia, are at the bottom of the scale.

Interprovincial differences in administrative spending are partly the result of differences in definitions and partly of differences in structure between the various provincial educational systems. For example, Quebec assumes a larger share of the funding of school boards than does Ontario. In addition, the Quebec Ministry of Education is generally more directly involved in the collective-bargaining process, and its higher administrative costs reflect its performance of these additional tasks.

The column on the far right of Table 5.8 shows the administrative expenditures per student adjusted to

Table 5.8
Spending per Student on Administration, 1986-1987 ($)

	School-board Expenditures	School-board and Education Department Expenditures	School-board and Education Department Expenditures (adjusted)
Canada	304	334	516
NF	191	237	478
PE	212	233	398
NS	166	191	408
NB	161	179	371
QC	398	440	579
ON	336	359	533
MB	355	384	564
SK	184	232	474
AB	257	284	530
BC	194	215	389

Source: Statistics Canada, *Financial Statistics on Education*, 1986-87, Catalogue No. 81-208 and *Education in Canada*, 1987, Catalogue No. 81-229 and author's calculations

include the salaries of school principals and vice-principals among administration costs (rather than with teachers' salaries, the convention followed by Statistics Canada). Since the positions of principal and vice-principal are primarily administrative, we added their salaries to administrative costs, using the number of teachers and school administrators in each province as a proxy. This calculation affects the ranking of the provinces only marginally, however. Quebec remains in first place, followed somewhat more closely by Manitoba and then Ontario. Except for Newfoundland, the Atlantic provinces and British Columbia remain at the bottom of the ranking.

Unquestionably, the provincial structure of school board expenditures can explain certain interprovincial differences in levels of spending. Several provinces in the Atlantic region, for example, devote a significant proportion of their spending to teachers' salaries. Quebec, on the contrary, allocates a fairly small proportion of its total spending to teachers' salaries, and that difference tends to slow the growth of its total educational spending. Ontario, on the other hand, spends very little on capital outlays.

Table 5.9
Spending per Student by Selected School Boards, Selected Canadian Provinces

	Nova Scotia 1989-90 Total	Nova Scotia 1989-90 Excluding Transportation	Quebec 1987-88 Total	Quebec 1987-88 Excluding Transportation	Saskatchewan 1988-89 Total	Saskatchewan 1988-89 Excluding Transportation	British Columbia 1989-90 Total	British Columbia 1989-90 Excluding Transportation
Urban Regions	4,663	4,597	4,629	4,243	3,968	3,897	4,210	4,160
Semi-urban Regions	3,783	3,616	4,845	4,319	4,257	4,014	–	–
Rural Regions	4,180	3,803	5,223	4,697	4,663	4,070	5,242	4,819

Source: Statistics Canada, *Education Statistics, Estimates,* Catalogue No. 81-220 and Catalogue No. 81-208

Intraprovincial Comparison

Even within a single province, there are major differences among school boards with respect to expenditures. Variables such as the size of the school board, its distance from urban centres, or the geographic area it covers can affect total expenditures. To examine the influence of such factors on school board expenditures, we calculated total expenditures per student in each of two urban, semi-rural, and rural school boards for four provinces for which we had data (Table 5.9). We determined that, except for Nova Scotia, the more highly urbanized the area in which the school board operates, the lower the expenditure per student. A number of factors may account for this.

Population density — the main factor that sets rural and urban school boards apart — has a major impact on transportation costs. One would expect per-student spending to be higher in rural areas because of the higher transportation costs per student. To test this hypothesis, we excluded transportation costs from total costs. Table 5.9 shows, however, that spending per student continues to decrease with the degree of urbanization even when transportation costs are excluded. These costs are, in fact, higher in rural areas but not enough to explain the difference in spending between rural and urban school boards.

Other categories of expenditure were also examined in an attempt to explain rural/urban cost differences. Generally, we observed the same pattern for each of these categories when expressed as a proportion of the number of students. On a per-student basis, administrative, operating, and maintenance expenditures, as well as salary expenditures, are all higher in rural school-boards. Rural/urban comparisons of student/teacher ratios explain some of the differences in salary expenditures. Our data suggest that urban school boards are generally able to maintain higher student/teacher ratios than their rural counterparts. This reduces urban school-boards' per-student salary costs.

The general explanation for urban/rural differences in all expenditure categories seems to be that urban school boards serve more students than rural boards, and that schools located in urban areas have more students than those in rural areas. Thus, the lower levels of expenditure per student in urban school boards tend to be the result of economies of scale. The more students a school board or school serves, the more efficient it is, and the lower its costs per student. Our econometric analysis suggests, moreover, that economies of scale also exist at the provincial level and that the greater the number of students in a province the more it can reduce its total spending per student.

The more students there are, the lower the cost of an item per-student, so major, fixed, per-student costs such as those represented by buildings drop as student numbers rise. A larger school handles administration and maintenance expenditures more efficiently because it can spread a relatively fixed service cost over a larger number of students.

Funding Sources for Educational Expenditures

The current debate on education is taking place in a climate of major budgetary restraint. Governments feel compelled to limit their spending in many areas, including education. Since funding methods also affect the ability of provinces to control educational costs, a review of funding methods and sources is relevant.

In Canada, the provinces exercise exclusive jurisdic-

Table 5.10
Sources of Funding for Elementary and Secondary Education, 1988–1989

	Total Spending ($ Millions)	Federal	Provincial	Municipal	Tuition Fees
Newfoundland	532	0	92.6	4.4	0
Prince Edward Island	99	1.8	97.4	4.4	0
Nova Scotia	782	1.9	82.2	13.5	0.8
New Brunswick	668	1.9	97.4	0	0.3
Quebec	6,350	1.4	89.6	3.6	3.0
Ontario	10,650	1.3	49.3	45.7	2.1
Manitoba	1,213	9.8	47.5	36.5	3.1
Saskatchewan	1,033	10.7	48.4	37.1	1.1
Alberta	2,410	4.1	56.0	34.9	1.5
British Columbia	2,536	3.2	78.3	12.4	2.9
Canada[1]	26,475	2.6	66.3	26.6	2.2

[1] Includes the Yukon and Northwest Territories.

Source: Statistics Canada, *Education Statistics Estimates*, Catalogue No. 81-220

tion over elementary and secondary education. Thus, provincial governments are the main source of educational funding, accounting for 66 per cent of total spending on education at the national level (Table 5.10). Municipalities fund just over 25 per cent of total educational expenditures; the rest comes from the federal government (2.6 per cent) and tuition fees (2.2 per cent).

Funds allocated to education vary significantly across provinces. East of Ontario, elementary and secondary education is funded almost entirely by provincial governments at a rate, on average, of more than 90 per cent. Local funding covers only a mere fraction of the total. West of Quebec on the other hand (except in British Columbia) the proportion of educational funding provided by provincial governments is often less than 50 per cent. Local funding is therefore more important in relative terms, reaching a high of 46 per cent in Ontario.

Provincial sources of financing differ widely, but funding arrangements are similar, representing variations on the equalization funding principle. The most common version is that of the *foundation program*, which has three components. The *foundation grant*, the first component, is generally a specific amount per student, based on criteria such as the classification of teachers according to provincial salary scales, distribution of children with learning disabilities, geographic isolation, and the presence of small schools. The second component, *categorical grants*, takes into account the specific needs of school boards with respect to such items as transportation, special programs, and language programs. The third component, *equalization grants*, helps school boards in a province to achieve certain equity objectives; these grants are generally based on the fiscal capacity of school boards as measured by the assessment of the value of their properties.

Although the foundation program approach is the most common funding arrangement, it has two major weaknesses. The first relates to the use of property taxes to generate funding for education. In some provinces, property taxes are a major source of funding, but the capacity of the local tax base to generate funds can vary significantly from one region to another. This is often a source of major redistribution problems. A school board located in an area where housing values are very high, for example, might receive only a small proportion of its funding from the provincial government, while a school board in an area where housing values are very low might receive a large share of funding from the province. Many consider this arrangement to be unfair.

The second major weakness of the foundation program approach results from cost-control problems. The foundation approach entails a major imbalance between the funding source and the source of demand for programs. Because the demand for special programs generally arises locally, provincial authorities, tend to be less sensitive to the importance of the demand and often allocate less money than required to meet it. This response increases pressure on local funding sources, ultimately resulting in a situation where locally funded expenditures rise at a much faster rate than provincially funded ones. This situation, in turn, generally leads to an increase in municipal taxes and, sooner or later, the provincial authorities come under pressure to relieve local homeowners of their onerous tax burden, thereby stimulating renewed demand for programs, which starts the cycle all over again.

There is one exception to the foundation program approach generally used by the provinces. The *resource-cost* model, which corrects some of the problems mentioned above, is based on the conviction that the provincial government should specify and fund program(s) that provide a basic level of education, and that any "extras" should be provided for and covered entirely by the local tax base. This approach requires that the desired service level be defined precisely, and that accurate costing of these levels be developed for each school district. Funding is then provided for that level of service. There is no set foundation level: each district has a unique funding level based on actual local costs of delivering the standard of basic services to the district. The resource-cost model stands in contrast to foundation plans, which frequently contain fiscal ceilings but do not spell out those limits in operational terms.

Local school districts retain significant autonomy in a resource-cost environment. The funds allocated to each school district are determined by establishing the basic standard costs of delivering educational services as mandated by the province. Local trustees and administrators retain the freedom to decide how funds are allocated to specific activities: increasing class sizes, for example, in order to provide funds for a special program. Programs specific to a given district can also be supported through local taxes. Because such special programs are financed in full through the local tax base, school boards are more accountable to local taxpayers. Financing through the local tax base may also mean, however, that poorer regions lack funds to develop special programs.

British Columbia is the only province that has implemented a resource-cost model. This approach, introduced in 1983-84, is still evolving. Strong fiscal controls were also introduced. Local school boards, for example, are not given access to the rich commercial-property tax base; provincially mandated program levels cannot be exceeded without a local referendum; and new services cannot be provided before service levels are established by the province. The first step British Columbia set for itself was to put into place the model's fiscal framework: an elaborate system of costing and accounting. The province has invested heavily in the development of output indicators, and the Ministry of Education hopes that future discussions will be concerned more with defining of appropriate service levels in light of the educational outcomes desired — and less with the accuracy of the costing of specific levels of instruction.

Private School Costs and Funding

The private school system obviously differs somewhat from the public school system: for example, the pressure of competition is much greater in the private system than in the public system. Generally, too, private school students come from higher level socio-economic groups. Some caution must therefore be exercised in comparing private and public school systems. Such comparisons are useful, nevertheless, not in order to set the private school system up as a model, but rather to observe the general direction taken by a more competitive educational system.

Approximately 5 per cent of Canadian elementary and secondary students are enrolled in private schools (Table 5.11), but this population is distributed very unevenly among the provinces. Quebec has the largest proportion of private school students, with 8.7 per cent, followed by British Columbia with 6.9 per cent, while each of the Atlantic provinces has a proportion of 1.1 percent or less.

Private school spending per student at the elementary and secondary levels is approximately $5,350, or approximately $200 *less* than the corresponding figure for public schools, which stands at is about $5,540. This public/private differential has changed somewhat since the early 1980s, but it has always remained in the private system's favour: that system's per-student expenditures have always been lower than the corresponding public sector figures.

At the provincial level, private school expenditures per student are generally lower than those of public

Table 5.11
Proportion of Students Enrolled and Total Spending per Student, Private Schools, Elementary and Secondary Levels, 1989-1990

	Enrolment as % of total student Population	Spending per Student ($)	Spending per Student (public schools)[$]
NF	0.2		
PE	0.3	3,803	4,819
NS	1.1		
NB	0.7		
QC	8.7	5,301	5,521
ON	3.3	6,071	5,801
MB	4.6	4,400	5,847
SK	1.4	6,370	5,074
AB	3.1	6,559	5,417
BC	6.9	4,089	5,179
Canada	4.6	5,350	5,536

Source: Statistics Canada, *Education Statistics, Estimates*, Catalogue No. 81-220 and *Education in Canada*, Catalogue No. No. 81-229

The various levels of government fund 31 per cent of total private school expenditures in Canada; provincial governments contribute most of this share. In Quebec, the provincial government funds nearly half of total private school expenditures, whereas the corresponding contributions are negligible in the Atlantic provinces and Ontario.

Other sources of funding account for approximately 18 per cent of total private school funding. Revenues from the lease and sale of schools and equipment provide most of these funds, but overall, private schools derive barely 3 per cent of their funding from this source.

Table 5.13 shows the distribution of expenditures by category for the private school system. Teachers' salaries account for just over half the total, but this proportion varies significantly from province to province, ranging from an average of nearly 56 per cent in the Atlantic provinces to 34 per cent in Saskatchewan. Spending on general administration accounts, on average, for 10 per cent of total expenditures. This proportion also varies from province to province, ranging from 15 per cent in Saskatchewan to 7 per cent in Quebec.

Parallels might be drawn between Table 5.7 and Table 5.13, which presents similar data for public schools, but the two systems are not really directly comparable because of differences in the definitions of the teaching and administration categories. In the public school system, for example, a "teacher" is defined much more broadly than in the private school system.

schools, except in Alberta, Ontario, and Saskatchewan where private school expenditures per student are highest. Although private schools in Quebec have a large student population, their average per-student expenditure is lower than the Canadian average.

In 1988-89, tuition fees accounted for almost half of private school funding (Table 5.12), compared with a corresponding contribution of virtually nil in public school systems. Tuition fees are proportionately highest in the Atlantic provinces and Ontario, and lowest in Quebec.

Table 5.12
Sources of Funding for Private Elementary and Secondary Schools, 1988-1989 (%)

	Tuition Fees	Public or Separate School Boards	Governments Provincial	Governments Federal	Other
Canada	47.5	3.7	30.4	0.6	17.8
Maritimes	69.8	0	1.0	0.7	28.4
Quebec	37.6	3.4	47.8	0.1	11.1
Ontario	67.9	6.1	0.2	1.0	24.8
Manitoba	44.9	1.4	18.6	1.3	33.8
Saskatchewan	42.8	5.9	17.3	0.5	33.5
Alberta	40.6	4.3	36.8	0.6	17.7
British Columbia	43.0	0	35.0	1.5	20.5
Canada, Public Schools	—	33.9[1]	63.3	2.8	—

[1] In the case of public schools, this column represents funding provided by school property taxes.

Source: Statistics Canada, Catalogue No. 81-002

Table 5.13
Private Elementary and Secondary School Expenditures, by Component and by Province, 1988-1989

	Teachers' Salaries	General Administration	Educational Services	Land and Buildings	Capital Assets and Debt	Other
Canada	51.6	9.9	5.9	11.5	6.6	14.5
Maritimes	55.8	9.2	2.5	16.6	7.6	8.3
Quebec	53.5	6.8	10.2	11.0	3.2	15.3
Ontario	48.9	12.4	2.6	12.9	8.2	14.9
Manitoba	51.1	10.6	3.6	11.3	12.1	11.3
Saskatchewan	33.7	14.7	2.7	12.0	7.6	29.3
Alberta	52.8	13.4	2.8	10.3	7.6	13.0
British Columbia	52.9	11.4	2.3	9.6	12.5	11.2

Source: Statistics Canada, *Financial Statistics, Private Elementary and Secondary Schools*, 1985-86 to 1988-89, Catalogue No. 81-002

Public-school administration costs, adjusted to include the salaries of principals and vice-principals were presented earlier (Table 5.8). The adjusted proportions of teachers' salaries and administration relative to total expenditures can be calculated on the basis of these new figures.

Public school boards spend approximately 56 per cent of their total budgets on teachers' salaries, compared with 52 per cent for private schools (Table 5.13). These figures apply to every province except Quebec, where the proportions are roughly equal. Table 5.14 shows that this difference cannot be explained by differences in student/teacher ratios. In fact, for Canada and for every province except Quebec, public school student/teacher ratios are always higher than the corresponding figures for private schools.

The adjusted figures also change the proportion of total public school spending allocated to administration. Public school administration expenditures now make up 11.2 per cent of the total. In all provinces except Ontario, Saskatchewan and Alberta, adjusted administration costs in the public school system are higher than corresponding costs in the private school system.

Table 5.14
Student/Teacher Ratio, Elementary and Secondary Levels, Public and Private Schools, 1989–1990

	Public Schools	Private Schools
Canada	17.7	16.4
Newfoundland	16.4	9.7
Prince Edward Island	17.9	12.7
Nova Scotia	16.6	8.3
New Brunswick	17.5	9.7
Quebec	17.9	18.1
Ontario	17.1	14.9
Manitoba	16.6	16.3
Saskatchewan	18.7	15.5
Alberta	19.0	17.3
British Columbia	19.1	15.9

Source: Statistics Canada, Education Statistics, Estimates, 1991-92, Catalogue No. 81-220.

Endnotes

1 This measurement therefore excludes private sector spending on education. In recent years, the OECD has added such spending to the public spending figures and concluded that the addition modifies the ranking of countries only slightly. Japan moves up in the ranking because it has a relatively large private education sector.

2 See Appendix for definitions of the levels of education.

Appendix

Definitions of Educational Levels[1]

- Elementary/secondary education: the elementary/secondary level of education as defined by each province.

- Post-secondary non-university education is equivalent to "the college sector"; this sector includes community colleges, regional colleges, and colleges of applied arts and technology (CAATs) in Ontario; institutes of technology, agricultural colleges, and similar institutions in Quebec; and similar institutions in other provinces.

- University education includes all public or private degree-granting institutions and their affiliates.

- Vocational training includes all vocational training programs offered by public and private trade or vocational schools, community colleges, institutes of technology, and similar institutions. The programs offered involve spending on human-resource training such means as apprenticeship and industrial training programs as well as allowances paid to trainees. Included in this category are the costs of training nursing assistants and aides in hospitals, providing government language courses, vocational training in provincial reform schools and federal penitentiaries, and other training expenditures by provincial and federal departments, private business colleges and trade schools, and other private schools.

---

[1] Based on Statistics Canada, *Financial Statistics on Education*, 1986-87, Catalogue No. 81-208.

6
Education and Training
An International Perspective

Most people believe that education, the labour market and the economy are closely linked, and that national wealth and economic development influence the resources that governments, businesses and individuals devote to education and training. Yet the reverse is also true: the extent and content of school curricula, post-secondary education, and vocational training affect economic performance. The skill level of the work force, therefore, is the intersection where education, the labour market, and the economy all meet.

Traditionally, the education system has been responsible for turning out young people with high levels of diversified skills that the nation then uses for the benefit of all. In the current climate of globalization, with its heightened competition and more permeable national borders, the ability of a country to compete successfully depends heavily on its having a highly skilled work force. It is becoming increasingly clear, for instance, that high levels of labour skills are a critical factor in the acquisition of new technologies — technologies that are necessary to secure productivity growth and improvements in living standards.

This chapter considers how Canada is faring with respect to educating and training its work force compared to other industrialized nations. On the basis of the relative rankings of all the countries, our conclusion is that *coherence* in national socio-economic systems is a keystone of economic success and higher living standards. Part of our effort here, therefore, is to identify the factors that favour such coherence in two of Canada's economic partners — partners who are often singled out as examples of economic success. Finally, we draw some lessons from our analysis for Canada.

Education, the Labour Market and the Economy: How does Canada Rate?

Analytical Method

For this section, we adopted a quantitative approach to assess the relative positions of various OECD countries — Canada's main competitors — with respect to three "systems": education, the labour market, and the economy.

In order to analyze the relationships between education, the labour market and economic performance, a statistical data base was developed around three groups of indicators — 16 for education, 16 related to the labour-market and 15 economic.

Primary sources for data included *Education in the OECD Countries, 1987-1988*, published by the OECD, UNESCO publications and *The World Competitiveness Report* published jointly by IMD International and the World Economic Forum. This latter publication provided two types of data: statistical data and data based on the *Business Confidence Survey* — a survey in which business leaders from around the world were asked to rate the performance of their country of residence in terms of a large number of factors. Such views are important because in the three systems — education, labour-market and economy — performance assessment by essential economic actors plays an important role alongside the more "objective" statistical elements, in determining behaviour. Some of the results of this survey have been incorporated into our analysis; in the text they are clearly identified as business leaders' opinions.[1] (In the detailed list of indicators shown on the following two pages, they are clearly identified by "(Survey)", and in Tables 6.3, 6.4 and 6.5, by an "(S)" following the relevant indicator.)

Within each group of indicators, variables were also selected that would strike a balance among three basic aspects of each system — resources, processing and output. The indicators selected for statistical analysis are listed on the following two pages.

Each country was ranked separately on the basis of each of the three groups of indicators as well as on the basis of its aggregate score. The following assumptions underlie the rankings:

- Each ranking depends heavily on the choice of indicator(s). Great care was taken to select indicators from all those available that best identified typical

Education Indicators

Accessibility to
Education
- Enrolment rate at age 17 [OECD, ED][2]
- Proportion of secondary students in technical/vocational programs [OECD, ED]
- Total number of students in higher education relative to the population of youth aged 20 to 24 [WCR91]
- Proportion of women among students in higher education [OECD, ED]

Academic Achievement
- Average years of schooling of total population aged 25 and older [HDR]
- Graduates of higher education [HDR]
- Proportion of women among graduates of long-term higher education [OECD, ED]
- Male graduates of higher education science programs [HDR]
- Female graduates of higher education science programs [HDR]

Financial Resources
- Public expenditures on education per capita [WCR91]

Performance of the
Education System
from the Labour Market
Standpoint
- Assessment of the availability of qualified workers (Survey) [WCR91]
- Assessment of whether compulsory education meets the needs of a competitive economy (Survey) [WCR91]
- Assessment of whether in-company training meets the needs of a competitive economy (Survey) [WCR91]
- Assessment of availability of competent managers (Survey) [WCR91]
- Ratio of employees in research and development to total employment [WCR91]
- Assessment of people's general economic knowledge (Survey) [WCR91]

Labour-Market Indicators

Labour Force
- Growth rate of the labour force [OECD, LF]

Employment
- Employment/population ratio [OECD, LF]
- Share of employment in industrial sector [WCR91]
- Share of employment in public administration [WCR91]
- Assessment of equal opportunity of employment, irrespective of race, sex or marital status (Survey) [WCR91]
- Assessment of how well women are integrated into the labour market (Survey) [WCR91]

Unemployment
- Rate of unemployment [OECD, LF]
- Youth unemployment (1980-88 average) [OECD, ECO]

Labour Cost
- Hourly wage paid to workers [WCR91]

Working Conditions
and Labour Relations
- Effective work week in manufacturing sector [WCR91]
- Assessment of effect of absenteeism on businesses (Survey) [WCR91]
- Assessment of contribution of labour relations to social harmony (Survey) [WCR91]
- Working days lost to labour strife [WCR91]

Personnel Management Practices of Firms	• Assessment of firms' freedom to adjust staff and wages to economic conditions (Survey) [WCR90] • Assessment of how strongly employees identify with company objectives (Survey) [WCR91]
Government Policy	• Assessment of whether personal income tax functions as a disincentive to work (Survey [WCR91]

Economic Indicators:

Growth Factors	• Growth rate of gross domestic product (GDP) [OECD, EMO] • Labour productivity in manufacturing [WCR91] • Share of gross fixed-capital formation in GDP [WCR91] • Share of gross domestic savings in GDP [WCR91]
Cost of Living	• Rate of inflation [WCR91]
Technology	• Firms' expenditures on research and development as a proportion of GDP [WCR91]
International Trade	• Openness to international trade in goods and services [OECD, NA] • Elasticity of imports relative to GDP [OECD, NA] • Exports of engineering products as a proportion of GDP [WCR91] International
Trade	
Quality	• Assessment of quality of domestically produced products (Survey) [WCR91]
Role of Government	• Assessment of capacity of banking and financial services to compete on deregulated world markets (Survey) [WCR91] • Assessment of government's flexibility in adapting its policies to new economic realities (Survey) [WCR91] • Direct taxes and social security premiums as a proportion of GDP [OECD, NA] • Growth rate of tax revenues [WCR91] • Assessment of government's ability to promote competitiveness (Survey) [WCR91]

patterns of behaviour in the countries selected.

- Ranking countries according to a particular indicator implies that the values for that indicator can be ordered in some way — which raises the question, "Given the objectives of the study, what are the implications of the relative values of the indicator(s) for competitiveness?"

- In order to compare countries' performances according to the various indicators and to ensure that the data are expressed in identical units of measurement, each indicator was subjected to a standardization procedure (ratio of deviation to mean standard deviation).

- All indicators within each group were given the same unit weight and standardized values were summed for each country. Countries were then ranked according to their total scores. The statistical analysis presented here is based on those standardized indicators.

The question of the indicators' relative values warrants further comment. Since our objective was to assess the contribution each indicator makes to economic competitiveness, most of the indicators posed no problem, (i.e., a high positive value denoted a positive effect on competitiveness and *vice versa*). Some indicators were not quite so clear cut, however, and required an assumption. Specifically:

- Proponents of opposing educational ideologies have long debated the value of introducing technical/vocational training at the secondary school level and the degree of emphasis that should be given to this type of training. We assume that providing such training at the secondary and post-secondary levels increases economic competitiveness. In particular, it broadens the base of students' options in school and provides them with an opportunity to choose the career path best suited to their aspirations and talents, and the diverse demands of the labour market.

- A high ratio (say, above 50 per cent) of women to men registered in (and graduates of) higher-education and long-term programs suggests that males are under-represented; a low ratio suggests that women do not enjoy the same opportunities as men. Both these situations, in our view, work against the objective of economic competitiveness. Accordingly, we compared the values of these indicators for each country with the overall proportion of women in the labour force and then standardized these values according to the absolute difference between the proportion of women in higher education programs (or among graduates of such long-term programs) and the proportion of women in the labour force. The resulting indicators reflect a more neutral judgement.

- The economic effect of having a large share of employment in the industrial sector was judged to be positive, given that competitiveness depends increasingly on the availability of larger numbers of workers for this sector. On the other hand, having a large share of employment in public administration was judged to have a negative impact, since this situation drains resources from the competitive areas of the economy.

- High ratings by business leaders (as drawn from the World Economic Forum survey) for equal employment opportunity and the integration of women into the labour force at the professional level were judged to be positive economic factors since they extend the potential number and improve the quality of available workers.

- A high degree of openness to international trade in goods and services was judged to be positive since international markets serve as a testing ground for a country's ability to compete. Conversely, wide fluctuation of imports related to fluctuations in GDP was considered to have a negative effect on competitiveness — all other factors being equal — since such a situation generally reduces the leeway to adjust national economic policies.

Separate assessments were made for each indicator independently of the other indicators (i.e., each assessment represents an independent judgement and was not dependent on any other indicator). Occasionally, however, a factor which, *in theory*, should have one result has virtually the opposite effect – especially when viewed in a particular national context. Such a factor is usually a by-product of the forces operating within a country which influence competitive. For example, Germany has very high wage costs which, *a priori* should work *against* competitiveness. This "weakness", however, is, if not a positive factor, at least a natural consequence of that country's emphasis on having a work force with certified skills and a capacity to "produce value-added". It is this value-added component that makes higher wages possible without reducing competitiveness.

How Does Canada Rank?

Table 6.1 recapitulates the ranking of the 18 countries selected according to their aggregated standardized scores as well as for their individual scores for each indicator.

Overall, Canada sits squarely in the middle, with a performance very close to average; its standardized score is just slightly above zero. Among the G-7 countries alone, Canada again places in the middle, behind Japan, Germany,[3] and the United States, but ahead of the United Kingdom, France, and Italy. In our group of 18 countries, Canada shares its mid-point ranking with Denmark, Sweden, Norway and the Netherlands, whose overall scores are virtually identical. Finland fares just slightly better. Japan, Germany and Switzerland lead the ranking with overall performances well above the average. The United States stands in fifth place, just ahead of Canada. The countries of southern Europe — Spain, Italy, France, and Belgium — and the other Commonwealth countries — the United Kingdom, Australia, and New Zealand — together make up the bottom half of the ranks, with overall performances ranging from slightly to considerably below average. It is tempting to see culturally-based patterns in these results.

The rankings on each of the three indicator groups for the 18 countries selected are shown in Table 6.1. Canada fares about the same in each of three indicator categories, achieving a standardized score very close to the 18-country average in each group. The three rankings are very close to one another; the correlation co-efficients between the standardized scores are all

Table 6.1
Ranking of 18 Countries, Overall and by Indicator Group

Overall Standardized Score Ranking	Score	Country	Education Score	Ranking	Labour Market Score	Ranking	Economy Score	Ranking
1	0.85	Japan	0.42	4	0.83	1	1.30	1
2	0.50	Germany	0.62	1	0.25	5	0.64	2
3	0.50	Switzerland	0.27	7	0.76	2	0.48	3
4	0.26	Austria	0.27	6	0.32	4	0.20	4
5	0.25	United States	0.21	8	0.49	3	0.06	7
6	0.23	Finland	0.61	2	-0.04	10	0.11	6
7	0.04	Denmark	0.31	5	0.12	7	-0.30	14
8	0.03	Sweden	0.60	3	-0.16	12	-0.36	15
9	**0.03**	**Canada**	**0.07**	**11**	**0.01**	**8**	**0.00**	**10**
10	0.02	Norway	0.12	9	-0.06	11	0.01	9
11	0.02	The Netherlands	0.06	12	-0.18	13	0.18	5
12	-0.12	United Kingdom	-0.48	15	0.15	6	-0.01	11
13	-0.14	Belgium	0.11	10	-0.59	17	0.06	8
14	-0.23	Australia	-0.30	14	-0.29	14	-0.10	12
15	-0.26	France	-0.24	13	-0.32	15	-0.22	13
16	-0.39	New Zealand	-0.54	16	-0.02	9	-0.63	16
17	-0.65	Italy	-0.78	17	-0.48	16	-0.69	17
18	-0.95	Spain	-1.33	18	-0.80	18	-0.73	18

positive and statistically significant (Table 6.2). It can be inferred that there are indeed strong links between the performances of the education system, the labour market, and the economy. Three of the six countries (Japan, Germany and Austria) are consistently in the upper third of the rankings – overall as well as individual. Canada and Norway fall within the middle group of rankings in each category, while France, Italy, and Spain consistently appear in the bottom third. This relative consistency of ranking (which is important because it supports the notion of the "coherence" of the systems being considered) does not appear to apply to only four countries — Denmark, Sweden, the Netherlands and the United Kingdom; these countries change their relative positions quite noticeably.

We shall now examine more closely the characteristics of each system as shown by our selected indicators.

Tables 6.3, 6.4, and 6.5 show how each country fares relative to the average situation of the 18 countries selected. The signs used in Tables 6.3 - 6.5 are to be interpreted as follows:

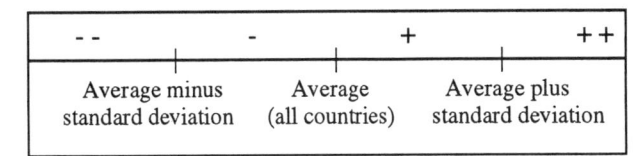

- -	-	+	+ +
Average minus standard deviation	Average (all countries)	Average plus standard deviation	

A double plus sign (+ +) or a double minus sign (- -) denotes that the indicator for that country is particularly high or particularly low respectively, relative to the average for all 18 countries.

EDUCATION

Applying the criteria for the education indicator, Germany, Finland and Sweden lead with practically identical scores. Although Japan still leads overall, it ranks fourth when evaluated against the education criteria and leads a group of countries with performances very similar to its own: Denmark, Austria, and the United States. Canada, in eleventh place, belongs to

Table 6.2
Correlation between Standardized Scores by Indicator Group

	Education	Labour Market	Economy
Education	1.0		
Labour Market	0.5907 (0.0098)	1.0	
Economy	0.6508 (0.0034)	0.7392 (0.0005)	1.0

Note: The degree of confidence is indicated in parentheses.

Table 6.3
Countries Ranked by Education Indicators

Ranking	Country	Enrolment at Age 17	Average Years of Schooling	Students in Secondary Technical/Vocational Programs	Enrolment Rate in Higher Education at Age 20 - 24	Women in Higher Education	Graduates of Higher Education	Graduates of Higher Education Science Programs - Men	Graduates of Higher Education Science Programs - Women	Women among Grads. of Long-term Higher Education	Public Expenditure on Education Per Capita	Response of Compulsory Education System to Needs of a Competitive Economy (S)	Response of In-company Training Programs to Needs of a Competitive Economy (S)	General Economic Knowledge (S)	Availability of Competent Managers (S)	Availability of Qualified Workers (S)	Research & Development Personnel
1	Germany	+	-	++	-	++	-	-	+	+	-	++	+	+	++	++	++
2	Finland	++	+	+	+	+	+	++	++	+	+	+	+	+	·	+	+
3	Sweden	+	+	+	-	+	+	++	++	+	++	·	+	+	·	+	++
4	Japan	+	+	·	-	+	+	-	·	·	++	++	++	++	+	+	++
5	Denmark	+	+	+	-	+	-	-	+	+	++	+	·	+	+	++	·
6	Austria	+	+	+	-	+	·	-	-	+	+	+	+	++	+	++	·
7	Switzerland	+	-	·	-	+	·	+	-	-	+	++	+	++	+	+	+
8	United States	-	++	·	++	·	++	-	-	·	+	·	·	+	+	+	·
9	Norway	·	+	+	+	+	++	+	+	+	++	+	+	+	+	+	+
10	Belgium	++	-	+	-	·	++	+	-	·	+	·	·	·	+	+	·
11	Canada	+	++	·	++	·	++	-	-	++	++	+	+	+	+	+	+
12	The Netherlands	+	-	+	·	+	+	+	+	+	-	+	·	+	+	+	+
13	France	+	+	+	+	·	+	+	+	·	·	+	·	+	+	·	+
14	Australia	-	++	·	·	+	+	+	++	+	-	·	·	·	+	·	-
15	United Kingdom	-	·	·	+	+	·	+	-	-	-	·	·	+	-	·	+
16	New Zealand	-	·	·	+	+	-	+	++	-	-	·	·	-	·	·	-
17	Italy	-	-	+	-	-	-	+	-	+	-	·	·	·	·	·	·
18	Spain	-	-	+	-	-	-	-	-	-	-	·	·	·	·	·	·

the next group, which also includes Norway, Belgium and the Netherlands. This accounts for the 12 countries with education systems that perform better than average. France is among the lower ranks, followed by the three other Commonwealth countries in sequence: the United Kingdom, Australia and New Zealand. Italy and Spain trail the field.

Each country has its own areas of relative strength and weakness. Presumably, the countries with high aggregate scores and high individual rankings have more strong points than countries with lower ratings. Our attention is therefore focussed on the strengths and weaknesses of the countries at the top of the lists, which by implication have found "winning combinations" that may offer lessons for Canada.

Germany's position confirms the high rating ascribed to its education system by that country's business leaders. As employers, they judge the school system by its "products". Their view is hardly surprising, given the extent of their direct involvement in the educational process through the "dual" system of vocational training. Their interest (and influence) is particularly reflected by the high proportion of students enrolled in secondary technical/vocational programs — 79.7 per cent of all students in upper secondary school.

The other side of this emphasis on technical/vocational training is evidenced by the relatively small proportion of young people (aged 20 to 24) who opt for higher education. However, those who do go on to university and other institutions of higher learning nearly always graduate from their chosen course of studies. Nonetheless, apprenticeship and adult vocational training programs remain the most common options, particularly for men, for obtaining qualification in scientific fields. This explains the relatively low proportion of higher-education graduates in scientific disciplines in Germany. Moreover, this arrangement is largely responsible for Germany *not* being among the countries with the highest public expenditures on education, since a substantial portion of early technical/vocational training is financed by private firms as part of industry's direct involvement in the dual system. The inherent logic of the system is apparent.

As in Germany, the Japanese educational system was given high marks by its own business leaders. This opinion appears to be widely shared outside Japan.

Again, private enterprise is very actively involved in training, although the mechanisms are quite different from Germany's. Nonetheless, the indicators for accessibility and academic achievement suggest that by North American and European standards certain aspects of Japan's education system leave something to be desired. For example, women are very poorly represented in long-term (over two years) higher-education programs and those women who do opt for post-secondary studies are unlikely to choose a science program. Yet, when all students in higher education are considered, women are well represented overall since large numbers are enrolled in short programs. Indeed, women account for more than 90 per cent of all students in the *tandai* or pre-university colleges, although they comprise only 25 per cent of enrolment at universities. While these patterns undoubtedly reflect the influence of history and tradition, economic constraints such as demographic changes and severe labour shortages may well effect changes in these patterns. Increasingly, businesses is finding it unwise to ignore the potential contributions of women.

Finland and Sweden separate Japan and Germany in our ranking. The two Scandinavian countries present almost perfect pictures in terms of our indicators, posting above-average performances under more indicators than all the other countries ranked. Their education systems would thus appear to be in tune with the requirements of a competitive economy.

Strengths and Weaknesses of Canada's Educational System

While we allow that our performance assessments of educational systems is based largely on a limited set of synthetic indicators, Canada's middle ranking nonetheless reflects a decidedly mixed performance. On the one hand, Canada can boast a high degree of accessibility to and sizeable public expenditures on education; on the other hand, it posts mediocre results according to the education indicators designed to measure the performance of the educational system from the labour-market standpoint.

Canada's education system shares some structural similarities with that of the United States, although its overall performance is poorer. The two countries register the highest average number of years of schooling although this figure should be adjusted to reflect their shorter academic year(s) compared, for example, with Japan and Germany. In addition, Canada and the United States have the highest rates of enrolment in and graduation from higher-education programs. Women enter universities in very large numbers and in a proportion higher than their representation in the labour force. For

110   Education and Training in Canada

**Figure 6.1
Educational Attainment**

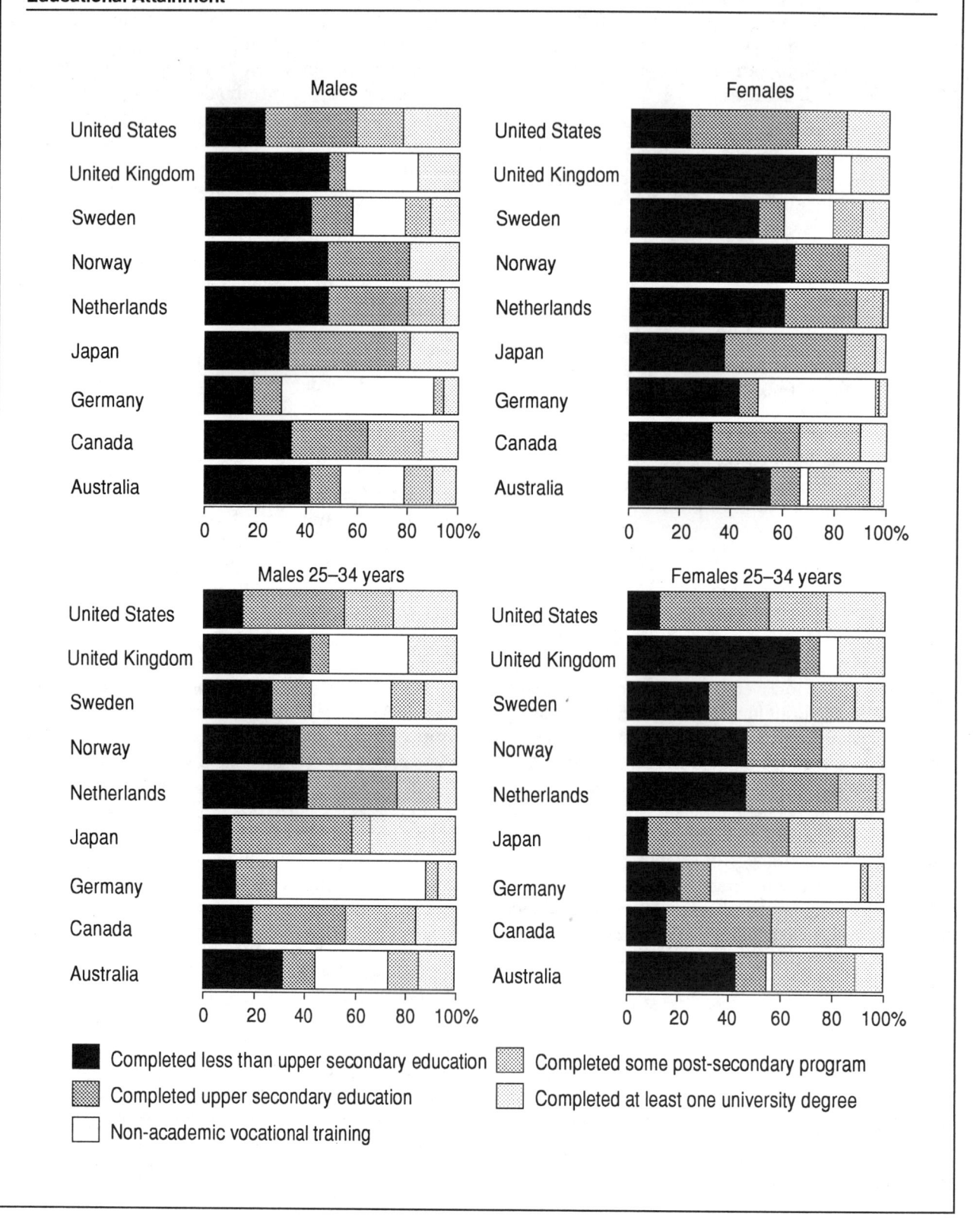

- Completed less than upper secondary education
- Completed upper secondary education
- Non-academic vocational training
- Completed some post-secondary program
- Completed at least one university degree

Canada as a whole, however, enrolment in science-oriented higher-education programs falls significantly short of the international average, for both men and women. So, while the educational *system* appears to be functioning relatively well, it is not producing either the numbers or the quality of output (i.e., the of graduates) that Canada needs – i.e., neither compulsory education nor life-long learning programs are responding adequately to the needs of a competitive economy. While this observation reflects opinions expressed largely by Canadian business leaders, their view is widely shared by Canadian educators and others.

To complement the foregoing, Figure 6.1 points up another pertinent comparison: the level of educational attainment of the population as a whole relative to the level of attainment of young people leaving the education system. The data indicate that:

- Canada and the United States are the only countries to show no significant difference by sex in educational attainment, both for the population as a whole and for young people.

- In all countries, the level of educational attainment of youth is higher than that of the population as a whole. Although Canada rates relatively well on this basis, it is nonetheless noteworthy that *between 15 and 20 per cent of Canadians aged 25 to 34 do not complete senior high school.*

- While Canadian students are more likely to go on to post-secondary studies than young people in most other countries, the proportion of Canadian students who actually graduate is relatively low.

- As with the United States, Japan, the Netherlands, and Norway, Canada lacks non-academic vocational programs that are integrated into the educational system as an optional study path. Germany is the outstanding example of a country where strong emphasis is placed on this type of training. In Canada, by contrast, a significant proportion of those who enrol in post-secondary courses previously attended a community college, where much of the instruction is more vocationally-oriented. Nonetheless, much of that training is still more academic than practical.

LABOUR MARKET

An analysis of the labour-market indicators also gives Canada mixed reviews (Table 6.4). Canada places eighth with a standardized score that is virtually the same as the 18-country average. Japan and Switzerland take top honours, followed by the United States (which rates considerably better here than Canada), Austria, Germany, and the United Kingdom. Canada shares the middle ground with the four Scandinavian countries and New Zealand.

Japan's first-place finish is attributable to a particularly strong showing with respect to: a public sector of limited size, a low (overall) unemployment rate, a low share of youth unemployment, a long work week, virtually no absenteeism, and harmonious labour relations that are undoubtedly linked to the strong identification of workers with the objectives and priorities of their firms. On the negative side, women do not fare well in the Japanese labour market, despite the 1986 *Equal Opportunity Act*.

The United States ranks third, thanks to the relatively strong growth of its labour force, the greater freedom that business leaders enjoy to adjust employment levels and wages, and a personal tax system that does not create disincentives to work. On the other hand, five indicators post below-average scores: employment in the industrial sector, the share of youth unemployment, the hourly wage cost, labour relations, and the identification of workers with their firms.

Germany drops from the first ranks, primarily because of the very weak growth of its labour force and its high labour costs. As noted earlier, this latter factor appears to have fewer negative consequences for Germany than for any other country. Because its firms try to maximize their productivity by using the best possible production technologies and optimal organization structures, they rely on highly qualified labour. Consequently, they can — and must — pay higher wages.

Strengths and Weaknesses of the Canadian Labour Market

Canada can boast some areas of excellence in its labour resources, notably strong labour-force growth and the recognition of women's right to equal opportunity and equal labour-market access. To a slightly lesser extent than in the United States, Canada's national business leaders enjoy some flexibility to adjust staff and wages. Flexibility, however, must be considered as a relative term because the seven countries judged to enjoy this advantage exhibit highly disparate patterns of institutional behaviour and organization.

Two distinct types of business adjustment are notable, each with quite different consequences for the firms themselves, the workers, and the economy. First,

112 Education and Training in Canada

Table 6.4
Countries Ranked by Labour-Market Indicators

Ranking	Country	Rate of Labour-Force Growth	Employment/Population Ratio	Share of Employment in Industrial Sector	Share of Employment in Public Administration	Equal Opportunity (S)	Integration of Professional Women (S)	Rate of Unemployment	Share of Youth Unemployment	Hourly Wage Paid to Workers	Effective Work Week in Manufacturing	Impact of Absenteeism (S)	Contribution of Labour Relations to Social Harmony (S)	Working Days Lost to Labour Strife	Firms' Freedom to Adjust Staff and Wages to Economic Conditions	Identification of Workers with Company Objectives and Priorities (S)	Impact of Personal Tax Burden on Disincentive to Work (S)
1	Japan	+	+	+	++	:	:	++	++	+	++	++	++	+	+	++	++
2	Switzerland	+	++	++	++	:	:	++	+	·	++	++	++	+	++	++	++
3	United States	++	+	·	+	+	+	+	+	·	+	+	·	+	++	·	++
4	Austria	·	·	++	·	+	+	+	++	+	:	+	+	+	·	+	+
5	Germany	·	+	++	:	+	·	+	++	++	++	+	+	+	·	+	+
6	United Kingdom	·	·	:	:	+	:	+	++	·	·	+	·	+	·	:	:
7	Denmark	:	++	:	:	+	++	+	+	++	++	+	+	·	++	+	++
8	Canada	++	+	:	·	+	+	·	+	·	+	·	·	·	+	·	·
9	New Zealand	·	·	:	:	+	+	·	+	·	+	+	·	·	+	·	+
10	Finland	·	+	·	:	++	++	+	·	+	·	+	+	·	+	+	++
11	Norway	+	+	·	+	++	++	++	·	+	·	·	+	+	·	+	·
12	Sweden	·	++	·	·	+	++	+	·	·	·	·	+	+	·	+	·
13	The Netherlands	+	+	·	+	+	+	+	·	·	+	·	+	+	+	+	·
14	Australia	++	+	·	+	·	·	+	·	+	+	·	+	+	·	+	·
15	France	:	:	+	+	·	·	+	·	+	+	·	·	+	·	·	+
16	Italy	:	:	·	·	:	:	:	·	+	+	·	+	+	·	+	:
17	Belgium	:	:	·	+	:	:	+	·	·	·	·	+	·	·	:	:
18	Spain	+	:	+	+	:	:	·	·	++	·	·	·	+	·	:	:

there is external flexibility, which allows employers to make short-term adjustments to staff levels in response to cyclical fluctuations in product/service demand. Second, there is internal flexibility, which enables a firm to retain its human capital by reshuffling its staff in response to economic shocks.

Since the current national and international economic climate tends to favour the production of high value-added goods and consequently the employment of highly qualified personnel, these two types of adjustment practices clearly differ in their effects on business competitiveness and general economic competitiveness. For example, even though Canadian, U.S., and Japanese business leaders give similar ratings to their (country's) capacities to adjust, evidence suggests that they are referring to different realities: primarily external flexibility in North American firms, and internal flexibility in Japanese firms.

Canada also shows some other points of weakness: its share of industrial employment is the lowest of all the countries surveyed; its labour relations are not at all conducive to social harmony; and, Canadian businesses lose a relatively high number of work days to labour strife. Predictably, when compared with employees in other countries, Canadian workers show little identification with the objectives and priorities of their firms, and absenteeism runs higher than average.

ECONOMY

The economic indicators identified in Table 6.5 show that Canada fares neither better nor worse in this category than in the other two — placing tenth with a standardized score of about average. Japan, Germany, Switzerland, and Austria hold the first four positions, and the United States comes eighth. Again, Japan's performance is far better than average in ten of the 15 indicators. Its only negative factors are its limited openness to foreign trade – it has the lowest rating the 18 countries – and its high growth of tax revenues; only Spain is higher (a high rating in this instance has a negative impact).

Although Germany does not rate as highly under the economic indicators today as it did before unification, it can still boast several strong points: very low inflation, a strong R&D effort, a high level of engineering exports, and high-quality domestic products. In addition, like Japan, Germany received very high marks from its business leaders for its government's efforts to direct public resources towards the promotion of industrial competitiveness. Both countries rate far ahead of all the others on this point.

Strengths and Weaknesses of the Canadian Economy

Although Canada's performance never moves far above or below the average with respect to any indicator, it achieves somewhat better ratings on the following bases: a moderate level of direct taxes and social-security premiums, a rate of economic growth that falls in the second rank of the G-7 countries, and banking and financial services that are judged competitive.

In contrast, negative ratings foreshadow some difficulties ahead: business leaders report that the government shows little flexibility in adapting legislation to economic realities; the commitment of the private sector to R&D is weak, and that weakness is not offset by above-average efforts on the part of the public sector to promote this important activity; and industrial productivity shows only weak signs of growth.

Competitiveness and the Coherence of Socio-economic Systems

> *The task for any government is to understand the underlying principles of national advantage and transfer them into policy initiatives that reflect the nation's particular circumstances.* (Michael Porter, *The Competitive Advantage of Nations*, p. 623.)

The foregoing analysis demonstrates that there is a close relationship between a country's educational system, its labour market, and its economic performance. Consequently, the situation of each country reflects the interrelation of its particular characteristics and the coherence of its socio-economic system. Clearly, every county has some sort of coherence. However, given that a major goal of every developed country is a sustainable pace of economic growth — resulting in an equitable distribution of its associated benefits — the rankings presented here indicate that some systems are coherent in a more *enviable* way than others.

These rankings also show that there is more than one recipe or model to achieve better economic performance. For example, while Japan and Germany exhibit a number of common features that help to explain their superior performance, the two approaches underlying those features are entirely different, and the education systems and labour-market conditions in the two countries reflect those differences.

By "coherence" we mean *the harmonious connection*

Table 6.5
Countries Ranked by Economic Indicators

Ranking	Country	Growth Rate of GDP Per Capita	Labour Productivity in Manufacturing Sector	Gross Fixed-Capital Formation	Gross Domestic Savings	Rate of Inflation	Firms' Expenditures on Research and Development	Openness to International Trade in Goods and Services	Elasticity of Imports to GDP	Exports of Engineering Products	Quality of Domestic Products (S)	Competitiveness of Banking and Financial Services in Context of Global Deregulation (S)	Governments' Flexibility to Adapt Legislation to New Economic Realities (S)	Direct Taxes and Social Security Premiums as Proportion of GDP	Growth Rate of Tax Revenue	Allocation of Public Resources for Promoting Industrial Competitiveness (S)
1	Japan	++	++	++	++	++	++	--	+	++	++	-	++	+	-	++
2	Germany	-	+	-	++	++	++	-	+	++	++	+	++	-	+	++
3	Switzerland	-	++	++	++	++	++	+	+	-	++	+	-	+	-	-
4	Austria	-	-	+	+	+	-	+	-	+	+	+	++	+	+	+
5	The Netherlands	--	+	-	+	++	+	++	+	-	+	-	+	-	++	+
6	Finland	++	+	-	+	-	-	-	+	-	+	+	+	+	-	-
7	United States	+	+	-	-	+	-	-	-	+	+	+	+	+	-	+
8	Belgium	-	+	-	-	-	-	++	-	-	+	-	-	-	+	-
9	Norway	+	-	++	++	+	-	+	++	-	-	-	-	-	++	-
10	Canada	**+**	**.**	**.**	**.**	**+**	**.**	**.**	**+**	**+**	**+**	**++**	**+**	**++**	**.**	**+**
11	United Kingdom	+	-	+	-	+	+	+	+	+	+	+	+	++	+	+
12	Australia	++	-	-	-	+	-	+	-	+	+	-	-	++	+	+
13	France	-	+	+	+	-	+	+	+	+	+	+	-	+	+	-
14	Denmark	-	-	-	-	-	-	+	+	+	-	-	-	-	+	-
15	Sweden	-	-	-	-	-	++	-	+	+	-	++	-	-	-	+
16	New Zealand	-	+	-	-	-	-	-	-	+	-	++	+	+	-	+
17	Italy	-	-	-	-	-	-	-	-	+	-	-	-	+	-	-
18	Spain	+	-	-	-	-	-	-	+	+	-	-	+	+	-	-

of the several parts of a system, so that the whole hangs together (Oxford Dictionary). For our purpose — that is, the relationship between a country's educational system and its socio-economic system — the concept of coherence has two distinct aspects. The first is the signals sent by the participants in the socio-economic system — including parents, teachers, guidance counsellors, employers, workers, labour unions, education officials and others — to the educational system and, more specifically, to the students. We can ask such questions as: Are those signals clear? Do they motivate students to strive for excellence in their studies? Do they convey the information students need in order to make critical choices in selecting their educational path? The second aspect relates to the people who receive those signals – primarily the students and the counsellors who guide them along their educational paths. Are they able to interpret the signals correctly? And are they responding in an appropriate manner?

The coherence of a system, then, should not be judged by that system's institutions,[4] but rather by the interaction among those institutions and the signals they send to one another. The *conduct* of the institutions represents an ongoing and continuous response to those signals. Analysing this behaviour, therefore, provides valuable information about both the signals and the coherence of the system.

The experience of a given country derives from its history — which has shaped its culture, created its institutions, and forged the links that enable its citizens to work together. Such an experience cannot be taken as a block and simply transplanted to another country. Nonetheless, the principles underlying the superior performance of other systems can be analysed in order to draw useful lessons for orienting future policy decisions. What follows, therefore, is an attempt to distill those principles from the experiences of Germany and Japan. Although lessons may well be drawn from the experiences of other countries, we have chosen Germany and Japan, because their superior performances induce interest in the underlying mechanics of their socio-economic systems and, second, because the significant differences between them illustrate how disparate coherent models can be.

Coherence in Germany

COOPERATIVE FEDERALISM
Like Canada, Germany is a federal state. This system of government adds another procedural level — and possibly additional obstacles — to the development of a coherent socio-economic system. Like Canada, Germany has not one, but several, school systems within its federal socio-political system. The division of powers under the "basic law" of 1949 (the German Constitution) only rarely assigns responsibility for a specific policy area to a single level of government; the usual arrangement is shared responsibility.

There is a high degree of interdependence between the federal government and the governments of the Länder (states), no single jurisdiction — not the federation, the Länder or the communes — is in a position to resolve major problems independently or to address major issues in their entirety. Nonetheless, in general terms, the federal government is responsible for legislation and the Länder are responsible for administration. Education, however, is one of the rare exceptions. In this field, responsibility for legislation, planning and funding, as well as the administrative authority rests principally with the Länder. Moreover, centralization has been pushed so far that within a particular Länder virtually all (educational) variation and the possibility of significant independent action on the part of the communes have been eliminated.

In each of the five sectors of the education system, the combination of responsibilities differs; the only constant is the central role of the Land. The Land and the communes share responsibility for nursery schools and for public primary and secondary schools. (About 6 per cent of students are enrolled in privately subsidized schools.) The federal government and the Länder share responsibility for universities. Vocational training is the responsibility of the Länder under federal legislation (the 1969 Vocational Training Act). Continuing education is the common responsibility of the Länder (for legislation), the communes (for providing services to adult training centres), and the Federal Employment Office (for funding).

Historically, education was the domain of the Länder alone. Even before the formation of the Federal Republic of Germany in 1948, issues related to regional interdependence, particularly the problems raised by inter-regional mobility and the desire to reduce regional disparities, led to the creation of a Standing Conference of the Länder Ministers of Education and Cultural Affairs (Ständige Konferenz der Kulturminister, KMK). Within this group, consensus was the rule in the decision-making process, but the federal government gradually gained influence in education policy and planning through constitutional amendments. In the late 1960s, the federal government entered the field of education directly when it began to promote scientific research and offer bursaries.

In 1970 a federal-Länder commission on educational planning and research promotion (*Bund-Länder-Kommission für Bildungsplanung und Forschungsförderung, BLK*) was established. At the time, the two levels of government concentrated on the links between education and other policy areas of federal responsibility, such as economic and social policy, and on the need to co-ordinate the actions of the two levels of government. In addition, the federal government accepted general responsibility for ensuring equal quality of life among all the Länder, even though such equality was not recognized as an objective in the Constitution, but rather as a means to guarantee inter-regional mobility. The Länder held, however, that the Standing Conference of Länder Ministers was the appropriate body to undertake the task. Thus, differences of opinion as to the function and extent of federal involvement in education policy emerged at an early stage.

The Länder continue to guard jealously their autonomy in education because they see education as one of their last important areas of responsibility and essential to their status as Länder. It is the resistance of the Länder to the federal government's attempts to encroach on this area that has prevented a major shift of educational responsibility to the federal government. While co-operation is extensive, it is still based on direct relations among the Länder.

BROAD SOCIAL CONSENSUS
ON THE IMPORTANCE OF EDUCATION

Diplomas and certificates are, unquestionably, one of the central elements of social life in Germany. The titles they confer signify not only knowledge in a particular subject area, but also broadly-based social recognition of that knowledge. Such awards also reflect the high esteem in which the associated education or vocational training is held. Young Germans probably spend more time in school than students anywhere else in the world. Schooling usually begins with two or three years of *Kindergarten;* 75 per cent of all children four to five years of age attend *Kindergarten.* Thereafter, full-time schooling is compulsory for nine or ten years (from the age of six until age 15 or 16), then there are two or three years of *compulsory part-time schooling* (from age 15 or 16 to age 18).

Germany has developed a veritable "training culture" that permeates society. One indication of the importance of this culture is the close involvement of parents in the operation of educational institutions and the number of members on the evaluation committees of vocational programs. Clearly, for a school system as selective as Germany's to work, there must be strong social consensus on the value of education. By promoting education as the guarantee of future success, German society exerts great pressure on its children. But as the education system strives to ensure academic success, it also tries to prevent academic failure by providing substantial safety nets, such as programs to teach basic skills within the apprenticeship system. The system takes for granted that every student can be trained to occupy a place in society as a productive, highly qualified, and well-paid worker.

The close involvement of German employers in education, particularly through the dual apprenticeship system, is highly praised. One of the employers' main motives underlying support for the system is the awareness of the social risk of allowing large numbers of youth to become "marginalized" through unemployment. Because of fierce competition for apprenticeship training, particularly in high-profile firms such as Siemens, IBM, Daimler-Benz and Bayer, young people are motivated to use 100 per cent of their abilities knowing that the key to their future success lies in the pursuit of excellence.

DIVERSITY OF OPTIONS
WITHIN THE EDUCATIONAL SYSTEM

The Bavarian Constitution requires that the State provide an educational system that "serves all the country's children in accordance with their intelligence, interests, and abilities". According to Bavaria's Minister of Education, the government has no choice, therefore, but to provide a diversified educational system – since a U.S.-style uniform or general-purpose system would be unconstitutional in Germany.[6]

In order to provide diversity, the German school system is selective (Figure 6.2). At the age of 10 or 12 years, when students graduate from primary school, they are directed to one of three types of school:[7] intermediate school (the *Hauptschule*), secondary general school (the *Realschule*), or grammar school (the *Gymnasium*). By the time students have reached this stage, their inclinations, skills, strengths and weaknesses are reasonably apparent to themselves as well as to their parents and teachers. The choice of career orientation made at this juncture is therefore not all that difficult, even though it represents a major decision and largely determines a student's future educational path.

Education and Training: An International Perspective 117

**Figure 6.2
The German Educational System**

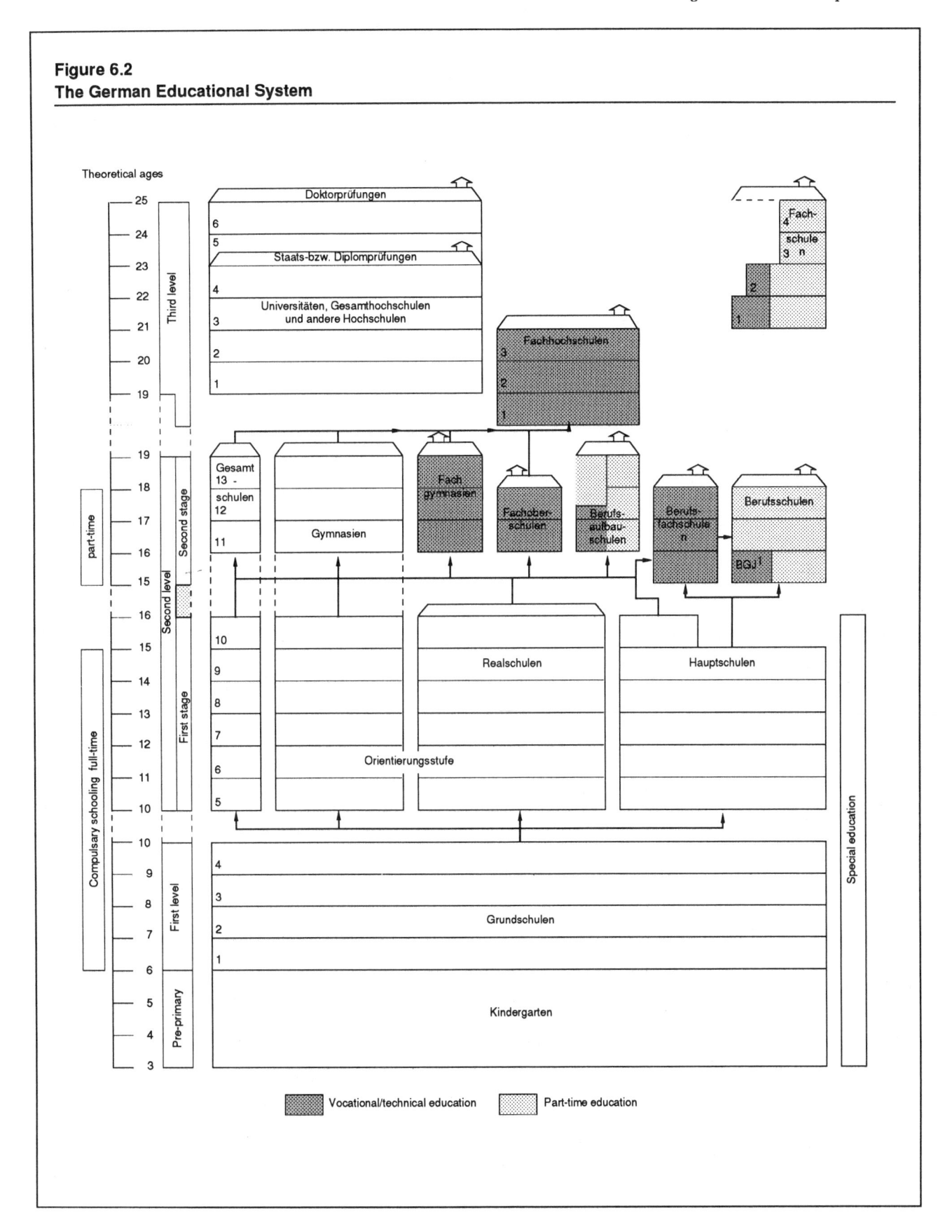

In theory, at least, the decision made here even affects the conditions of the student's labour-market entry.

While it may appear that adolescents are under tremendous pressure to choose a career early, the education system is sufficiently flexible to allow students to change orientation at a later date. Although making such a change is by no means easy, it is possible for a student to move from one type of school to another, In theory, at least, the decision made here affects the conditions of the student's labour-market entry.

While it may appear that adolescents are under tremendous pressure to choose a career early, the education system is sufficiently flexible to permit students to change orientation at a later date. Although making such a change is by no means easy, it is possible for a student to move from one type of school to another, provided that the academic prerequisites are met. In fact, such changes occur fairly frequently.

Each of the three types of school mentioned above has a different curriculum. The *Hauptschule* is intended to prepare students for apprenticeship by the end of their years of compulsory full-time schooling. The *Realschule*, provides students with an extra year of schooling during which science, mathematics and foreign languages are stressed. The *Gymnasium* offers a nine-year program that takes students to age 18 or 19 and leads to the *Abitur* certificate, which is usually the ticket to higher education.

Taking all students in Grades 7 to 9 into account, approximately 35 per cent attend the *Hauptschule*, 30 per cent attend the *Realschule*, and slightly more than 30 per cent attend the *Gymnasium*. The *Realschule* option is growing in popularity, since it offers instruction that is appropriate both for the labour market and for higher education, and is an alternative to the more elitist *Gymnasium*. A little more than a third of apprenticeship trainees in 1989 held a *Realschule* certificate. Whereas barely 22 per cent earned the *Abitur in 1980*, almost 36 per cent did so in 1989.

The *Gesamtschule* should also be mentioned. This integrated school combines the three streams at one institution, offering some courses to all students. Barely 6 per cent of students in Grades 7 to 9 attend this type of school, however. Only a few Länder with governments dominated by the Social Democrats have developed extensive *Gesamtschule* networks.

In Germany, apprenticeship is not regarded as the option of failure, nor are entry-level vocational training programs considered to be dead ends or second-best options. These programs are designed to offer students a combination of vocational and academic instruction with the option of going on to university or to higher-level vocational schools. Indeed, students in all streams are required to achieve a high level of general education and the combinations of academic and vocational training which are tailored to the labour market are highly regarded by employers. The increasingly diverse academic backgrounds of students entering apprenticeship programs testify to the value of this type of training, since there have been simultaneous shifts in the relative use of the various educational pathways (Table 6.6).

A recent survey conducted by the Federal Institute for Vocational Training determined that 72 per cent of students who left the general school system in 1987 entered the dual system, including 86 per cent of *Hauptschule* graduates, 81 per cent of *Realschule* graduates, and 36 per cent of *Abitur* holders.[8]

At the post-secondary level, Germany has a variety of institutions of higher education. Besides the universities and colleges with varying degrees and areas of specialization, there are vocational training schools that can grant, for example, credentials in engineering. The number of students enrolled in all these post-secondary institutions passed the million-and-a-half mark in 1989, equalling apprenticeship enrolment for the

Table 6.6
Educational Background of Young People in Dual Training Program (%)

	Completion of *Hauptschule* (with or without certificate) and Undeclared	Mittlere Reife (*Realschule* Completion Exam)	Abitur	Vocational Training and Pre-Vocational Schooling
1970	79.8	18.9	1.3	—
1989	34.2	34.1	15.8	15.9

Source: Basic and Structural Data — Federal Ministry of Education and Science, 1990–91; "Formation professionnelle et emploi : un lien plus marqué en Allemagne," Économie et statistique, No. 246–247, septembre–octobre 1991

first time; enrolment has since surpassed that figure. This phenomenon, of course, reflects the rising number of young people holding *Abitur* qualifications and the growing trend of entering university via apprenticeship programs. Indeed, a modest but growing number of students enter institutions of higher learning through ways other than the traditional *Gymnasium* system.

The variety of educational programs and their relative flexibility are important factors in the diversity of career paths open to young Germans. Through the transitional conduit of the dual system, the educational system is directly "plugged into" the diverse needs of the labour market. Students are motivated to attend school by their perception of a direct relationship between education and future employment. No effort is spared to make this perception a reality. As in Denmark and Sweden, students in Germany begin to learn about the various occupational options and the educational programs associated with them as early as the seventh grade, when employers and labour-market representatives visit schools to hold employment-information sessions.

TRANSITION FROM SCHOOL TO LABOUR MARKET: A BROAD PARTNERSHIP

Since schooling, at least on a part-time basis, is compulsory in Germany until age 18, the school-to-labour-market transition is simply one more step along the academic path of students enrolled in the *Hauptschule* and the *Realschule*. This has a definite — and, of course, positive — influence on the youth-unemployment rate. Structured information about the labour market is made available very early and is disseminated by such means as "career days", meetings with occupational representatives, and field trips to companies. Young people quickly realize that they must rely on themselves to find an employer willing to take them on as trainees. Thus, they learn very early what job-hunting entails.

The dual system is the key element — a corridor — in the transition of German youth from education to working life, and approximately 70 per cent of all students pass through it. The system involves various kinds of duality.

- **Duality of location.** Apprenticeship training takes place partly in a vocational school and partly in a firm. While the time spent at each site varies, trainees generally spend about 40 per cent of their time in school and 60 per cent with the firm.

- **Duality of knowledge and course content.** This follows from duality of location. Generally, student trainees receive their general academic and theoretical instruction in school. Many Canadians would be surprised at the level of sophistication of the topics covered. Learning is complemented by practical instruction received within the firm, on the job, under the supervision of a *Meister*, a professional certified to act as a trainer. The two places of instruction are usually separated, although certain large corporations with their own training centres provide on-site locations for the theoretical part of technical/vocational training.

- **Duality of status.** Trainees are both students and employees. As students they attend an educational institution; as employees they are paid for their contribution to the firm's operations while they acquire the practical part of their education. Starting wages are low (ranging from 20 to 27 per cent of the wage paid to a fully qualified worker), but payment increases gradually to close to 50 per cent by the final year of training. This simply reflects the strong qualifications-based hierarchy that is built into German society. The wage cost for the firm training students is small. The system works because students enter the apprenticeship system at an early age and they usually live at home and need not support a family. Young people are taught that they are contributing financially to their own education by accepting low wages. At the same time, they know what they can eventually expect to receive, and so they value highly the apprenticeship program and their chosen occupation. By the end of the apprenticeship period, trainees are fully qualified to practise their profession. At that point they receive their certification papers, the *Gesellenbrief*, without which no one can work in that occupation.

- **Duality of responsibility.** The Länder governments are responsible for the training provided in the school system, while employers and their professional associations (the "Chambers of Industry and Commerce" and "Chambers of Crafts") are responsible for in-company training. School training thus falls under the purview of public law; in-company training is under the jurisdiction of private law.

The dual system mobilizes and co-ordinates the efforts of many players, who work as partners. Thanks to close co-operation between schools and employers, academic instruction provides a strong foundation for

Figure 6.3
The Organization of the German Dual Apprenticeship System

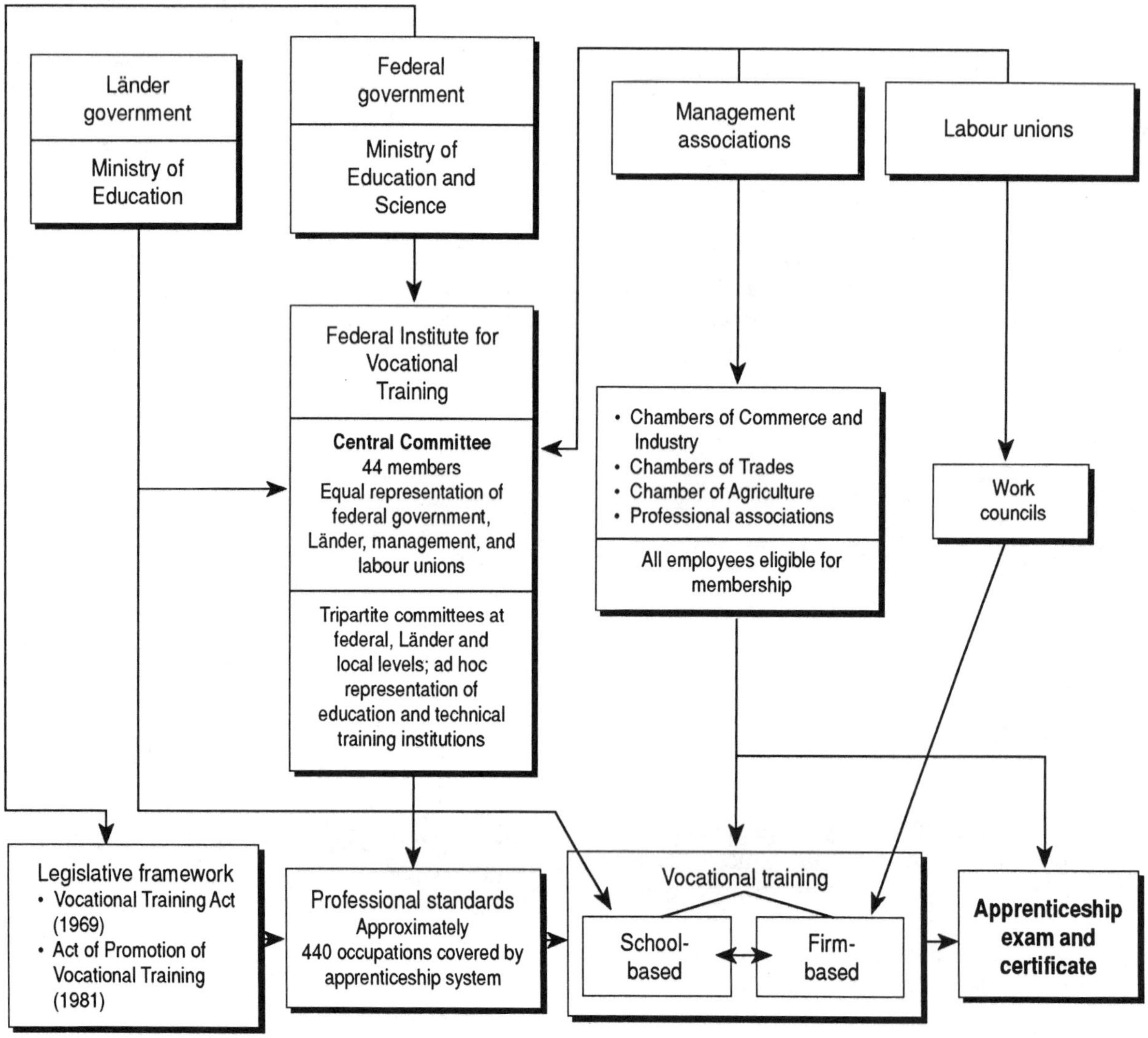

Source: C. Lane, "Vocational Training and New Production Concepts in Germany: Some Lessons for Britain," *Industrial Relations Journal*, Vol. 21, no 4, Winter 1990.

practical experience, and student/trainees enjoy the benefit of being able to pursue both at the same time. But the co-operation and co-ordination go well beyond the simple delivery of training; they encompass all aspects of the system.

As can be seen in Figure 6.3, the legislative framework of the apprenticeship system is established by the federal government while professional standards, which constitute the foundation of the system, are set by the Federal Institute for Vocational Training. The Central Committee of the Federal Institute includes representatives from the federal and Länder governments, business, and labour unions.

Professional standards, which specify the precise qualifications required for some 440 different occupations, also serve as the basis for both the practical in-company training and the academic school-based training programs. Supervision by the Chambers of Commerce, the company Work Councils and the Ministries of Education ensures that all the programs conform to professional standards. At the end of their academic studies and practical training, trainees receive what amounts to a "passport" into their chosen profession: certification papers entitling them to practise their chosen occupation anywhere in the country.

An important by-product of Germany's on-the-job apprenticeship program is the employee loyalty it engenders among the trainees towards the training firm with the result that a high percentage of trainees remain with their training company as permanent employees after completing their programs.

CONSTRUCTIVE PERSONNEL MANAGEMENT

In Germany, personnel management is part of a dynamic, comprehensive process that takes into account the changes that occur in production systems and work organization. It does so by encouraging the speedy adoption of new work organization and production methods. This process may be referred to as the "virtuous circle" generated by the vocational training system.

The dual system for initial vocational training is part and parcel of a learning continuum that maintains continuity between initial training and continuous learning, by offering employees a broad spectrum of possibilities to advance their careers throughout their working lives. After students have completed their secondary studies at about the age of 18 or 19 years, they continue learning, often on a formal basis, after they enter the work force. Night schools are open to certified apprentices who wish to develop specialities or take courses that may eventually allow them to move in a different career direction. Entering university remains a possibility for certified apprentices who succeed in obtaining the necessary credits through night school. In addition, after working for three to five years in the trade in which they are qualified, new workers may apply for entry to the teachers' school (the *Meisterschule*), where they can take courses leading to a certificate as a Master of Training. Those who complete their courses successfully can then train apprentices in their own right.

More than one out of every four heads of German companies started out as a trainee, and close to half of these returned to school to earn a post-secondary diploma. One out of every three German companies trained its own chief executive officer. It is a standard practice within German companies to develop and promote staff from within the company (another aspect of corporate coherence). Firms that emphasize training and back it up with adequate funding (Siemens, for example, which spends 8 per cent of its total wage bill on apprenticeship and continuous education programs) are truly nurturers of practical skills and knowledge. Such firms are the backbone of the training and certification market. The fact that German firms make educational background their prime consideration when selecting senior managers reflects the direct link between firms' internal promotion systems and the training system. Vocational training is perceived as a way to prepare an individual for a series of practical responsibilities in a specific field, and each career step is preceded by a new training period.[9]

In Germany, work methods stress worker autonomy and superior qualifications. As a general rule, workers contribute to the firm's organizational planning and are consulted on major investment decisions and work-related plans. Because of the close working relationship between workers and management, many German firms are able to practise the most productive forms of work organization based on the latest technologies. As a result, the firms can pay high wages commensurate with the well-developed skills and operational flexibility of the work force.

Figure 6.4 depicts this "virtuous circle", from which a number of points emerge clearly:

- vocational training plays a critical role in ensuring a homogenous work force that shares a common conviction as to the value of the established structures of qualifications

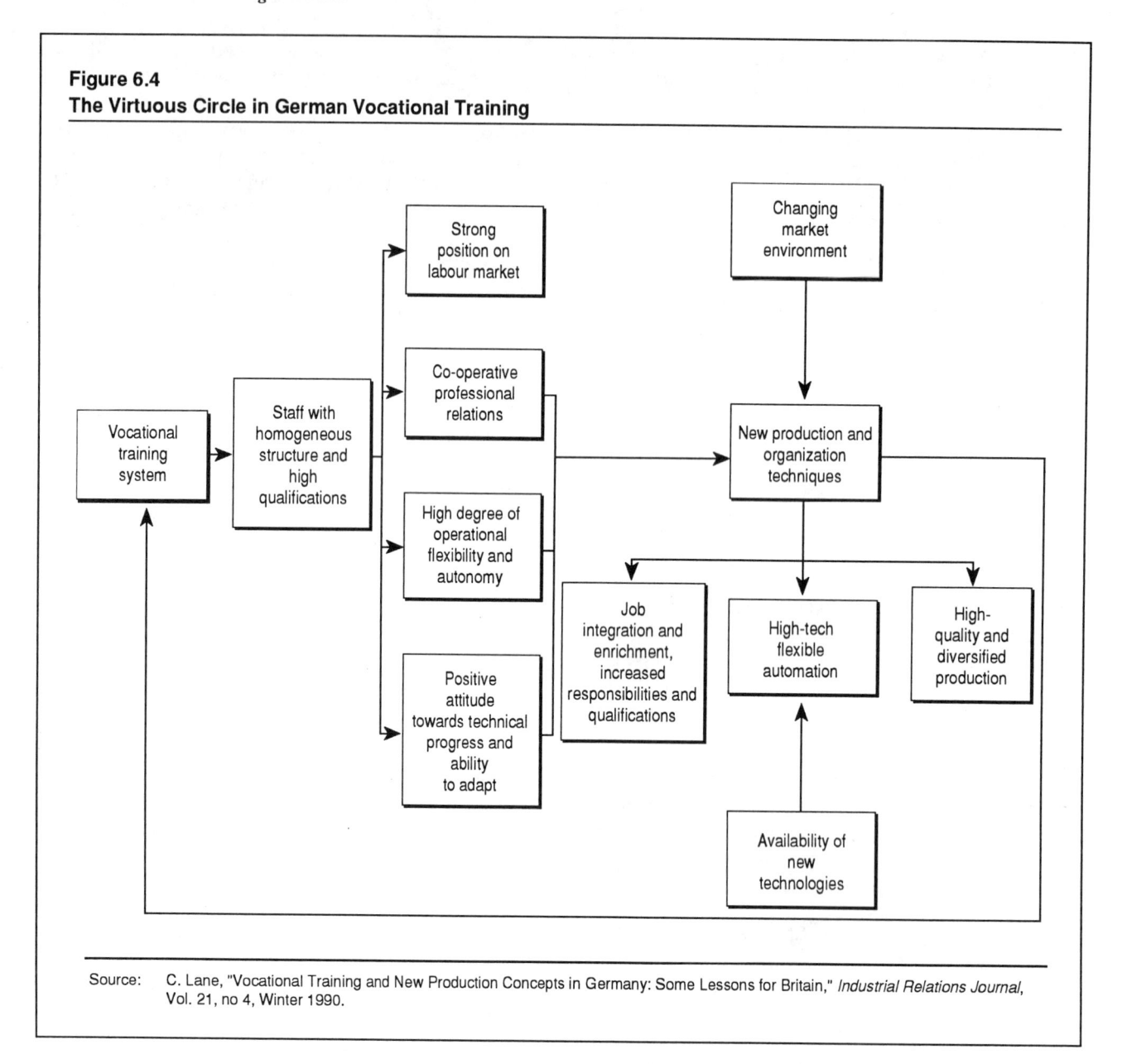

Figure 6.4
The Virtuous Circle in German Vocational Training

Source: C. Lane, "Vocational Training and New Production Concepts in Germany: Some Lessons for Britain," *Industrial Relations Journal*, Vol. 21, no 4, Winter 1990.

- there are notable advantages for the firm — as well as for the worker if he/she should eventually decide to leave the firm
- firms enjoy increased opportunities because of their highly qualified staff
- productive personnel policies come full circle with the continuing demand for additional training generated by the need to adjust constantly to changing labour-market needs and to advances in production and organizational techniques.

THE STATE AS LABOUR-MARKET PARTNER

Germany's federal government works actively in collaboration with its labour-market partners. Through the Federal Institute for Vocational Training, it helps to develop detailed generic job descriptions and corresponding training programs for the approximately 440 different occupations covered by apprenticeship programs in the dual system. Employers, however, have so far strongly resisted every attempt by the federal government to establish professional standards comparable to those that exist for the apprenticeship programs. They oppose the government's efforts because they are determined to preserve the freedom they enjoy in this area in contrast with the strict regulations governing apprenticeship.

A summary of public expenditures on labour-market programs (Table 6.7) shows that while Germany and Canada both spend roughly the same amount relative to GDP, Germany devotes twice as much to "active" measures such as training as opposed to "passive" programs such as unemployment insurance. In Germany, active measures account for almost 50 per cent of labour-market programs compared to less than 25 per cent in Canada. To complement employers' efforts on behalf of their employees, the German government also undertakes direct, positive action to assist workers experiencing difficulty entering or re-entering the labour market.

Coherence in Japan

THE FOCUS ON EDUCATION

In Japan acceptable behaviour among its citizens is judged according to rules established by social consensus that explicitly delineate standards of behaviour. The Japanese have long recognized education as the key to industrial development, national unity, political stature on the world stage, personal development, moral force, cultural continuity, and the creation and maintenance of satisfactory interpersonal relationships. As early as 1870, around the beginning of the Meiji era, 43 per cent of all boys and 15 per cent of all girls aged 15 had attended school and knew how to read. These figures are considerably higher than the corresponding figures for Europe, where the movement towards universal access to education was only in its earliest stages. At that time, Japan was essentially a rural society. Only 20 per cent of its population lived in urban areas; its industrial revolution had barely begun.

Japanese parents today make substantial financial contributions towards the cost of their children's education, and they — especially the mothers — take a strong direct personal interest in school activities. Private spending on education accounted for 1.4 per cent of Japanese GDP in 1988, and has been growing at a considerably faster rate than public spending — which itself is only three times larger than private spending. Besides paying for private schooling (which most often occurs beyond the years of compulsory school attendance) families also pay high fees to enroll their children in supplementary programs (known as *juku* or *yobiko*) in order to help prepare them for the critical points of education experience: the entrance exams for senior secondary school and for university. Most Japanese children are enrolled in such supplementary schools at some point in their school-age years.

Many Japanese parents also pay another kind of price in the cause of educating their children. As a kind of counterbalance to their job security within the firm, employees are often asked to transfer to another location. This is the practice of *tanshin funin*, which involves moving alone, leaving the family behind, and returning home only on weekends or perhaps three or four times a year, depending on the distance involved. The chief rationale for this practice is to avoid disrupting the continuity of children's schooling.

RESPONSIBILITY FOR ACADEMIC EDUCATION AND VOCATIONAL TRAINING

In Japan it is the school's responsibility to provide students with a high-quality general education and to mould proper social behaviour; it is the firm's responsibility to provide its staff with vocational training. Firms therefore do not expect schools to turn out graduates with fully developed occupational skills ready-tailored to their needs. Nonetheless, employers have a very clear notion of what they want in new employees. Of the criteria that companies use in recruiting high-school graduates, the foremost is "zeal and willingness to work" (cited by more than two out of every three firms), then "good health and vigour", "a cooperative attitude", and "good general knowledge". Fewer than one employer in five mentioned "high marks", and barely one in ten considered "specialized knowledge or professional qualifications" to be worth mentioning.

Table 6.7
Government Expenditures on Labour-Market Programs (%)

	Expenditure as % of GDP	Share Allocated to "Active" Measures*
Canada (1989/90)	2.08	24.5
France (1989)	2.65	27.5
West Germany (1990)	2.18	46.8
Italy (1988)	1.52	52.6
Japan (1990/91)	0.45	28.9
Sweden (1990/91)	2.25	70.2
Great Britain (1990/91)	1.49	39.6
United States (1990/91)	0.85	29.4

* Administration and employment services, vocational training, youth-oriented measures, hiring-assistance measures, and measures to support disabled workers.

Source: *Employment Outlook*, OECD, 1991

When employers recruit university graduates, they often specify among their essential requirements "the ability to understand and make decisions", and for more technical jobs, "specialized knowledge or professional qualifications" and "creativity and planning ability" (cited by only slightly more than a third of all employers).

In summary, a firm expects its young recruits to have a positive attitude towards work, an ability to work co-operatively, good health, and extensive general knowledge. Employers consider these traits to offer the best guarantee that new employees will adapt successfully to the firm's work environment and corporate culture.

Because firms' recruiting criteria are widely known, they serve as a guide for both teachers and their students. The educational system responds to these criteria by acting as a filter, screening its "output" according to the rules of a rigid institutional ranking system. The rank or rating of each grammar school or college[10] is based on the number of graduates it has sent on to higher levels of education. For a college, this means having the highest possible number of its students pass the entrance exams of highly-regarded grammar schools. Similarly, private and public grammar schools trumpet the number of their students accepted through entrance exams for first-rank universities run either by the state, like the Universities of Tokyo and Kyoto, or privately, like Waseda or Keio. Finally, a first-rank university prides itself on the number of its graduates that find employment with the largest corporations or the most important government ministries: Finance, International Trade, or External Affairs. Thus the ultimate goal poised at the top of the education pyramid is a job with a major corporation or government ministry.[11]

Generally speaking, Japanese firms have little regard for vocational schools. Such institutions are considered suitable only for students with poor academic prospects because of low marks earned during their years of compulsory schooling. Whereas more than one firm in three recruits its office and general workers from among "regular" secondary-school graduates, only one firm in six recruits from among vocational school graduates.

Japan is a society where university study absorbs a substantial proportion (about 40 per cent) of an entire age group. There is a strong and widespread drive for university-level education, and the financial means to attend university are widely available. Predictably, therefore, students do everything in their power to improve their chances of university access and are unwilling to follow any educational path leading away from that goal.[12] Nonetheless, the intent of Japan's educational system is not simply to skim off the cream of outstanding students; rather, the system serves to classify young people according to their intellectual abilities and ambitions. While the system is unquestionably selective —rigidly so in fact — no student is rejected or shunted into a dead-end. Each finds his or her place as determined by intellectual abilities, ambitions and financial means.

As in many other countries, Japan's educational system is currently weathering a crisis. It has been severely and widely criticized for being rigid and oppressive, and for failing to meet contemporary needs for diversity, flexibility and creativity.[13] As with educational systems everywhere, the Japanese system faces great challenges. But while the issues are far-reaching, the country remains well equipped with an efficient system rooted in a social context that is open to gradual, consensus-based change.

A SEAMLESS SCHOOL-TO-LABOUR-MARKET TRANSITION

Firms recruit young workers through direct contacts with the educational institutions and universities and with students themselves. Firms accomplish this by making a special effort to build long-lasting relationships with educational institutions so that in keeping with the Japanese code of loyalty, they will receive preferential treatment from guidance counsellors who advise students on career choices. Thanks to the long-term nature of these relationships, employers often adjust their needs and schools their responses on the basis of the previous years' experience. Firms planning to hire secondary-school graduates[14] simply advise one or more schools of the number and kinds of jobs they wish to fill. As long as the schools are satisfied with the range of job offerings, and the firms are satisfied with the students recommended by the schools, these "semi-formal" contracts remain very solid, and firms continue to take great pains to maintain good relations with the educational institutions, even in times of economic downturn.

Recruitment of university graduates follows a similar pattern. Corporate personnel departments establish direct links with university professors who make recommendations to their graduating (usually fourth-year) students. This hiring strategy is most common in scientific fields and at second-rank universities. Such universities often have a special administrative office that acts as a clearing house for job offers. In the larger universities, students are inundated with prospectuses and letters of invitation from firms as soon as they reach their fourth year of study — which over 90 per cent of them do.

One characteristic of the Japanese economic system establishes the context of its labour market and the general tone of employee recruitment from the education system: it is a full-employment economy. This characteristic works to the benefit of the labour supply, since employers are anxious to avoid future labour shortages and therefore actively court workers. On average, each Japanese citizen under the age of 20 may choose (a career path) from among roughly three job offers. (Although these data relate specifically to October 1988, labour has continued to be in high demand for several years.) The situation is even more favourable for graduates of the major universities who, depending on their area of specialization, are each offered from three to ten jobs.

TRAINING IN THE WORK-PLACE

Although Japanese personnel directors rarely mention their companies' training programs, the importance generally accorded human-resource development and management training is directly related to the (substantial) investments in employee training made by most firms. It is taken for granted that a firm will provide training, inasmuch as the concept of a comprehensive "training culture" is inherent in Japanese business, and business is the driving force behind the steadily rising level of skills in the Japanese work force. Every effort is made to provide workers with opportunities to improve their skills. Of course, the nature and extent of training, the amount of money devoted to it, its particular format and target group(s) depend on the size of the firm involved. Training is inextricably bound up with the operations of the firm. Much importance is attached to training at all levels of the business hierarchy. In many of the larger firms responsibility for training is assigned to a separate department and is not simply an extension of the personnel department.

A high proportion of new Japanese recruits are post-secondary graduates, all of whom possess a well-rounded general knowledge. Only rarely is an individual hired for a specific job. Rather, new recruits are hired for a lifetime career in a firm, and the firm does not expect them to have learned occupational skills during their academic years. Irrespective of the size of the firm, the overwhelming majority train their own employees in one way or another. Statistically, 100 per cent of firms with more than 300 employees provide their own training, as do 91 per cent of firms with 100 to 299 employees, and 78 per cent of small companies with 30 to 99 employees.[15]

As Table 6.8 shows, however, there are some significant differences in the kinds of training provided and the goals of that training by firm size:

- Clearly, larger firms provide a much broader spectrum of training than smaller firms. Size, therefore, is a critical factor in determining the kind of training made available to employees.

- While Japanese employers traditionally consider on-the-job training to be most important, it is formally planned in only one-quarter of all cases. Most often, on-the-job training is given on an *ad-hoc* basis at the instigation of the immediate superior or senior employees. This applies particularly in small businesses.

- Off-the-job training is very common, particularly among smaller businesses that lack the resources to

Table 6.8
Type of Training by Size of Firm
(%; Multiple Responses Allowed)

Type of Training	All Firms	Firms with More Than 1000 Employees	Firms with from 30 to 99 Employees
All Firms	100.0	100.0	100.0
In-house Off-the-job Training	58.6	96.8	52.0
External Off-the-job Training	45.9	62.0	41.8
Planned On-the-job Training	25.8	69.5	20.8
Support for Self-instruction	22.8	66.5	19.1
Paid Education Leave	8.0	9.7	7.8

Source: Ministry of Labour, *Survey of Vocational Training in Private Enterprises*, 1985

maintain their own training establishment. Small businesses also receive extensive assistance from the government for this purpose. (At one time, several very large corporations operated training centres for their own, and occasionally their subcontractors' exclusive use. Such firms actively recruited outstanding students whom they withdrew entirely from the regular school system to train themselves. As the duration of schooling has increased, and the level of education of young entrants to the labour market has improved, these firms have either closed their parallel schools or transformed them into continuous-education facilities.)

- Support for self-training is becoming a more popular option, particularly among large corporations. Executives recognize that they can save money by having their employees invest their own time and money to stay abreast of developments in their particular areas of interest.

- Although paid education leave is still uncommon, it occurs as often in small firms as in large corporations.

The same survey showed that only one firm in four has a formally-structured, preplanned internal training program for its employees. Of the firms surveyed, only 7 per cent guaranteed systematic training throughout an employee's career, from recruitment to retirement. However, this group is composed almost exclusively of large companies, as 53 per cent of firms with more than 1000 employees offer such training programs. Since 1985, the government has encouraged companies to appoint an individual to oversee in-company training, and has offered financial assistance for that purpose.

Although the better-educated workers have the best chance of benefitting from additional training during their careers, surveys show that the great majority of Japan's workers believe they receive the training they need. Overall, three out of every four workers in firms with more than 30 employees reported receiving some additional training at some point during their working lives. Of course, there are inequalities hidden in this average. Although 80 per cent of all men received additional training, only 61 per cent of women received training. In firms with more than 1000 employees, 90 per cent of employees received additional training, compared to 60 per cent in firms with from 30 to 99 employees. On an industry basis, 85 per cent of the employees in the financial, insurance, and real estate sectors received additional training, compared to only 60 per cent in the textile industry.

According to recent research, when training budgets are considered by themselves, the total amount spent on employee training by Japanese firms is not particularly high compared with the amounts spent by industries in other countries. Nonetheless, Japanese firms consider training to be fundamental and they use a variety of on-the-job methods, such as job rotation, quality circles, and unstructured training by supervisors. Training is a concept totally integrated into the every-day activity of the firm. Instead of reducing their training budgets when recession hits, most Japanese firms take the opportunity to send their surplus staff on skill-enhancement courses to prepare for better days ahead. When the yen fell suddenly in late 1985, retraining was one of the main strategies adopted by Japanese industry. Clearly, employers' respect for the principle of job security is a critical factor in making such a decision.

GOVERNMENT SUPPORT OF PRIVATE-SECTOR DEVELOPMENT

While the Japanese business and industrial sectors are the primary providers of vocational training, the government also plays an important supportive role. Although there is no legislation requiring minimum levels of vocational training, government initiatives through the Ministries of Labour and Education are closely co-ordinated with the employer-based system: a common arrangement in Japan. Through its minimal but realistic framework policies, its institutions, and its subsidy program, the government strives:

- to guide firms' training decisions in the best interests of society

- to improve the access to education of disadvantaged individuals and firms

- to support the efforts of small- and medium-sized businesses and initiatives on behalf of special target groups such as the disabled and the elderly

- to provide recognized national certification standards to administer qualifying exams.

The *Vocational Training Act* was passed in 1969 and revised in 1985, at which time it was renamed the *Act for the Promotion of Human-Resource Development*. This *Act* sets out the basic principles of national policy in this area. It stipulates that the upgrading of occupational skills shall be a systematic and incremental process spanning an individual's entire working life. It also specifies that the individual's aspirations, abilities, experience, and various other personal factors, shall be taken into consideration as well as such external factors as developments in the industry and labour market, technological and structural change, and the nation's increasing participation in the world economy.

The *Act* also specifies that vocational training and certification are among the most important means to develop occupational skills, and stresses that employers primarily are responsible for providing their employees with adequate training and additional opportunities for professional development. Responsibility for encouraging and helping employers to fulfill these obligations and for administering training programs in regulated occupations rests with the national and local governments. In accordance with these general principles, the Ministry of Labour regularly draws up long-term human-resources development plans.

The *Employment Insurance Act*[16] provides the Japanese government with the financial means to implement its vocational training policy. A percentage of insurance premiums (0.35 per cent of the wage bill), representing the employer-funded portion, is earmarked exclusively for government programs in four areas: employment stabilization, improvements in employment structure, human-resource development, and welfare services for workers.

The administration of tests and certification procedures constitutes one of the main activities of the Ministry of Labour in the area of vocational training. The aim of the government is not only to ensure public safety, as is common elsewhere, but also to improve national efficiency. The list of occupations for which national testing is available was first drawn up in 1959 when the system was introduced. It has since been reviewed and revised regularly by the Ministry. In October 1989, 133 occupations were subject to testing. Between 1959 and 1990, 3,860,000 candidates (at all levels) applied for certification; 1,620,000, or 42 per cent, passed the certification examinations. The highest numbers of certificates were awarded in the construction and machinery-operation trades.

While certification is recognized at the national level, workers appear to seek it not so much to improve their job prospects in the external labour market as to improve their qualifications and chances of promotion within the company. A certificate itself does not guarantee a particular job, but it does testify to the worker's level of qualification and may qualify him or her for a better position as an instructor in the employing company or a training centre.

Many employers encourage their employees to sit the national exams purely in order to increase their motivation. Most companies — particularly major corporations — make no commitment to award raises or promotions to employees who pass the tests. Workers do not expect such recognition and seem to share their employers' attitude. Their main purpose in taking the tests is not to achieve immediate promotion or monetary gain, but to increase self-motivation and personal pride.

Occupational training centres are administered by the Ministry of Labour and regional governments and the public served by these institutions is diverse — an indication of their capacity to adapt to the requirements of their environment. Occupational training centres offer courses, generally without charge, to individuals who are seeking a job and who need retraining. They also assist employers in a variety of ways, by setting up training programs on demand, by lending out their instructors, and by allowing private companies to use their facilities upon request. The centres strive to maintain close links with local firms in order to enlist their co-operation in hosting practical training sessions and in securing job openings for their students. By nurturing these contacts, they can evaluate current needs on an on-going basis and adapt their training programs accordingly.

While their impact falls far short of in-company training, these public occupational training centres make an important contribution. During the 1990 fiscal year (April 1990 to March 1991), they provided a total of 380,000 training places. According to a 1989 survey on private-enterprise vocational training, however, only 37 per cent of Japanese firms used public occupational training centres as a source of outside training, while 51 per cent relied on private training institutions. Predictably, smaller companies made greater use of public training facilities than did larger firms, but the difference was fairly small: 39 per cent and 30 per cent respectively.

Some Lessons for Enhancing Coherence in Canada

National institutional systems are strongly rooted in their historical and cultural contexts. Obviously, Canada would gain little by attempting simply to duplicate the institutional arrangements or the successful formulae used by other countries. There is more than one strategy for achieving economic success. A better approach would be to emulate the emphasis on coherence which is found among the socio-economic players in those countries with outstanding performance records, as well as some of their methods for achieving that coherence. Educational systems within the context of a country's larger socio-economic system must ensure that they (the educational systems) receive clear signals and that those signals are accurately transmitted in order to guide students effectively in their curriculum choices and occupational orientation.

The analysis presented here suggests five critical ways by which greater coherence may be imparted to the Canadian educational system. They are described below in general terms, so they may be considered as guiding principles for sustained, long-term, future action rather than as recipes for a "quick fix".

- A high level of education among the population as a whole can be achieved only as part of a broad general acceptance by the population of the value and relevance of education within society and the economy. In other words, Canada must establish a training culture. In its statement *A Lot to Learn*, the Economic Council of Canada pointed out a number of ways in which Canada is falling significantly short of this goal.

- In order to make the education system relevant to the labour market and to the economy, we must develop a capacity to respond to the double diversity of students' aptitudes and preferences and to the skill needs of the labour market. As it now stands, Canada's educational system is "out of sync" with the reality of the times. It offers students little in the way of genuine choice, relying on general academic instruction to satisfy everyone's needs. Thus our current education systems fail to meet the expectations of young people who are better suited to technical/vocational training than to academic instruction. It also fails to respond adequately to the diverse needs of the labour market.

- In the present socio-economic context, in which education and work are inextricably linked, it is essential for employers to participate in general and vocational training. Their participation can take a variety of forms. Existing partnership models both at home and abroad provide many good examples that are worth developing further.

- In response to current and future economic challenges, employers must transform their business operations into "learning enterprises". Without radical change in employers' attitudes towards vocational training for their employees, Canada has little hope of meeting future challenges successfully. Employers must understand that the quality of human resources is a key factor in the nation's relative competitiveness as well as essential to their own survival. Moreover, the importance of this factor will continue to increase.

- Whatever constitutional and administrative arrangements emerge from the current debate, governments must assume a deliberately proactive role in facilitating the adjustments and initiatives required. Canada has a tradition of government labour-market programs, but these are primarily passive measures and they represent a substantial financial burden. Only through systematic co-ordination of their efforts can the various levels of government achieve the kind of program coherence needed to ensure that government policy initiatives will generate efficiency and synergy.

Endnotes

1. Unfortunately, the authors of the *World Competitiveness Report* do not provide any information that would allow us to evaluate the "statistical validity" of their survey of world business leaders.
2. The abbreviations refer to the source of the data as follows:
   OECD, ED: *Education in OECD Countries 1987-88*, Paris, 1990.
   OECD, LF: *Labour Force Statistics 1969-89*, Paris, 1991.
   OECD, ECO: *Economic Outlook, Historical Statistics, 1960-89,* Paris, 1991.
   OECD, NA: *National Accounts*, Volume II, *1977-89*, Paris, 1991.
   WCR90: *The World Competitiveness Report 1990*, IMD International and the World Economic Forum, June 1990.
   WCR91: *The World Competitiveness Report 1991*, IMD International and the World Economic Forum, June 1991.
   HDR: *Human Development Report 1991*, United Nations Development Programme, New York, 1991.
3. Throughout this study, "Germany" refers to the Federal Republic of Germany prior to unification.
4. "Institution" must be taken here in its widest sense: i.e., to encompass school, parents of students, the business sector, the government, and society as a whole.
5. See in particular Heinreich Mäding, "Federalism and Education Planning in the Federal Republic of Germany," *Publius: The Journal of Federalism,* 19, Fall 1989.
6. According to William E. Nothdurft in *Schoolworks,* The Brookings Institution, Washington, DC, 1989.
7. The first two years of secondary school are increasingly lumped together -- in the Orientierungsstufe -- to delay early streaming.
8. Cited in «Formation professionnelle et emploi : un lien plus marqué en Allemagne,» *Économie et statistique*, No. 246-247, septembre-octobre 1991.
9. See *L'Expansion*, «En Allemagne un patron, ça se forge en entreprise. En France, dans le tout-État,» 9/22 janvier 1992.
10. Corresponding to senior and junior high school respectively.
11. Jean-François Sabouret, *L'État du Japon*, La Découverte, Paris: 1988, pp. 206-07.
12. Ronald Dore and Mari Sako, *How the Japanese Learn to Work*, London: Routledge, 1989.
13. See Jacques Lesourne, *Éducation et société : les défis de l'an 2000*, La Découverte et Le Monde, Paris, 1988.
14. See, for example, James E. Rosenbaum, and Takehiko Kariya, "From High School to Work: Market and Institutional Mechanisms in Japan," *American Journal of Sociology*, May 1989.
15. Ministry of Labour, *Survey on Employment Management*, 1984.
16. Note the positive connotations of the title of this Act, formerly the 1947 Unemployment Insurance Act. The name was changed in 1974, in the midst of recession.

Bibliography

ASHTON, D. and G. Lowe (eds.), *Making Their Way - Education, Training and the Labour Market in Canada and Britain* (Toronto: University of Toronto Press, 1991).

Canadian Labour Market and Productivity Centre, *Établissements et politiques de formation au Royaume-Uni, en Allemagne et au Pays-Bas* (Ottawa, November 1990).

DORE, R. and M. Sako, *How the Japanese Learn to Work* (London: Routledge, 1989).

Foreign Press Center, Education in Japan, "About Japan" Series, No. 8 (Tokyo, March 1988).

HEGE, A., "Apprentissage et insertion professionnelle en RFA," *La Note de l'IRES*, No. 12, 2nd quarter 1987.

ISHIKAWA, T., *Vocational training.* Japanese Industrial Relations Series No. 7 (Tokyo: The Japan Institute of Labour, 1991).

L'Expansion, "En Allemagne un patron, ça se forge en entreprise. En France, dans le tout-État," 9/22 January 1992.

LANE, C., "Vocational training and new production concepts in Germany: some lessons for Britain," *Industrial Relations Journal*, Vol. 21, No. 4 (Winter 1990):247-59.

MÄDING, H., "Federalism and Education Planning in the Federal Republic of Germany," *Publius: The Journal of Federalism*, Vol. 19 (Fall 1989).

MAURICE, M., et al., *Politique d'éducation et organisation industrielle en France et en Allemagne, Sociologies* (Paris: Presses Universitaires de France, 1982).

Ministry of Education, Science and Culture, *Education in Japan, 1989 - A Graphic Presentation* (Tokyo: The ministry, 1989).

MÖBUS, M. and P. Sevestre, "Formation professionnelle et emploi : un lien plus marqué en Allemagne," *Économie et statistique*, No. 246-247 (September-October 1991).

NAKAJIMA, F., *A comparative study on choice of first-job and early occupational history in Japan, the United States and Great Britain,* photocopy, Tokyo, Japanese Institute of Labour, 1990.

National Center on Education and the Economy, *America's Choice: High Skills or Low Wages,* The Report of the Commission on the Skills of the American Workforce (Rochester NY: The Center, June 1990).

NORTHDURFT, W.E., *Schoolworks - Reinventing Public Schools to Create the Workforce of the Future* (Washington: The Brookings Institution, 1989).

OECD, "Le niveau d'instruction de la population active," in *Employment Outlook*, Chap. 7 (Paris, July 1989).

PAYEUR, Christian, S'engager pour l'avenir - Formation professionnelle, éducation et monde du travail au Québec, Centrale de l'enseignement du Québec, March 1990.

ROSENBAUM, J. E. and T. Kariya, "From High School to Work: Market and Institutional Mechanisms in Japan," *American Journal of Sociology* (May 1989).

SABOURET, J.-F., L'État du Japon, *La Découverte* (Paris, 1988):206-07.

SILVESTRE, J.-J., "La professionnalisation : l'exemple allemand," *Pouvoirs,* No. 30 (Paris, 30, 1984):39-46. [Cited in Problèmes politiques et sociaux, No. 504, 25 January 1985.]

STONE, N., "Does Business Have Any Business in Education?", *Harvard Business Review* (March-April 1991)46-62.

U.S. Congress, Office of Technology Assessment, *Worker Training: Competing in the New Economy* (Washington, U.S. Government Printing Office, September 1990).

WHITE, M., *The Japanese Educational Challenge - A Commitment to Children* (Tokyo and New York: Kodansha International, 1987).

7
Conclusions and Policy Recommendations

Many Canadians are not well served by their education system. For example, secondary-school programs are heavily geared to the needs of the 30 per cent of students who will go to college or university. Most of those students will graduate and find interesting jobs and decent incomes. But what about the other 70 per cent of young Canadians?

Our research shows a woeful lack of pragmatic technical and vocational programs to prepare young people for the world of work. There are very few exceptions. So it is hardly surprising that about one third of secondary-school students drop out and spend haphazard periods of casual work and joblessness. The failure to provide these students with basic skills means that nearly a quarter of young Canadians are both illiterate and innumerate. *If present trends continue, our schools will release one million more illiterates into the work force by the year 2000.* When they do find a job, their employers are unlikely to offer them world-class on-the-job training.

Our findings point to two other weaknesses of the education system. First, the performance of Canadian students on international tests in mathematics and science – essential subjects in the 1990s – is mediocre. These lacklustre academic results, combined with the poverty and paucity of secondary-school vocational programs, gives us the worst of both worlds. Second, the substantial differences in achievement among the provinces suggest serious inequalities in learning opportunities across Canada.

The Council believes that Canadians as a society *and* as individuals must now give an urgent priority to improving the overall performance of their learning system. We propose ways of doing so here. We set out targets for the system, suggest indicators to assess progress towards these targets, and recommend four directions for systematic improvement in elementary and secondary education and in workplace training. The success of these, or indeed of any other, proposals for improvement depends on coherence in education and training.

As suggested elsewhere in this report, coherence is a coordinated system of communication based on clear signals, effective incentives and appropriate responses. In practical terms it means, for example, that students (and their parents) receive a consistent set of signals and can easily grasp how to respond to them. This does not happen at the moment. Information about employers' expectations is hard to get and often confusing; students receive little help in their transition to the workplace. High achievement is not always rewarded, and credits are often nontransferable. Some of the most useful courses are underfunded, and those who teach them are often held in low esteem.

To change this situation we need, first of all, a broad consensus among Canadians on the role and value of learning. Next, stakeholders must commit themselves to improving the coherence of the system. Employers in all sectors must articulate their needs and expectations clearly; school boards, counsellors, and teachers must find it to their advantage to interpret and respond to employers' needs; the numerous programs and levels within the education system must fit together so that they offer predictable pathways to students. This entails a wide spectrum of groups working together to diffuse information, design and implement programs, and adjust incentives. Figure 7.1 shows how complex the interactions between students and other players are. In a coherent system, these interactions complement each other; in an incoherent one, they confuse and demotivate the student, and often lead to the costly trial-and-error training and job search that is the norm for too many young Canadians.

How can we turn things around? Clearly, the very nature of coherence rules out recourse to a governmental "grand design." The $40-billion learning system is too large – and the needs of Canadians, too diverse – for that. So, neither creating a centralized federal education department nor strengthening the authority of provincial departments would solve the problem. Nor would convening a Canada-wide meeting to draw up educational goals and targets. Rather,

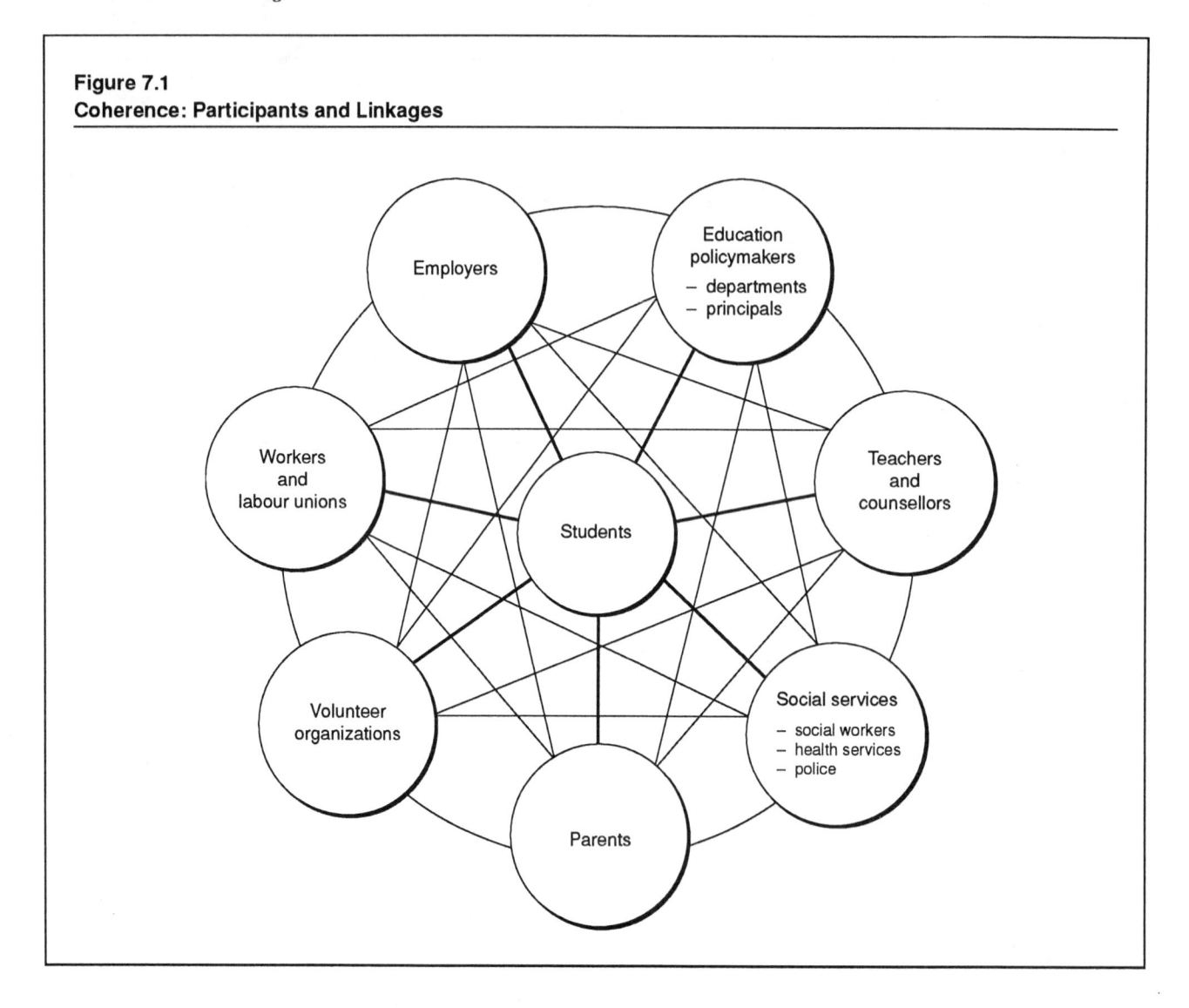

Figure 7.1
Coherence: Participants and Linkages

Participants (circles): Employers; Education policymakers – departments, principals; Workers and labour unions; Students; Teachers and counsellors; Volunteer organizations; Social services – social workers, health services, police; Parents.

Canadians must establish mechanisms to engage the stakeholders – departments of education, teachers, employers from all sectors, unions, parents and students, and social and voluntary agencies – in the pursuit of coherence on an on-going basis.

Such mechanisms have long escaped us in Canada, but there are welcome signs of change. The Council of Ministers of Education is moving towards broad consensus on objectives, indicators, and student testing. The Canadian Labour Force Development Board, which will assess various aspects of the learning system and its links with the labour market, is bringing together a broad spectrum of employers, unions, and educational and social constituencies. And the "learning" component of the federal government's Prosperity Initiative represents an effort to emphasize the national importance of education and training, and to canvass the widest possible cross-section of Canadians. Provincial initiatives — such as the Ontario Training and Adjustment Board and the proposed *Société québécoise pour le développement de la main-d'œuvre*, for example – are a further reflection of a growing understanding of the importance of enhancing our learning potential in a concerted way. A convergence of such initiatives will be an important step towards coherence. Indeed, the emergence of a coherent learning system would represent, in our view, a powerful form of social compact.

In the following pages, we set out some targets, as well as four broad directions for change that would, we believe, improve performance, enhance coherence, and move us closer to these targets.

Targets

The targets (see box below) are intended to provide a broad framework for policy making. In some cases – such as literacy, numeracy, and drop-outs – we propose numerical targets. In other cases, only broad, general objectives can be stated. The list is not exhaustive, but we hope it will set a benchmark for provinces, for school boards, and for individual schools. In some cases, tougher – or simply different – objectives will be appropriate, depending on circumstances and ambitions.

In defining these targets, we have been very mindful that they should be ambitious yet attainable, and we have worked to strike a balance between the two. In our research, we determined where Canada stands currently with respect to a number of indicators of performance of the education system. We then identified targets and goals being set in various jurisdictions – some of these targets are very similar, if not identical, to targets set in some provinces recently – and consulted widely with experts and advisors in the community.

We do not claim that this set of targets is immutable: it is expected that the targets will change through time as progress is made in achieving them. And not all jurisdictions will give equal priority to all targets. In terms of specifics, different provinces and even different regions within provinces face different challenges, and they may well prefer to focus on one problem over another; for example, drop-out levels

The Council's Proposed Targets

Targets	Current Status
1 By the year 2000, all 16-year-old Canadians (except for the mentally disabled) should be functionally literate and numerate.	In 1989, some 28.5 per cent of 16 to 24-year olds did not reach Functional Literacy Level 4 and 44.5 per cent did not reach Numeracy Level 3.
2 Increase the proportion of graduates among high-school leavers by 3 per cent per year.	The apparent drop-out rate of high-school students is estimated at 30 per cent.
3 Increase enrolment in mathematics, science, and engineering at university and in technology subjects at the college level; increase the retention rate in advanced maths and sciences at the end of secondary school to 30 per cent by the year 2000 and 40 per cent by 2010; encourage girls and young women to enter these fields.	Full-time college enrolments in engineering and applied science have fallen steadily since 1983; typically, fewer than one fourth of senior high-school students enrol in advanced mathematics and science.
4 Improve achievement, especially of the weaker provinces, and improve Canadian students' performance on international tests.	Literacy, numeracy, and student achievement in mathematics and science show large interprovincial differences; Canadian students' results on international mathematics and science tests are mediocre.
5 Improve the image and content of vocational secondary-school programs and encourage partnerships and cooperative programs.	Only about 10 per cent of Canadian secondary-school students are in vocational programs.
6 Overhaul the apprenticeship system to make it more relevant and responsive.	The coverage of the system is highly concentrated in traditional trades and a few low-skilled service occupations.
7 Improve the quality and quantity of industry-based training.	On a per-employee basis, spending on formal training by private firms in 1987 was less than half that in the United States.
8 Enhance articulation of the education system to simplify transfers among institutions.	Recognition of, and accreditation for, past programs and related experience is piecemeal.
9 Enhance accessibility by raising retention rates and enrolment rates of the disabled, women, and aboriginals to the average of the general population.	Grade 12 retention rates for aboriginals are only about 45 per cent; women are underrepresented in technical fields of study; the disabled are underrepresented in postsecondary programs.

may be very high in one region, while another may find that although drop-out rates are relatively low, achievement levels are unsatisfactory.

We do strongly believe, however, that the set of targets that we have identified serves to outline, accurately and fairly, the core dimensions of the challenges faced by education in Canada in the 1990s. We therefore urge all stakeholders – from schools, parents, and students through school boards and provincial education ministries to employers, unions, and the community at large – to examine their own performance in order to see how well it measures up and to assess where their energies should be directed to effect improvements in education performance.

Indicators

Indicators enable us to monitor progress towards attainment of the targets. A vast array of indicators would be necessary to provide a comprehensive assessment of the education and training systems. The criteria that one invokes to judge performance depend on the objectives of the evaluators: parents, students, teachers, administrators, governments, taxpayers, employers. Each group has expectations of the system that may not always coincide. Moreover, many important outcomes of the system – such as tolerance, civility, fairness, independence, flair, and love of learning – are intangible. We tend to measure what we can, and to report it.

A number of useful indicators can be considered that could be helpful in monitoring progress towards goals. Ideally, one would like to see a highly readable "digest" or "scorecard" of the relevant data on a regular basis (perhaps every five years) so that progress could be assessed. A suggested set of such indicators is shown in the frame on this page.

Such a set of targets and indicators would, we believe, help school administrators, teachers, parents, employers, students, and policymakers judge the performance of the system and, most importantly, their own performance within it. It could do much to heighten public awareness and, thereby, help in the setting of appropriate expectations. Together, heightened awareness, challenging goals, and measures of performance are likely to enhance a crucial ingredient of the system – namely, motivation.

Directions for Change

Four directions for change will, in our view, result in a system of education and training that is:

The Council's Proposed Indicators

Achievement
- Literacy and numeracy test results should be published every five years.
- Drop-out rates should be published regularly; they should be refined to take account of those who "drop back in."
- Student achievement in basic skills should be assessed regularly for early detection of deficiencies.
- International, interprovincial, and intraprovincial test results – and results over time – should be assessed in order to permit important comparisons.

Preparation for the Labour Market
- Enrolments in secondary-school vocational courses show progress towards a more relevant range of programs.
- Graduates' occupation by field of study, and placement success, indicate the employment relevance of initial preparation.
- Type and amount of employer-based training data help gauge the industry's commitment to skill formation.
- Supplies of highly qualified personnel show how well the education system responds to the skill needs of the information economy.

Accessibility
- Female enrolment and graduation in various disciplines indicate women's progress in nontraditional fields.
- Secondary-school retention rates of aboriginal children and participation rates of the disabled help monitor progress for important minority groups.
- Socio-economic status of students shows how well the system serves different groups.

- *comprehensive* – addresses the needs of all students
- *open* – encourages innovation, differentiation, and greater parental involvement
- *responsive* – adapts to social change and individual needs
- *relevant* – i.e., recognizes the skill needs of the information age.

Towards a Comprehensive System

Canada must move towards a system that provides a closer integration of school, work, and training. The wholehearted commitment and active participation of employers in all sectors – public and private, goods-producing and service-producing – are absolutely essential to the success of such an approach. Employers must continually identify and clearly articulate their needs; communicate their

expectations to students, parents, and educators; and commit themselves to active collaboration with educators and with the wider community in the design and delivery of programs.

In this regard, certain approaches look promising. These include partnerships between employers and the schools (including co-operative education programs) and the integration of a revitalized and expanded system of apprenticeship with secondary-school programs.

Promote Partnerships

Partnerships between employers and schools may take a variety of forms — from informal exchanges of information and student visits to the workplace, to highly sophisticated ventures involving jointly-planned curricula and credit programs integrating school and work/training experience. Two obervations are appropriate in this context. First, such arrangements often depend on the energy and initiative of visionary individuals, so that momentum may be lost when they move on. Thus it is important that shcool boards come to view such arrangements as a matter of policy; as well, the active involvement of industry and employers' associations and of unions is also needed to provide a context of continuity. (The efforts of the Canadian Chamber of Commerce set a good example in this regard.) A commitment to employer/education partnerships must be institutionalized as one of the essential components of a system in which economic agents and the education system work together in a coherent framework. Partnership is a key ingredient of coherence — one consistent with the Canadian market economy.

Second, partnerships should be defined widely so as to involve not just employers (whether business or non-profit organizations like hospitals), unions, and the schools, but the wider community of stakeholders, including parents, social agencies, and the voluntary sector. This would enhance awareness and support, promote continuity, and overcome the isolation from the everyday world felt by many teachers and students.

While partnership can take many forms, two – cooperative education and apprenticeship – are particularly important.

Expand Cooperative Education

While formal evaluations of cooperative education are few, the evidence to date strongly suggests that all parties benefit. The beneficial effects in terms of reducing absenteeism and drop-out rates may be particularly important. Cooperative programs at the secondary-school level have been developed in Ontario, British Columbia, and Alberta; however, the overall percentage of students involved is very small (less than 10 per cent). Furthermore, with few exceptions, such programs have tended not to focus on the skilled trades. The positive contribution of cooperative education should be encouraged through an expansion in the number of students and in the range of programs. To that end, provincial education authorities should set targets for cooperative programs, giving school boards incentives to seek out the best practice from across Canada and to work with employers and unions to put cooperative education programs in place at the secondary-school level. These efforts should include greater emphasis on exposing students to the skilled trades.

Link Formal Schooling and Apprenticeship Training

Fundamental to the creation of greater coherence is the closer integration of secondary-school education and apprenticeship training. Closer links between education and training at the secondary-school level would address two concerns – the academic bias of the secondary-school system and the low status of apprenticeship training.

There is a wide and growing consensus that a fundamental flaw in the Canadian educational system is the excessively academic orientation of the typical secondary-school curriculum. While such an approach is appropriate for the 30 per cent of students who go on to postsecondary studies – though, as we point out elsewhere, we are concerned that even that 30 per cent is not being as well-served as it should be – it fails to serve the needs of the remaining 70 per cent. For the latter, two outcomes are apparent. A disturbingly high proportion drop out of school altogether, whether because of a lack of interest or a lack of ability, or because they are drawn by the prospects of employment. And the remainder who do complete school but do not go on to postsecondary studies find that they have limited job skills. They know little about the labour market and are not equipped to succeed in it.

Our belief that apprenticeship training must be more closely integrated into Canadian secondary schools also arises from concerns about the apprenticeship system itself. Apprenticeship training has a low status in the minds of many Canadians. That reflects faults within the apprenticeship system as well as the fact that most Canadians know little about the types of training apprenticeship offers. As noted earlier, Canadian apprentices are much older than those in other countries. Too often in Canada, people turn to the apprenticeship system only after they realize that they have few skills to offer potential employers. Part of the reason for that, we suspect, is that many students and new entrants to the labour market are simply unaware of what the skilled trades do and what apprenticeship training provides. Earlier exposure to vocational programs, coupled with relevant work experience, would do much to overcome these problems.

Experience to date with apprenticeship programs at the secondary-school level appears to be very positive. In this context, Ontario's Secondary School Workplace Apprenticeship Program, now offered by 25 boards, bears examination. SSWAP students gain credits both towards apprenticeship qualifications and towards secondary-school graduation. We note that almost half of all secondary-school students work part-time; that proportion is higher in the higher grades. Partnerships offer an opportunity to tailor a student's work experience to vocational programs in a systematic way.

Earlier in this document we pondered the question of whether, given global competitive realities, Canada could continue to maintain a learning system markedly different from the most successful models of coherence. While insufficient data have as yet been amassed to permit conclusive evaluations, the apprentice-like alternating of work experience and education that characterizes co-op programs may be a promising move towards a Canadian variant of the dual system – one that is consistent with our overall market orientation. This opportunity should not be ignored. Clear and direct links to the regular adult apprenticeship system are of critical importance.

Broaden the Range of Apprenticeship Training

The first step towards the closer integration of secondary-school education and apprenticeship training must consist of a broadening of apprenticeship in Canada. Canadian apprenticeship is highly concentrated in a few occupations, primarily in the goods sector. Given the changing nature of the Canadian economy, such a focus is too narrow. Furthermore, the provinces have tended to develop their apprenticeship programs and standards independently, leading to uncertainties about comparability and transferability. Our research reveals that the number of trades granting Red Seals to a majority of their apprentices has been low. The adoption of agreed-upon standards for a skilled trade serves notice to prospective employers that the person certified to that standard has commonly accepted skills, and equally important, can work to recognized safety standards. We do not envision a system involving the imposition of standards upon provinces; but we do see a great deal of scope for wider agreement between provinces on certified apprenticeship standards. Worker mobility within and between provinces would be enhanced, and that in turn could help to shape a labour market that is more flexible in the face of globalization, technological change, and shifts in the industrial structure of employment.

We need a master plan to expand the apprenticeship system, in terms both of the range of occupations covered (including new types of jobs in the service sector) and of standards that are recognized across provincial boundaries. That will require the collaboration of several groups. Currently, certification standards are agreed upon by the Canadian Council of Directors of Apprenticeship, which consists of representatives of each of the ten provinces. But extending the range of certified occupations requires broader input – from the Canadian Labour Force Development Board and its provincial counterparts, the proposed *Société québécoise de développement de la main-d'œuvre*, the professional associations, and the unions.

The creation of closer links with a modernized, expanded, and consistent apprenticeship system is essential for coherence in the school-to-work transition, for students' understanding of the nature of work skills demanded in the labour market, and for their decisions regarding occupational choice and the pursuit of postsecondary studies. A master plan to revamp apprenticeship training in Canada, then, should include the creation of links with secondary-school education. Students should receive credits for any apprenticeship training they complete while in school, and those school programs should be linked to graduates' next stage of training.

Upgrade the Status of Secondary-School Technical/Vocational Education

In many respects, the status of vocational training at the secondary school level has been the victim of a vicious circle. Students considered to be "the best and the brightest" are prepared for postsecondary studies while their academically weaker or more discouraged peers are steered towards vocational programs (when they are available). In a system biased towards academic content and composed largely of teachers with university degrees, vocational teachers, most of whom are the product of apprenticeship programs, are at a disadvantage, irrespective of the quality of their teaching. Shop facilities and equipment often are lacking or outdated – a further reflection of the lower status given vocational training by the educational system and society as a whole. We can no longer afford to shortchange 70 per cent of the secondary-school population. In order to attract more able students, we must improve the status of technical training. Formal linkages to postsecondary apprenticeship training can do much in this respect. Rounding out the preparation of technical teachers to include literacy and numeracy skills where these are weak can also help to improve their status. Partnerships between schools and employers have an important role to play as well by helping students to see that employers regard technical training as useful, relevant, and rewarding.

Strengthen Career Counselling in the Schools

Counselling is a critical element in a coherent system, especially given the rapid and complex evolution of Canada's occupational structure and its associated skills, and the need for most individuals to make multiple occupational changes throughout their working lives. Students, adults entering or re-entering the labour force, and those facing a change in occupation, need much better exposure to the range of possibilities in the labour market.

Too often, counsellors in the secondary schools have little formal preparation and many schools give career counselling a very low priority – a reflection of their focus on academic preparation for postsecondary studies. Career counselling must become an integral part of a student's education and a key adjunct to labour-force entry and re-entry. All counsellors should be required to complete a standard core curriculum, to meet provincial standards for certification, and to have regular contact with employers and, if possible, work term assignments. "Career courses" should become a compulsory part of the secondary-school curriculum. Students should receive some exposure to information on career options early in their secondary-school years so that they may be aware of occupational requirements in advance of course selection in later years. At the senior-high-school level, students should be given career counselling to assist them in choosing cooperative programs, apprenticeship training, or academic preparation for postsecondary education.

Special attention should be paid by educators, employers, and governments to those groups whose "learning continuum" traditionally has been interrupted most severely – women, Natives, and the disabled.

Towards an Open System

The educational system will have to change in order to improve its overall performance. Change must involve the recognition of differences among schools and among teachers, as well as the injection of opportunities for students and parents to make free choices. To that end, the local organization (school board, school, etc.) must assume leadership and primary responsibility in education. Education ministries should act to support the local organization and set strategic goals for education within the province.

The public education system is a large monopoly that is heavily bureaucratized on both the employer and employee sides. The Council believes the system would perform better if it were more open and flexible. It would then be better placed to build upon its strengths and correct its weaknesses. However, we believe the system can be opened up without taking drastic measures to privatize. But it should offer more choice and more scope for differentiation. The measurement of school performance is a critical component of a school system based on choice. We believe the teaching profession could be opened up as well by the explicit recognition of differences among teachers and by professionalizing teaching.

Introduce School Choice

In many respects, the education bureaucracy, in its attempt to treat all participants equitably, has ended by treating all equally – regardless of ability, interests, or performance. Thus most students are offered academic courses with few technical/vocational options, and most children attend their neighbourhood school. A more transparent system — one that allowed more *choice* and differentiation — would help to involve parents and students more than does the rather inflexible system that is currently in place. In our view, provincial policy and school-board practice should be designed to increase the opportunity of choice of school for all parents and their children within the public school system.

Vancouver and Edmonton are examples of two jurisdictions that have introduced school choice, and their experiences have been very positive. Of course, the opportunities for choice are greater in larger cities than in rural areas and small towns; in the latter cases, differentiation would more often be confined to program offerings within schools, but it could also be improved through distance education.

The advantages of freedom of choice among schools in the public system include increased accountability of principals and teachers for educational outcomes. It would place a high value on excellent teaching. It would help to decentralize responsibility to local schools and to parents. And it would help to identify weak spots in the system so that remedies could be introduced to upgrade schools that are performing poorly; these might include the need for a new principal, for involvement of social agencies to address students' problems, for stepping up remedial classes for students who are falling behind, or for changes in the teaching staff, for example. School choice would also offer the opportunity for, and means of assessing, differences in teaching approaches, in school ethos, and in school organization, and other factors that affect educational outcomes.

Taken further, a system based on school choice would encourage greater differentiation among schools, enabling students to achieve a closer match of their interests and abilities with program offerings. Some schools might attract students who are especially strong in maths and sciences, while others might offer excellence in technical or artistic studies or other important avenues for personal and intellectual development. The important thing is that programs not aiming to prepare students for college or university should be providing clear pathways to future training and employment opportunities. And regardless of their focus, all schools must strive for excellent literacy and numeracy skills.

Measure School Performance

Parents and students can choose intelligently only if reliable information is consistently available regarding schools' educational characteristics and achievement. Provincial authorities and school boards should, therefore, provide continuous comparable information on the performance of all fully and partially funded schools in their jurisdictions on the basis of selected relevant educational indicators. Such information must be comparable across schools and through time, and must be made public. The Quebec ministry of education already publishes an array of achievement indicators for the secondary-school level, showing, for example, average student test scores by subject and by school board.

In a system characterized by differentiation of program offerings across schools, it would be necessary to develop a range of indicators that might include, for example, drop-out rates, average scores on standardized tests, the percentage of students going on to university, the percentage of students completing the secondary-school stage of apprenticeship training, and the percentage placed in advanced apprenticeship training programs. While such information would be absolutely essential in a system based on school choice, it would also be highly desirable in the current system.

Professionalize Teaching

Given the important role played by teachers in Canadian society, we must ensure that the quality of those entering teaching is high. Many factors affect an individual's occupational choice. Among those are the status and pay associated with any given occupation. On average, teachers in Canada are relatively well paid, compared with teachers in other countries and with other occupational groups in Canada. However, they face a fairly flat earnings scale: earnings are relatively high at the lower end of the scale and level off by mid-career. A related concern has been expressed about the appeal of teaching as a profession. The education system is heavily bureaucratized, and little distinction is made between good teachers and poor ones. Too often, the rewards and incentives for outstanding performance are absent; equally, sanctions against poor performance are rarely applied, if at all.

Elementary and secondary teaching is in need of professionalization. Career planning should become an integral part of the relationship between teachers, principals, school boards, and ministries of education. Currently, teachers' careers progress more or less in lock-step fashion, with salary increases being determined according to a standard formula based on years of teaching experience and educational background, including additional qualifications. Means must be found to motivate all teachers to perform to their full potential, to reward superior teachers so that they stay in the classroom, and to urge poor ones to leave it. Career-path planning would facilitate the more careful deployment of the teaching force: superior teachers could, in addition to teaching, act as role models for other teachers and help to train student-teachers; good teachers would, as now, provide the backbone of instruction; and poor teachers would be encouraged to seek opportunities in other fields. Attention to the portability of teachers' pensions will help to ease the transition out of the classroom and into other employment for those for whom teaching is no longer attractive.

Progress towards the greater professionalization of teaching could be achieved through the introduction of categories of teachers, differentiated by performance and ability, education/training, salary, and responsibility. We envision a model based on three levels of teachers: instructors, career teachers, and lead teachers.

The *instructor* level would consist largely of beginning teachers undergoing a two-year period of induction, after which, if successful, they would receive full accreditation as teachers. They would combine a smaller teaching load than certified teachers with study, observation and critical self-appraisal, and would work under the supervision of a senior teacher.

Career teachers would be those who have successfully completed the requirements for certification and taken on the full responsibility for teaching students.

Lead teachers would be those who have consistently shown superior performance and ability, motivation, and commitment; they would act as mentors and role models for other teachers in their schools; and they would play an active role in shaping instruction in the school.

Teachers do differ in ability; some would move more quickly than others from level to level, and some would never reach the senior ranks. At the same time, incentives and reward systems would be in place to recognize the contributions of the best teachers, giving them a route to advancement that keeps them in teaching rather than, as is now the case, forcing them to seek administrative positions that, while placing them on a new career path, take them out of the classroom where they are most needed.

Establish Teacher Registries

The process of matching teacher supply and demand is poorly organized. If an interested and available teacher with the required skills does not happen to see a job vacancy advertised in a given location, then the best hiring decision may not be made. Teachers may leave the profession for either the short or the long term for a variety of reasons, but once no longer employed with a school board, contact with them is often lost. And it is vitally important that teachers be well trained in the fields in which they teach. To match teacher demand and supply more closely and to have consistent information over time regarding teacher supply and demand trends, each province should maintain a "central teacher registry." Such registries would allow the tracking of practising and nonpractising teachers and their records of certification. School boards could register their teacher requirements with the provincial central registry, which could then play an important brokerage role in matching teacher supply and demand.

Rationalize and Restructure

Finally, given the funding and cost constraints reported earlier on, efforts to improve the overall performance of the system must be accompanied by redoubled efforts to control costs. School boards and provinces should closely examine the organization of education within their jurisdictions with a view to rationalizing structures and reducing administrative overhead and duplication of services.

The educational system in Canada consists of a multiplicity of school boards divided along linguistic, religious, and geographic lines. At the same time, school boards exhibit differences in cost structures, including the share accounted for by administration costs. We cannot help but believe that, given the size of the educational bureaucracy, a great deal of scope exists for reducing wasteful duplication of services within and across school boards. Throughout Canada, governments and industry alike face the necessity of controlling expenditures, restructuring, and rationalizing their operations. The educational bureaucracy is no different. We urge provinces and school boards to examine closely their own organizational structures in order to identify opportunities to reduce costs. Such opportunities may range from sharing transportation services to amalgamating school boards in some areas.

Towards a Responsive System

In addition to broad directions for change, there is a need to focus on specific targets, notably reducing drop-out rates and increasing literacy and numeracy.

In our assessment of the quality of the learning system, we have observed an array of new and complex factors that pose major problems for educators. Our research into the characteristics of students in major

Canadian cities, for example, reveals a wide diversity in their ethnic, cultural, and linguistic backgrounds. Special efforts are required by teachers, parents, and the students themselves to help them realize the potential of the learning environment.

Be Ready to Learn

In addition, we have observed the increasing need for teachers to deal with a variety of social problems – drugs, pregnancies, unstable home environments, and child poverty – that were formerly handled by other institutions such as the family and the church. We learned of an alarming need to provide breakfast programs in the schools: too many Canadian children come to school too hungry to learn. For a variety of demographic and socio-economic reasons, therefore, readiness to learn may be a problem at any age. A fully coherent system must place learning firmly in the context of a wider social environment and ensure that the role of the school has the support of other social and community services.

Since learning is a cumulative process, however, we especially emphasize the importance of readiness to learn at a very early age. We therefore urge provincial governments to pay special attention to preschool programs of the Head Start variety.

Adopt Remedial Measures

We observe that "dropping out" is not a clear-cut, instantaneous event. Rather, it is a process that begins when a child first "drops behind." All provinces, school boards, and schools should undertake regular *diagnostic assessment* of children's performance in basic skills from the earliest years of schooling. A variety of remedial measures should be developed to prevent students from falling behind. One promising approach is to recognize explicitly that different students progress at different rates, so that some need more time than others to master a particular skill. Rather than giving slower students easier material, they could be given additional time. Other approaches include special tutoring by teachers, teachers' aides, and/or parents; mentoring — which might involve, for example, a more advanced student; supplementary study-groups; and the time-differentiated learning approach described above. This remedial work is the area that should be given the highest priority in allocating new funds and where cutbacks should be avoided.

Recent Statistics Canada surveys of literacy and numeracy have demonstrated that some 3 million Canadians are functionally illiterate and innumerate. If the performance of the school system does not improve and if the drop-out rate does not decline, at least a million new young illiterates will be released into the labour force during the 1990s. *Such an outcome must be avoided at all cost.* Accordingly, provinces and school boards should increase the required credits in compulsory subjects, enrich the opportunity to learn in these subjects, and reduce the number of elective subjects.

Towards a Relevant System

Canadians must commit themselves to continuous upgrading of skills in the workplace, in educational and training institutions, and in the home.

To succeed in fiercely competitive global markets, Canadians will have to be innovative and flexible enough to exploit new technologies. This means that they must have good foundation skills and that they must continually extend and upgrade their range of specialized skills. In addition, however, it is clear that the new skill requirements place a heavy premium on scientific and technological literacy.

Improve Performance in Mathematics and Science

In this context, the school system has an important role to play, both in giving all young people a certain basic level of understanding of how science and technology affect their lives and in fostering an interest in pursuing postsecondary studies in these fields. That is why we have set as an important target the retention of more students in advanced maths and sciences at the senior-high-school level and the attraction of more students to postsecondary studies in those fields. We note, in particular, the need to encourage more young women to enter the science disciplines.

Of course, the quality of those science and mathematics courses will have a bearing on the level of students' interest in enrolling in them and in working to do well. But many school boards are experiencing difficulties in recruiting sufficient numbers of teachers qualified to teach science, mathematics, and technical courses. Often, the result is that underqualified teachers are asked to teach these subjects or that, especially in the case of technology, the courses simply are not offered. Special measures are needed to address these shortages, which are expected to persist. Faculties of education should focus especially on undergraduate students in science and mathematics when recruiting. In addition, they should set targets for the recruitment of potential teachers in those subject areas where shortages exist so as to better balance supply and demand in each area.

Increase Workplace Training

Formal schooling and the inculcation of good foundation skills represent the earlier stages of the learning continuum. Equally important is training for new skills that come with new technology or that enable employees to perform their jobs better. Learning must be regarded as a continuum that extends throughout an individual's lifetime. Workplace training can run the gamut from highly sophisticated in-house programs with resident instructors to informal learning-by-doing. Whatever the form, it should reflect the conviction that the strategic planning of the enterprise must involve the clear identification of skill needs and that success — for individuals, firms and society — will depend in large part on the continuous upgrading of skills.

Canada's record on workplace training compares unfavourably with that of its major trading partners. Some observers contend that a significant portion of Canada's training effort is not measured by surveys because it is of the informal learning-by-doing variety, and that it would compare more favourably if this were taken into account. There is little reason to assume, however, that other countries do significantly less than Canada in this regard. The calls for much greater emphasis on development of a *training culture* appear appropriate. But of all the reasons for employer reluctance to invest in human-resource development, the outstanding one is still the issue of what economists call "externalities": the possibility that a firm's investment in people will be captured by a "pirate". This is particularly the case for small firms which may lose workers to larger organizations that can offer a broader choice of opportunities for advancement. The federal and provincial governments, in collaboration with the Canadian Labour Force Development Board and its provincial/regional equivalents, should examine ways to create institutional arrangements in order to provide greater incentives for human-resource investments in small firms and to enhance the targeting of training-assistance funds to small firms.

Several models have been proposed to help stimulate more training in industry. One scheme to address the pirating problem is the Employee Training Loan Insurance Scheme, which involves a loan advanced jointly to employer and employee to cover training costs. Repayment is the employer's responsibility so long as the employee does not leave the firm voluntarily. If the employee does leave, then the repayment is the employee's responsibility, with the option to arrange compensation from the new employer. Australia has adapted an alternative arrangement in the form of the Training Guarantee, introduced in 1990. This requires all but very small firms to incur training expenditures equivalent to at least 1.5 per cent of their payroll. Firms that do not meet this minimum target are required to pay the difference to a government fund that will be used to support training. A third model that should be examined closely is Quebec's recent scheme of reimbursable tax credits for training.

Concern about Canadian employers' apparent weak commitment to workplace training is not new. In fact, the Council has raised this issue on a number of occasions in the past, most recently in *Good Jobs, Bad Jobs* (1990) and *Making Technology Work* (1987), where we outlined the benefits of formal training arrangements such as paid educational leave and training vouchers. We again urge employers to examine their records of commitment to training and to develop employee training programs that will enhance their performance.

Build on the Potential of Distance Education

In concluding our comments on the importance of lifelong learning and the development of a "learning culture", we draw attention to the potential offered by distance education as a learning tool. This alternative delivery mechanism for the learning continuum is often overlooked by both public and private sectors, although Canada's strength in this area is recognized throughout the world. Further development of distance education might usefully involve the creation of networks of community-based learning centres providing access not only to a range of technologies but also to other learning tools, including libraries, instructional software, and tutorial and counselling services. Information on distance education is sorely lacking, however, and we urge Statistics Canada to include on a regular basis data on the characteristics of courses, costs, and numbers of students among its educational statistics data.

Concluding Remarks

During our work, we have frequently been struck by the paucity and poverty of data. While we have enjoyed good cooperation from the provinces in the provision of information, we note considerable variation in the type of data, level of detail, accessibility, and presentation. We have noted the need for better, regular information about distance education, private-sector provision of vocational education and training, training in industry (especially the magnitude of on-the-job training), and vocational education at the secondary-school level. The Council of Ministers of Education should work to create greater harmonization and complementarity in the collection and analysis of data by the provinces.

To obtain more detailed data on the learning continuum, the Council of Ministers of Education, in cooperation with Statistics Canada and a task force of relevant stakeholders, should explore the feasibility of establishing a longitudinal database covering individuals from (say) the age of five through completion of "foundation" education and ten years into the labour force. A database comparable to the Swedish Malmö longitudinal study (which now extends over 50 years) would provide a cornucopia of interesting, relevant and important findings, ranging from the effect of preschool conditions on educational achievement and on labour-market success to the effect of educational methods and reforms, and including information on the effect of education on career development, job satisfaction, and life enrichment.

In this study, we have attempted to assess the ability of Canada's education and training systems to meet the challenges that lie ahead. We have drawn attention to a number of areas where we have found those systems wanting. We repeat the need for commitment and concerted effort by well-motivated students, well-informed parents, enlightened employers and trade unionists, and dedicated teachers to ensure a solid investment in the future. It is not just a question of paying our taxes and waiting for the system to produce. For sound investment, we must be more demanding, and we must also be active participants. There is no better way, in our view, to secure the present and improve the future prospects of our children. In the words of Confucius: "If you think in terms of a year, plant seed; if in terms of ten years, plant trees; if in terms of a hundred years, teach the people".

Bibliography

ANDERSON, L. W. and T. N. Postlethwaite. "What IEA studies say about teachers and teaching" in *International Comparisons and Educational Reforms* (q.v.).

BARRO, S. M. and L. Suter. *International Comparison of Teachers' Salaries: An Exploratory Study*, National Center for Education Statistics, Washington (D.C.), U.S. Department of Education, 1988.

Canadian Federation of Independent Business. *Skills for the Future: Small Business and Training in Canada*, Toronto, 1989.

Canadian Labour Market and Productivity Centre. "Rapport des groupes de travail sur la statégie de mise en valeur de la main-d'œuvre", Ottawa, 1990.

CROCKER, Robert K. "Science achievement in Canadian schools: National and international comparisons," Working Paper No. 7, Economic Council of Canada, Ottawa, 1990.

DESLAURIERS, Robert C. "The impact of employee illiteracy on Canadian business," Conference Board of Canada, Human Resources Development Centre, Ottawa, August 1990.

Employment and Immigration Canada. Labour Market Policy Analysis, "EIC study on high school vocational education in Canada," Ottawa, February 1992.

FULLAN, M. and F. M. Connelly. *Teacher Education in Ontario: Current Practices and Options for the Future*, Toronto, Ministry of Colleges and Universities, 1987.

GOODLAD, John I. *A Place Called School: Prospects for the Future*, New York, McGraw-Hill, 1984.

Government of Ontario. *People and Skills in the New Global Economy*, A Report by the Premier's Council, Toronto, Queen's Printer for Ontario, 1990.

HANUSHEK, Eric A. "The impact of differential expenditures on school performance," *Educational Researcher*, vol. 18 (May 1989).

IEA. *The Classroom Environment Study*. L. W. Anderson, D. W. Ryan et B. J. Shapiro, (eds.), London, Pergamon, 1989.

————. *International Comparisons and Educational Reforms*. Alan C. Purnes, Association for Supervision and Curriculum Development, Alexandria, VA, 1989.

KIFER, E. "What IEA studies say about curriculum and school organization," in *International Comparisons and Educational Reforms* (q.v.).

KRAHN, Harvey and Graham S. Lowe. "Young workers in the service economy," Working Paper No. 14, Economic Council of Canada, Ottawa, January 1991.

LAPOINTE, Archie E., Janice M. Askew andt Nancy A. Mead. *Learning Science*, Prepared for the National Center of Education Statistics, U.S. Department of Education and the National Science Foundation, Washington (D.C.), 1992.

NAKAJIMA, Fumiaki. *A Comparative Study on Choice of First-Job and Early Occupational History in Japan, the United States, and Great Britain*, Tokyo, The Japan Institute of Labour, 1990.

Nelson Canada. "Canadian tests of basic skills: Form 5 & Form 7 equating study, 1980-1987," Report to the Economic Council of Canada, 1991.

Organization for Economic Cooperation and Development. Education in OECD Countries *1987-88*, Paris, 1990.

Porter, Michael E. *The Competitive Advantage of Nations*, New York, Free Press, 1990.

Québec, Ministère de l'Éducation, Direction générale de la recherche et du développement, *Indicateurs sur la situation de l'enseignement primaire et secondaire, 1991*, Québec, 1991.

REES, R., W. K. Warren, B. J. Coles and M. J. Peart. "A study of the recruitment of Ontario teachers," Social Program Evaluation Group, Queen's University, Kingston (Ont.), March 1989.

ROBITAILLE, David F. and Robert A. Garden. *The IEA Study of Mathematics II: Contexts and Outcomes of School Mathematics, International Studies in Educational Achievement*, London, Pergamon Press, 1989.

Rutter, Michael. "School effects on pupil progress: research findings and policy implications," *Child Development*, vol. 54, 1983, p. 1-29.

SELLIN, N. and L. Anderson. "The student variable model," in *The IEA Classroom Environment Study*.

Siemens Electric Limited. "Apprenticeship training: Canada vs. Germany," a paper persented at a Labour Canada seminar, Ottawa, 18 June, 1991.

Statistics Canada. "Distribution report: Human resource training and development survey," Ottawa, 1990.

United Nations Development Program. *Human Development Report*, 1991, New York: United Nations, 1991.

World Competitiveness Report, 1990, 10th edition. S. Garelli, (ed.), Lausanne and Geneva: IMD International and World Economic Forum, 1990.

World Competitiveness Report, 1991, 11th edition. S. Garelli, (ed.), Lausanne and Geneva: IMD International and World Economic, 1991.

Authors and Consultants

The authors of the Economic Council research reports are the staff economists and, in some case, outside researchers working under contract for the Council. Education and Training in Canada is the product of the contributors listed below.

The closing of the Economic Council was announced by the federal government in February 1992 and the Council officially ceased work on June 30, 1992. Readers who may have questions or comments regarding the research presented in this report can reach most former Council staff members through the Government of Canada telephone directory.

Authors

Chapter 1   Keith Newton, Principal Author, with Thomas Schweitzer and Gilles Mcdougall

Chapter 2   Thomas Schweitzer

Chapter 3   Keith Newton, Principal Author, with Tom Siedule

Chapter 4   Kathryn McMullen

Chapter 5   Gilles Mcdougall

Chapter 6   Patrice de Broucker

Chapter 7   Staff of the Economic Council of Canada

Consultants

Bill Ahamad and Miles Wisenthal, Ahamad Consultants Inc.

Barbara Brunhuber, University of Ottawa

Robert Crocker, Memorial University

Jane Gaskell, University of British Columbia

Bertha Joseph, Aboriginal Management Consultants

Graham Lowe & Harvey Krahn, University of Alberta

Nelson Canada

David Robitaille, University of British Columbia

Tim Sale, Tim Sale and Associates

Robert Sweet, Lakehead University

François Vaillancourt, Université de Montréal

Special thanks are also due to Lucie Marier, Secretary, and the staff of
the Economic Council's Informatics, Publications, and Public Affairs Divisions.